EDUCATION AND RACISM

DAMES
Dansk Center for Migration
og Etniske Studier

**EUROPEAN RESEARCH CENTRE
ON MIGRATION & ETHNIC RELATIONS**

Education and Racism
A cross national inventory of positive effects
of education on ethnic tolerance

Edited by
LOUK HAGENDOORN and SHERVIN NEKUEE
European Research Centre on Migration and Ethnic Relations
Utrecht University

LONDON AND NEW YORK

First published 1999 by Ashgate Publishing

Reissued 2018 by Routledge
2 Park Square, Milton Park, Abingdon, Oxon OX14 4RN
711 Third Avenue, New York, NY 10017, USA

Routledge is an imprint of the Taylor & Francis Group, an informa business

Copyright © Louk Hagendoorn and Shevrin Nekuee 1999

All rights reserved. No part of this book may be reprinted or reproduced or utilised in any form or by any electronic, mechanical, or other means, now known or hereafter invented, including photocopying and recording, or in any information storage or retrieval system, without permission in writing from the publishers.

Notice:
Product or corporate names may be trademarks or registered trademarks, and are used only for identification and explanation without intent to infringe.

Publisher's Note
The publisher has gone to great lengths to ensure the quality of this reprint but points out that some imperfections in the original copies may be apparent.

Disclaimer
The publisher has made every effort to trace copyright holders and welcomes correspondence from those they have been unable to contact.

A Library of Congress record exists under LC control number: 99073639

ISBN 13: 978-1-138-31262-3 (hbk)
ISBN 13: 978-1-138-31263-0 (pbk)
ISBN 13: 978-0-429-45810-1 (ebk)

Contents

List of Figures vii
List of Diagrams viii
List of Tables ix
List of Contributors xii
Acknowledgements xiv

1 Introduction: A Model of the Effects of Education on Prejudice and Racism
  Louk Hagendoorn 1

2 Education and Prejudice against Immigrants
  Pierangelo Peri 21

3 The Effect of Education on the Expression of Negative Views towards Immigrants in France: The Influence of the Republican Model Put to the Test
  Florence Haegel 33

4 'Everyday' Racism in Belgium: An Overview of the Research and an Interpretation of its Link with Education
  Hans De Witte 47

5 The Impact of Education on Racism in Poland Compared with Other European Countries
  Aleksandra Jasinska-Kania 75

6 Explaining Individual Racial Prejudice in Contemporary Germany
  Jürgen R. Winkler 93
  Appendix 128

7 Dynamics of Political Values: Education and Issues of Tolerance
  Paul Sniderman & Erica R. Gould 137
  Appendix 158

8 Education, Attitudes towards Ethnic Minorities
  and Opposition to Affirmative Action
  Geneviève Verberk & Peer Scheepers 163
  Appendix 203

Author Index 211

Subject Index 215

List of Figures

6.1 Level of racial prejudice: by structural disposition and contact intensity   117

6.2 Level of racial prejudice: by socio-cultural insecurity and contact intensity   117

6.3 Level of racial prejudice by age and level of education   120

7.1 Political choice: symmetrical activation effects for judgements for governmental guarantees of equal opportunity for women and for blacks as a function of education and ideology   150

List of Diagrams

1.1	Model of the possible effects of education on prejudice	19
2.1	Causal relation between education and prejudice mediated by 'conformism', 'traditional values' and 'professional status'	27
2.2	Form of causal model between education and prejudice mediated by 'conformism', 'traditional values' and 'professional status'	28
2.3	The 'best' model	28
2.4	The 'worst' model	29
4.1	First model explaining 'everyday' racism	57
4.2	Second model explaining 'everyday' racism	59
6.1	Causal relation of scales and items to the dependent theoretical constructs	97
6.2	A model explaining racial prejudice	124
6.3	A model explaining racial prejudice (less highly educated people)	126
6.4	A model explaining racial prejudice (more highly educated people)	126
7.1	A schematic model of value activation	144
7.2	Racial tolerance: education's multiple roles	146
8.1	Theoretical model for hypotheses 4 and 7	183
8.2	Structural equation model of the effects on opposition to affirmative action controlled for gender, age, religious denomination, and region and degree of urbanisation of place of residence	200

List of Tables

3.1	The various items of the 1997 CEVIPOF survey	35
3.2	Social factors influencing a negative attitude towards immigrants	37
3.3	The role of religion	38
3.4	Full or partial agreement with 'There are too many immigrants in France'	40
3.5	Those holding a diploma lower than a BAC who fully agree that there are too many immigrants in France	42
3.6	Those holding a diploma higher than a BAC who fully agree that there are too many immigrants in France	42
3.7	Relationship between a negative attitude towards immigrants and authoritarianism, political preference and insecurity about the future	44
4.1	Rating of items concerning everyday racism	50
4.2	Distribution and content of the four 'ethnic types'	52
5.1	Perception of different groups as belonging to the same race as Poles	76
5.2	Education and perception of different groups as belonging to the same race as Poles	77
5.3a	Those who do not want to have members of other ethnic groups as neighbours: Western Europe	81
5.3b	Those who do not want to have members of other ethnic groups as neighbours: Eastern Europe	81
5.4	Socio-demographic predictors of social distance towards various ethnic groups in Europe	84
5.5	Attitudes predicting social distance towards various ethnic groups in Europe	86

5.6	Socio-demographic predictors of social distance towards various ethnic groups in Poland	87
5.7	Attitudes predicting social distance towards various ethnic groups in Poland	88
6.1	Racial attitudes in Germany: 1980–1996	100
6.2	Negative attitudes on immigration to Germany	101
6.3	Regression of racial prejudice on socio-demographic variables	104
6.4	Regression of racial attitudes on socio-cultural insecurity variables	108
6.5	The effect of socio-cultural insecurity on racial attitudes	109
6.6	Regression of racial prejudice on socio-demographic variables and socio-cultural insecurity	110
6.7	The effects of structural dispositions on racial attitudes	113
6.8	The effects of socio-cultural insecurity and structural disposition on racial prejudice	114
6.9	Contact and the level of racial prejudice	116
6.10	Regression of intergroup attitudes	121
6.11	Regression of intergroup attitudes (those with lower levels of education)	122
6.12	Regression of intergroup attitudes (those with higher levels of education)	123
6.1a	Dimensions of racial attitudes	128
6.2a	Scale: general prejudice and stereotypes	130
6.3a	Scale: anti-Semitism	130
6.4a	Scale: social distance	130
6.5a	Scale: attitudes towards immigration	131
6.6a	Scale: attitudes towards equal rights for racial minorities	131
6.7a	Scale: personal agreement to discrimination	131
6.8a	Demography and racial prejudice	132
6.9a	Socio-cultural insecurities and racial prejudice	133

List of Tables xi

6.10a	Structural dispositions and racial prejudice	134
6.11a	Contact intensity and the level of racial prejudice	134
7.1	Normative choice: asymmetrical activation effects on positive evaluative judgements of blacks as a function of the interaction between education and political tolerance	148
7.2	Political choices: The immunising effects of support for 'Open Housing' in the face of competing values as a function of education and ideology	155
8.1	Aspects of blatant and subtle negative attitudes of the ethnic majority towards ethnic minorities	175
8.2	Ethnocentrism (answer categories: agree entirely; agree; do not agree, do not disagree; disagree; disagree entirely; never thought about)	186
8.3	Ethnocentrism: frequencies, factor analyses and reliability	187
8.4	Perceived threat of competition: items frequencies, factor analyses and reliability	190
8.5	Authoritarianism: items, frequencies, factor analyses and reliability	191
8.6	Political intolerance: items, frequencies, Mokken scale analyses	192
8.7	Opposition to affirmative action: items and frequencies	193
8.8	Percentage of agreement with blatant and subtle negative attitudes and percentage of opposition to affirmative action by education	196
8.9	Percentage of agreement with blatant and subtle negative attitudes and percentage of opposition to affirmative action by social class	196
8.10	Standardised parameter estimates of the structural equation model of the effects on opposition to affirmative action controlled for gender, age, religious denomination, and region and degree of urbanisation of place of residence	199
8.1a	From theoretical model to empirical model: actions and fit of the model	203

List of Contributors

Erica R. Gould is working towards her Ph.D. in the Department of Political Science at Stanford University, USA. She is working on a dissertation on the International Monetary Fund and a paper on post-war Germany and Japan. She completed her undergraduate at Cornell University, USA, from which she graduated *magna cum laude* with distinction in all subjects.

Florence Haegel is a tenured research assistant in the Fondation nationale des sciences politiques and is working in the CEVIPOF (Center for studies on French political life). She also teaches at the the Institut d'études politiques des Paris. Her current research focuses on political attitudes and activities in an urban context and on political parties (mainly rightwing). She has published a book *Un maire à Paris*, Paris (Presses de la Fondation nationale des sciences politiques, 1994).

Louk Hagendoorn chairs ERCOMER, the European Research Centre on Migration and Ethnic Relations, and is professor in the Faculty of Social Sciences, Utrecht University, the Netherlands. His research focuses on the social psychology of inter-group relations, political psychology and cross-cultural studies. Recent publications include: *European Nations and Nationalism* (edited with G. Csepeli, H. Dekker and R. Farnen, Ashgate, in press) and *The Perception of Russians* (co-authored with H. Linssen and S. Tumanov, forthcoming).

Aleksandra Jasinska-Kania is professor of sociology and head of General Sociology in the Faculty of Philosophy and Sociology, Warsaw University, Poland. She has held many visiting professorships in the USA and Europe. Publications include: 1 authored, 1 co-athored, 1 edited and 2 co-edited books, the most recent being *Nation–Power–Society* (edited with J. Raciborski, Warsaw: Scholar, 1996); 25 articles in English, and over 50 in various Polish publications. Her research focuses on comparative studies of value systems, national identity, nationalism and ethnic stereotypes. She is a member of the 'Democracy and Local Governance' international research programme steering committee, and head of the Polish group for the *European Values Study*.

Shervin Nekuee graduated in sociology from Utrecht University where he is working towards his Ph.D. He is also conducting an extended survey, to be completed in 2000, on prejudice towards migrants in the Netherlands. He is particularly interested in the development of explanatory models for prejudice and ethnic exclusion. He contributes to the public debate with articles in policy journals and newspapers. His most recent publication is: 'Subjective well-being, discrimination and cultural conflict: Iranians living in the Netherlands' in *Social Indicators* (with M. Verkuyten, 1999).

Pierangelo Peri lectures in methodology and techniques for social research in the School of Sociology, University of Trento, Italy. He has worked extensively in the field of cultural studies, mass media research, and racial prejudice with particular attention to methodological issues. Recent publications include: 'Italy: an Imperfect Union', in *European Nations and Nationalism* (Ashgate, in press).

Peer Scheepers is associate professor of sociology and special professor of social prejudice in the Faculty of Social Sciences, University of Nijmegen, the Netherlands. He has published extensively on (longitudinal trends regarding) ethnic prejudice and discrimination as well as on political and religious attitudes and behavior.

Paul Sniderman is professor of political science, Stanford University, California, USA (1969–). He has received numerous academic awards, including the American Political Science Association's Gladys M. Kammerer award for best political science publication in the field of US national policy (1998), the Gustavus Meyers Center award for outstanding book on the subject of human rights (1994), the International Society of Political Psychology's Harold D. Lasswell award for distinguished scientific life-time contribution to the study of political psychology (1998), and the Woodrow Wilson Foundation Prize (1992). He is the author of numerous publications, the most recent of which include *The Outsider* (with P. Peri, T. Piazza, and R. di Figuerido, in press), *Reaching Beyond Race* (with E.G. Carmines, 1997), and *The Clash of Rights: Liberty, Equality and Legitimacy in Liberal Democracy* (with J.F. Fletcher, P.H. Russell, and P.E. Tetlock, 1996).

Geneviève Verberk tutors and conducts research in the Department of Methodology, University of Nijmegen, the Netherlands. After graduating *cum laude* in sociology she completed her doctorate in 1998 on attitudes towards ethnic minorities. Her research focuses on the conceptualisation and measurement of the unfavorable attitudes that members of the ethnic majority have towards ethnic minorities, as well as investigating the causes and consequences of these attitudes.

Jürgen R. Winkler lectures in political sociology, political systems and comparative politics at the Institute of Political Science, Johannes Gutenberg University of Mainz, Germany. His main interests are elections, party systems, political extremism and comparative research. Recent publications include: *Sozialstruktur, politische Traditionen und Liberalismus* (1995), *Rechtsextremismus* (with J. Falter and H.-G. Jaschke, 1996), and *Jugend, Politik und Rechtsextremismus in Rheinland-Pfalz* (with S. Schumann, 1997).

Hans De Witte Ph.D. in psychology, head of the Labour Section of the Higher Institute of Labour Studies (Hoger Instituut voor de Arbeid (HIVA)), and staff member of the Centre of Community Psychology at Katolieke Universiteit-Leuven. His research fields include: racism and right wing extremism (attitudes, voting behaviour, participation in right wing organisations); working class culture, class consciousness; psychological consequences of unemployment and job insecurity for the individual and society; participation in trade unions. Recent publications include: *Bestrijding van racisme en rechts-extremisme. Wetenschappelijke bijdragen aan het maatschappelijk debate* (1997, Ed.); 'Strijd om klassen. Discussies over de relevantie van het klasse-begrip', *Tijdschrift voor Sociologie*, Special issue, nos 1&2 (1997, edited with I. Glorieux); and 'Belgium: a Diversity in Unity', in *European Nations and Nationalism* (Ashgate, in press).

Acknowledgements

This book is the result of a project initiated by the Dutch *Ministry for Public Health, Welfare and Sports*. The Ministry was interested in the preventive and corrective effect of education on racism and in the nature of such a possible effect. It was also concerned to know whether a general cross-national model could explain racism in Europe.

With these two questions in mind scholars from Belgium, France, Germany, Italy, the Netherlands, Poland and the USA were invited to present a paper based on data from nation-wide surveys in their countries. The invited participants, and contributors to this book were Erica R. Gould, USA; Florence Haegel, France; Louk Hagendoorn, the Netherlands; Aleksandra Jasinska-Kania, Poland; Shervin Nekuee, the Netherlands; Pierangelo Peri, Italy; Peer Scheepers, the Netherlands; Paul Sniderman, USA; Geneviève Verberk, the Netherlands; Jürgen R. Winkler, Germany; Hans De Witte, Belgium.

All these scholars were prominent in the field of research on prejudice, racism and ethnic relations, or were writing dissertations on these topics. The expert conference was organised by José Pepels and Shervin Nekuee and took place in October 1997 in Utrecht.

The papers from this conference formed the basis for the chapters in this book. We are grateful to Rachel Kress for correcting the English and preparing the texts for publication. We would like to thank Polskie Wydawnictwo Naukowe (Polish Scientific Publisher) for permission to use an extract from the 1996 *Nowa encyklopedia powszechna PWN* (New General Encyclopaedia), vol. 5, in Chapter Six of this book.

Louk Hagendoorn & Shervin Nekuee
Utrecht, September 1999

1 Introduction: A Model of the Effects of Education on Prejudice and Racism

LOUK HAGENDOORN

Education reduces racism

Imagine meeting a person who in commenting on the economic situation concludes that many things would be better if there were not so many foreigners in the country. Feeling uncomfortable, we might politely try to convince this new acquaintance that maybe other factors than just migrants contribute to the existing economic problems and, moreover, that the social costs of accommodating migrants are an unavoidable aspect of today's open economies. Such counter-arguments would at least signal our lack of sympathy for racist views. We might have reason to doubt, after all, that it is possible to really change such views because bigots are, after all, often rather persistent.

This is one side of the picture of prejudice: bigotry is hard to correct. There is also the reverse image of prejudice, however, that education can act as a remedy against prejudice. These two views of prejudice, that bigots are incurable and that education remedies prejudice are, of course, inconsistent. The 'incurable' view suggests that bigotry is deeply ingrained in personalities. The 'educational' view suggests that prejudice can be changed by proper education. Maybe the full picture, encompassing both these views, is that prejudice generally emerges at a young age and reflects the worldview of parents and family but that education can correct prejudice in a second stage of socialisation. A more dramatic role for education is hardly conceivable. The question is, however, whether this view of education is correct. To answer this question we asked scholars in the field of racism to provide an inventory of the factors contributing to prejudice in seven countries and to indicate the role of education in this process.

The following simple model summarises the results found on the effect of education on prejudice. Education seems to provide people with cognitive skills that allow them to better understand the world of nature and human interaction. These cognitive skills refer to the categorisation of events and entities, to the understanding of causal relations and to being able to predict the effect of an intended course of action. In principle, such knowledge is neutral and technical. In addition education transmits ideas about desired states of the world. This refers to values and norms. Generally, this aspect of education is less explicit. Hence, while education improves the cognitive abilities of people, it also provides people with specific goals to orient their abilities to. These two aspects, although fairly general in nature, may affect the specific ways in which people learn to think about a variety of specific subjects. One such subject is the presence and acceptance of migrants in society. Education affects their views on this topic by enhancing understanding of the background to ethnic and cultural differences and by presenting the presence and acceptance of migrants as a positive state of affairs.

This is the mechanism by which education is assumed to affect prejudice. The assumption is that the lower the level of education undergone by a given individual the lower the level of knowledge and cognitive skills he or she will possess with which to understand migrants and culturally deviant ethnic groups. Understanding is important because people are generally afraid of things that are unintelligible and alien. Moreover, the lack of appropriate cognitive skills may affect people's ability to comprehend the causal nature of social processes and thus migration in modern societies. This effect of education, a more adequate understanding of causal processes, can be called intrinsic in the sense that it emerges essentially from the educational process itself. People with a lower level of education express a greater reluctance towards immigrants because they lack enough information with which to perceive them as familiar as well as the level of cognitive skills to adequately understand the causes and effects of their presence.

However, there is another reason why people with lower levels of education may be aversive or negative with respect to migrants. Migrants are often over-represented among the less highly educated segments of society and therefore people in these strata expect, may, or will have to compete with migrants on the labour market. Thus, in so far as migrants are, rightly or wrongly, perceived as competitors, and in so far as less highly educated people are more likely to perceive them as such, the relationship between a lower level of education and prejudice will be reinforced. The reason for this additional effect may be either instrumental, people feel migrants to be a threat to their material interests, or psychological, in the sense that those less highly educated feel more easily threatened by alien groups. Yet, apart from its nature, the effect of perceived competition seems, given the place of migrants in the labour market, to reinforce the prejudices of less highly educated people in particular. Thus, technically speaking, this effect *interacts* with education.

In contrast, a higher level of education has a reductive effect on prejudice. Having further developed their cognitive skills, such people have a greater awareness of the complexities of the presence of migrants in modern societies and are therefore less amenable to prejudice. Moreover, the benefit of more education may be that people are more likely to value cultural diversity, tolerance and egalitarianism and to apply these values to specific choices and situations. Finally, more highly educated people are, precisely by virtue of their greater exposure to education, more sensitive to the high value placed on tolerance specifically towards minorities and the concurrent public rejection of prejudice and are therefore generally more aware of the negative consequences of blunt expressions of prejudice. In other words they will be more eager to conform to the norm of ethnic and racial tolerance. In summary, the more highly educated are less prone to prejudice because of their cognitive sophistication, because they have learned to appreciate values opposed to prejudice, because they are more able to apply values to decisions in specific situations, and due to their increased sensitivity to the norm of ethnic tolerance.

However, the positive effect education has on diminishing prejudice needs to be dealt with in greater detail. There are factors that may reinforce, or worse, undo the positive effects of cognitive skills or learned egalitarian values. For example political preferences that have their roots in earlier socialisation or which develop parallel to, but unaffected by, the educational process may immunise people against the positive effects of education mentioned above. Such political preferences then moderate the effect of education on prejudice. However, in the case of higher levels of education these moderator effects may not only affect the relationship between education and prejudice but also the form in which the prejudice is expressed. This regards the issue of so-called blatant and subtle prejudice. The idea is that more education may not reduce prejudice but only the manner in which prejudice is expressed. More highly educated people may simply have better learned to express themselves in accordance with shared norms about tolerance without actually sharing the feelings that should motivate that tolerance.

This issue of blatant and subtle expressions of intolerance requires a little more elaboration. It emerged post WWII in the United States when it appeared that racism, expressed through large-scale surveys, had consistently declined. Many scholars took this positive change at face value. Others doubted whether the change merely reflected the public's increasing awareness that racial prejudice was objectionable and thus the actual feelings behind the more careful expressions about ethnic groups had changed less than was suggested by the data (Kleinpenning & Hagendoorn, 1993). It was suggested that the more highly educated, in particular, were more sensitive to expressions that might otherwise be interpreted as racist. Hence the alarming hypothesis emerged that although the expressions of blatant and subtle racism were confusingly different, the feelings behind them were dangerously similar. Even more alarming was the observation that in comparison to blatant racism seemingly innocent expressions of subtle racism were indistinguishable from apparently acceptable political views. For example, the view that government assistance for minorities should be rejected. Such a viewpoint is similar to conservative political views favouring restraint in government intervention in general, including government assistance for minorities in particular. In contrast to these latter views, which are expressions of sincerely held political convictions, subtle racism expressed, through such views, a deeper lying apprehension towards minorities (Dovidio, 1993). The confusion created by the concept of subtle racism stems from the suggested similarity of the latent content of blatant and subtle racist beliefs, which blurs the distinction between politics and prejudice (Sniderman & Tetlock, 1986).

If we accept the possibility that education may change the expression of prejudice rather than the content, then our summary should include two possible additional interactions to the relationship between education and prejudice. The first reflects a learned sensitivity to a socially acceptable expression of socially unacceptable attitudes towards minorities. The second reflects an acceptable effect of political values, in particular of conservative views regarding government intervention. While the first effect is the result of an increased sensitivity to socially desirable behaviour resulting from a higher level of education, the second is an effect of conservatism persisting in spite of this.

Next to the crucial effect of education only a few other factors appear to affect prejudice significantly. Some of these factors interact with education. Social class, professional status, age, gender and contact with minorities affect prejudice independently from education, but most of these effects are not strong. More substantial is the effect of perceived economic threat, personality dispositions and value preferences. These three factors, however, interact with education and either reinforce the effect of being less highly educated or reduce the effect of a higher level of education. A third category of effects regards specific attitudes that mediate the effect of education, such as conformity, alienation, and localism. A higher level of education, for example, reduces alienation, conformity and localism. These attitudes, in turn, are linked to personality factors such as authoritarianism and thus indicate barriers faced by those wishing to use education to decrease or eradicate prejudice.

General education, or specific lessons on tolerance?

If education is, under most circumstances and in most countries, the social institution which effectively combats prejudice and, if more highly educated people are the least racist, does this imply that it could be more effective still to introduce special programmes about the dangers of racism into the educational system? The answer to this question is not obvious. One reason to doubt the necessity of special programmes is that a positive effect of education on tolerance was already apparent in surveys held in the decades immediately after WWII. At that time ethnic and racial tolerance was hardly a public issue, if at all, and there was no explicit content devoted to the teaching of racial tolerance. After this period, especially in the US, there were explicit efforts to address the issue of racial tolerance and to use the educational system to drive it home as a value. Although there is no empirical evidence that educational programmes on racial tolerance have been counterproductive, there is no evidence that they have been especially effective either. Moreover, in spite of such programmes data from the US shows that recently educated youth are no more racially tolerant than their post-war peers. Although many factors may have contributed to this outcome, it should also be considered that many of the programmes addressing the issue of racial tolerance may have politicised the racial issue instead of solving it, thereby contributing to emerging feelings of resentment.

Why an effect of education?

That education plays an important role in reducing prejudice does not indicate which aspects of education evoke the effect. Let us make an inventory of the possible aspects that may play a role. In the first place a higher level of education implies more accumulated knowledge. This refers to the time invested in transmitting this knowledge, hence to the duration of the education, indicated by the number of years spent in education. More education can also imply more advanced knowledge, depending on the type of schooling followed. In many countries there are various levels in the school-system into which students enter and leave at roughly the same age. For example, the secondary school system in the Netherlands has three parallel levels beginning after primary school: general secondary education (MAVO), higher secondary education giving access to further professional education (HAVO), and preparatory academic secondary education giving access to university (VWO). Futhermore, education can differ in teaching methods, the mix of courses on offer and in the degree of active and critical participation required of the pupils. The effect of such aspects is suggested by evidence that education which does not stimulate pupils' critical capacities has no effect on narrow-minded attitudes, in spite of the number of years of education (Vogt, 1997, p.73). Finally curricula can differ in content. For example, history courses in the curriculum may implicitly transmit nationalistic values while courses on the multicultural society, or on political and social tolerance can be used to redress prejudice.

Most research on education and prejudice uses the total years spent in formal schooling as an indication of the level of education acquired. What is clear is that the number of years of formal schooling is directly related to ethnic and racial tolerance (Hyman & Wright, 1979; Nunn, Crockett & Williams, 1973). There is also evidence that the effect of education differs with the level achieved (Ekehammer et al., 1987; Mattyssen et al., 1986). Much less is known about the effect of different teaching methods and the content of the curriculum. However, the existing evidence is sufficient to conclude that there is an intrinsic effect of education on prejudice, intrinsic in the sense that it is not specifically the content of the acquired knowledge and skills which affect prejudice, but rather the amount and quality of them. It is remarkable that in spite of the substantive evidence for this intrinsic effect of education there is no research indicating which mechanism leads to this outcome. Instead we have to work with the interpretation suggesting that the crucial factor is that education teaches people how to categorise theoretical and empirical entities and understand their causal relations. In other words education leads to cognitive complexity and cognitive sophistication. This makes it possible to apply more sophisticated cognitive frameworks to ethnic and race relations in modern societies and thus to be able to understand the complexities of the situation of ethnic and racial minorities (see also Vogt, 1979). Whereas much prejudice consists of the application of faulty causal schemes, the improvement of understanding complex causal processes can redress the faulty conclusions as well. However, the essential role played by cognitive skills in the effect education has on prejudice, has, remarkably enough, not yet been tested explicitly.

Thus far the model explaining the effect of education on the reduction of prejudice emerging from the contributions in this book. The model seems valid across a number of European countries as well as the US. We will now illustrate how the specific contributions of the various authors fit the model.

Education and cognitive sophistication

The thesis that education leads to cognitive sophistication and thereby to a more adequate understanding of the reality of migrants and ethnic minorities in modern societies and thus reduces prejudice is brought forward by *Pierangelo Peri*. But, *Peri* also mentions a secondary effect, that education also transmits values and norms counteracting prejudice. In modern democratic societies these transmitted values are equality, individual freedom and tolerance for different opinions and lifestyles. Yet there are not only intrinsic but also extrinsic effects of education that may affect prejudice. Less highly educated people often have to compete with migrants and other minority groups on the labour market and in other spheres of life such as housing and education. The perceived competitive relationship to minority groups may reinforce existing prejudice. Hence, prejudice in *Peri's* view originates from two sources, first a lack of appropriate cognitive skills and values and second, an economic threat.

These possible intrinsic and extrinsic effects of education on prejudice were tested on data from a representative sample of 2000 Italians in 1994. It appeared, first, that more years of formal education leads to substantially less prejudice towards migrants. This effect was partially direct, signalling an intrinsic effect of education, probably due to increased cognitive sophistication. But the effect was also partially indirect, namely due to reduced conformity and conservatism. Moreover, professional status exerted a small effect indicating that increased competitive capabilities also reduce prejudice. The results thus show that education is important for reducing prejudice: its effect is substantial and, moreover, mainly intrinsic. In other words education reduces prejudice by increasing cognitive sophistication and by stressing the value of independent judgement. In addition the higher professional status made possible by a higher level of education, which probably reduces the perceived threat of minorities, also reduces prejudice.

Acquiring values through education

Just how important education is for the transmission of values is elaborated in chapter three by *Florence Haegel*. She examines how the French school system socialises pupils in the so-called 'republican model', a system of values centred around equality, tolerance and universality. Republican values articulate the individual relationship between citizens and the state and thereby deny the relevance of ethnicity. They aim to integrate all inhabitants of France as equal citizens. *Haegel* posits that formal education is not enough to redress prejudice but that the transmission of republican values is the crucial factor. By the same token, however, the transmission of values at school is not an unequivocal process. The transmitted system of republican values may either match the value system into which the individual is socialised at home or not. Education will be more effective in reducing prejudice among pupils who have learned values at home consistent with the egalitarian republican model than among those who have learned contradictory values.

Based on data from surveys of the Centre d'Etude de la Vie Politique Francaise (CEVIPOV) in France in 1988, 1995 and 1997 *Haegel* shows that education is the strongest predictor of prejudice. Compared to education the effects of age, socio-economic background, profession, religion and gender are marginal. However, education affects people whose parents have right wing political preferences far less than those with parents whose political preferences lean to the left. Yet, this effect is pertinent only for those with a higher level of education; among less highly educated people the parents' political values exert hardly any effect on prejudice. Among more highly educated people the parents' right wing preferences seem to neutralise the effect of the republican values taught in school while left wing ones reinforce the effect of education. This suggests that primary socialisation interacts with the effect of education. Another indication that primary socialisation is important for the effect of education is that more highly educated generations born before WWII, when republican values were associated to a greater degree with nationalism and colonialism, are more prejudiced than are those born post WWII. In summary, *Haegel* shows an important interaction between education and pre-existing political preferences and values and their effect on prejudice.

Why cognitive sophistication counteracts prejudice

The main reason why education counteracts prejudice is, as we saw before, that it leads to a more adequate understanding of reality. Education transmits information and cognitive skills that correct wrong ideas and simplistic attributions. The hypothesis is that people who have these skills will also be able to analyse the situation of migrants and minorities in modern societies with a greater degree of sophistication and therefore be less prejudiced. Convincing as this may sound it is rather abstract and may be naive. The assumption is that those who have learned the insights and skills will also apply them to the context of migrants. In chapter four *Hans De Witte* considers an alternative effect, that by increasing knowledge and cognitive skills education implicitly transforms attitudes related to prejudice. This thesis is analysed using two representative surveys done in Belgium in 1989 and 1991.

It appears that the effect of education on reducing prejudice is massive. It completely overshadows the effect of other factors such as social class, gender, age, or living in an urban environment. But it also appears to coincide with the change of specific attitudes related to prejudice. The results of one survey suggest that the effect of education is to transform these attitudes, those of the other survey suggest that there is also a direct effect of education on prejudice. The interpretation of these results is that formal schooling leads, possibly in three different ways, to more tolerance. First, education contributes to the development of cognitive skills and sophistication. This in turn adds to the understanding of the causal dynamics of social life, the causes and effects of migration and thus undermines oversimplified representations of migrants. Second, education informs pupils about the complexity and variety of social life. Information contributes to feelings of efficacy, control and the ability to understand and properly evaluate different behavioural and cultural models. This also reduces prejudice. Third, education transmits values such as equality, justice and solidarity. Such values are inconsistent with prejudice and therefore tend to reduce prejudice.

The effect of education is general across countries

That increased formal education reduces prejudice in most European countries is an effect also found in Poland. *Aleksandra Jasinska-Kania's* analysis of Polish opinion surveys, in chapter five, confirms the model found in most Western European countries, in which education is the most important factor explaining prejudice (after urbanisation). In Poland highly educated Poles perceive fewer national groups as different from the Poles, maintain less social distance from them and feel less negative towards them.

The analysis made by *Jasinska-Kania* of the *European Values Study* held across a large number of European countries in 1990 indicates that in all countries formal education leads to greater tolerance towards migrant groups and ethnic minorities. The crucial factors affecting tolerance are educational level, professional status and occupational opportunities. In harmony with the intrinsic and extrinsic effects of education mentioned above, more highly educated people are less prejudiced because of increased intellectual capabilities, increased occupational opportunities and a decreased fear of professional competition. Less prejudiced people also appear to be more trustful and less focused on their local sphere of activity.

However, there are also effects that differ from the general model. This regards reactions towards specific groups such as Jews and Muslims. On the whole, it is not education but gender, professional status and urbanisation that determine social distance towards these groups. This outcome suggests that although the pattern of factors associated with prejudice is similar across countries, it may differ for specific behavioural consequences of prejudice, as well as for specific groups and under specific circumstances. In other words, the model is valid for prejudice in general and groups in general, but it may differ if any of these categories is specified. This conclusion is also borne out in terms of the characteristics of prejudice and tolerance. People may be tolerant in general and express that attitude generally, but this does not mean that they are always tolerant in all respects to all groups in all possible situations (Sniderman, Tetlock, Glaser, Green & Hout, 1989). This raises the question whether these aspects of prejudice and tolerance, general, situational and specific, should be differentiated and how important this would be for understanding the dynamics and consequences of prejudice.

Prejudice and categorisation

Prejudice reflects a specific, generally negative, attitude towards groups that *differ* in *significant* aspects from the group one belongs to. The question is what is significant and which differences count? For an answer to the first question we refer to theories on inter-group perception as developed by Turner and Oakes (Turner, Hogg, Oakes, Reicher & Wetherell, 1987; Oakes, Haslam& Turner, 1994). Here we will concentrate exclusively on the second question, which refers to the object of prejudice, namely the target group towards which a person is prejudiced. The answer is seemingly simple because the object is migrants, ethnic minorities, or foreigners. However, on reflection, these 'objects' are not so 'objective'. First, within these general categories numerous more specific group distinctions can be made, added to which people seem to use more general or more specific categorisations in a flexible manner as befits their prejudiced purposes. Second, who is coded a migrant or foreigner is to a certain degree subjective. Is a Jew whose parents came to the Netherlands in the seventeenth century to be considered a migrant? Is a Moroccan whose parents came in the 1970s, but who speaks Dutch and holds a Dutch passport a foreigner? These examples suggest that prejudice itself may affect the narrowness of the categories used by affecting how strict the criteria of difference applied will be. Prejudiced people generally have a narrow definition of who belongs to the ingroup and are less concerned about what are perceived as minor differences among outgroups. In that sense their evaluations of different outgroups are often interchangeable.

The idea that prejudiced people do not differentiate much in their evaluations of outgroups does not only fit a common sense view of prejudice, it is also the view of famous scholars in the field of prejudice (for example see Adorno, Frenkel-Brunswik, Levinson, & Sanford, 1950; Allport, 1954). Their idea was that the essence of prejudice is precisely its unspecific nature, unspecific even to the extent that prejudiced people will react in a prejudiced way towards purely imaginary groups if the label indicating such groups sounds exotic or alien. Hence, in this view prejudice always refers to outgroups or aliens in general and the attitude towards these groups is more or less similar.

Yet, this is only half the truth. Who could deny that there are actual social and cultural differences between ethnic and national groups and that almost everybody is aware of them? Hence collective representations of typical group characteristics reflect the reality of these differences. These representations may provide a prototype of the outsider per se but also unavoidably define who are outsiders and to what degree. Such representations naturally vary across countries and in time. The question is should these representations be taken into account in understanding the nature of prejudice?

In one sense the answer is yes, in another sense it is no. It is yes in the sense that the study of these collective representations is the task of anthropologists (Hagendoorn, 1995). It is no in the sense that the development of general theories about the causes of negative attitudes towards outsiders is the task of sociologists, social psychologists and political scientists. General theories should be general; in other words they should apply to a wide range of specific groups categorised as outsiders. What can be explained is why people have negative attitudes towards these outsiders, of whatever kind, and act in accordance with these and the limitations of the particular situation. The intrinsic abstractness of that which has to be explained—prejudice—implies that the consequences of prejudice may be specific, but the causes should be general. This implies, in turn, that it is necessary on the one hand to determine the common denominator of all related manifestations and consequences of prejudice, while, on the other, it is equally necessary to be as specific as possible about the different causes of prejudice. If this is a sensible approach then the first equally sensible question is whether or not there is a common denominator of prejudice.

The abstract nature of prejudice

Jürgen Winkler addresses this question in chapter six, using nation-wide survey data collected in Germany in 1996. The survey measured different aspects of prejudice with regard to a large number of minority groups namely: stereotypes, negative attitudes towards minorities and immigration, social distance, granting rights to foreign groups and discriminatory behaviour. Questions referred to foreigners, asylum-seekers, German immigrants from Eastern Europe, Turks, Jews and Italians. It appeared that the aspects were indeed different, forming seven separate internally consistent attitude clusters. But one component, referring to generalised prejudice and stereotypes, was dominant. This indicates that more specific attitudes crystallise around generalised prejudice, specifying feelings about possible consequences and behavioural reactions evolving from the core attitude. Obviously the core and the specific attitudes are differently affected by external factors. For example education reduced negative attitudes towards immigration to a greater degree than it diminished general prejudice. But by the same token the core and the specific attitudes have much in common. After determining the common denominator using secondary factor analysis, subsequent regression indicated that only education, age, region, urbanism and occupation had a significant affect on (this common denominator of) prejudice. The most important effect was that in Germany older and less highly educated individuals are more prejudiced than younger and more highly educated individuals.

Dispositions are not easily modified by education

In line with prevalent theories on prejudice *Winkler* assumed that prejudice is in essence the result of two types of factors, namely socio-economic insecurity and authoritarian attitudes. The core of the socio-economic insecurity complex was determined using secondary factor analysis of more specific attitudes with regard to work, the economy, economic position, economic threat and trust in society, politics and justice. In a similar way the essence of the attitudinal disposition was determined by locating the common denominator of authoritarian values, right wing beliefs and national pride. Subsequently the effect of these two powerful predictors, as well as the demographic factors, perceived group differences and contact with migrants, was assessed. The result was a net effect of only five factors on general prejudice: education, attitudinal disposition, socio-structural insecurity, perceived group differences, and contact.

In so doing the place of education in this model was clarified. Education had only a small direct effect on prejudice. Its effect via socio-structural insecurity and attitudinal disposition was much stronger. In other words, education intrinsically reduces prejudice, but does so mainly by removing feelings of socio-structural insecurity and undermining conservative, authoritarian dispositions. It appeared that if less highly educated people were prejudiced they were more insecure and authoritarian, while among more highly educated people prejudice was determined by an authoritarian disposition alone. Thus demonstrating that education affects prejudice, but in specific ways. First, education directly reduces prejudice, possibly through the development of cognitive skills. But this effect is small. Second, education reduces socio-economic insecurity and breaks down authoritarian dispositions. Third, education is not always effective in breaking down authoritarian dispositions: among the more highly educated such dispositions may persist, counteracting the reduction of prejudice.

These elegant results nicely fit the 'double interaction model' elaborated above. Having a lower level of education causes people to feel more vulnerable to (perceived) competition by migrants and this reinforces prejudice. A higher level of education provides the skills necessary for understanding the situation of migrants in society, changing attitudes and values accordingly, and provides an entry-ticket to the labour market, altogether resulting in less prejudice. But education is not always effective in socialising the more highly educated in values which diminish prejudice and this is when prejudice and racism persist.

When values matter

Generally values acquired through socialisation are rather abstract. Freedom, tolerance and equality are principles that have a wide range of application. Moreover, one value can contradict another value and often choices have to be made. Hence, endorsing a certain value does not necessarily mean living by it. This leads to the question of whether education, apart from transmitting values, also teaches people how to apply them as guiding principles in speci-

14 *Education and Racism*

fic circumstances. *Paul Sniderman* and *Erica R. Gould*'s focus in chapter seven is therefore not so much on whether education transmits values leading to tolerance, but rather on whether education furthers the ability to translate abstract values into concrete choices.

Sniderman and *Gould* argue that choices are of two types: normative choices which are by definition one-sided (good or bad/wrong or right) and political choices which are by definition two-sided (good and good). Values regulate these choices. Tolerance is a one-sided normative choice, principally regulated by the value of political liberty. Education may contribute to understanding that the abstract notion of political liberty concretely implies tolerance towards ethnic minorities. In contrast to one-sided normative choices there are two-sided political ones, for example, a choice for the left or for the right. Here the pressure of education towards logical consistency does not work in one direction but can work either way. The implication of this bilateral structure of choice is that a higher level of education might immunise (some) people against values which do not fit with their political preferences, even if these values imply tolerance.

Using fascinatingly designed experiments in their survey *Sniderman* and *Gould* try to determine the effect of education on the consistent application of values to choices. They confront respondents with the choice to react positively or negatively to blacks in specific situations. The question being how does education affect the choice made: by promoting the value of racial tolerance; by promoting the more fundamental value of political tolerance; or, by increasing the likelihood that people will apply the idea of political tolerance to race relations. The last of these three possibilities refers to an interaction effect in which a higher level of education increases the likelihood that the principle of political tolerance will be consistently applied in situations and will result in a specific choice for racial tolerance. The experiments indicated that more highly educated people do indeed manifest all three of the effects mentioned: they were more politically tolerant in general, more tolerant in racial matters, and more readily applied the concept of political tolerance to issues of race. This was dramatically shown when respondents had to choose between favouring or rejecting government assistance for blacks and women. It appeared that among the less highly educated respondents, conservatives as well as liberals reacted in a discriminatory way, favouring government assistance for women more than for blacks. But the more highly educated respondents favoured government measures for blacks and women equally, although liberals were more likely than conservatives to favour government assistance for both blacks and women. Hence, education stimulated liberals as well as conservatives to apply their political values more consistently to the specific issue of government assistance for blacks and women.

However, there also appeared to be limits to the application of learned values to specific issues. In a third experiment conservatives and liberals were asked their opinion about a law forbidding homeowners to take the racial characteristics of potential buyers into account when selling their house. In two versions of the question (two experimental conditions) the respondents were asked to consider either homeowners' freedom to handle their property as they wished, or the responsibility of the government to guarantee equal treatment of blacks on the housing market. This articulated one of two possible values: property rights versus government responsibility for attaining equality. The idea was that more highly educated people in particular would take these values into account, especially when the values coincided with pre-existing political beliefs (conservative beliefs with property values and liberal with government responsibility). It appeared that more highly educated liberals were indeed immune to the evocation of property values. However, more highly educated conservatives were not immunised against the evocation of government responsibility, rather this evoked value had no effect at all. Hence, merely relying on the evocation of a value is not enough, as an individual's pre-existing political beliefs may hold more sway. Sound arguments are required for an evoked value to have an effect on the evaluation of an issue, otherwise the value will not be applied at all.

The *Sniderman–Gould* experiments illustrate how a higher level of education contributes to relating abstract values to more specific issues such as those of minorities, and thereby reduces prejudice. However, the experiments also indicate just how confusingly prejudice and political choices may be intertwined. People may object to government assistance for minorities either because they object to the presence of minorities, or because they simply object to government assistance. If the objection is categorised as prejudice without taking into account the reason for the objection then this leads not only to mistaking a political choice for a moral one, but also to overlooking the positive effects of a higher level of education.

The limits of prejudice

Some researchers are certain that racism has increasingly concealed itself behind ostensibly acceptable objections against assistance for minorities from the public purse, as we saw above (Crosby, 1994). Others reject that view and argue that what some perceive as hidden manifestations of racism actually are legitimate political choices. They say that people may reject affirmative action programmes because they object to government assistance of minority groups, or are against government intervention across the board, or because they are against the idea of a multicultural society in which different groups have different rights.

The issue of subtle racism reflects directly on the relationship between education and racism because it is the more highly educated who, perhaps able to read the sign of the times, have become more careful in their expression of racism. Hence there are two questions to address. First, are obvious expressions of subtle racism really racism, and second, are subtle forms of racism more prevalent among the more highly educated. If subtle racism is indeed racism and if more highly educated people support subtle racist views to the same extent as less highly educated people support blatant racist views than the seemingly positive effect of education on ethnic tolerance might be a chimera. If subtle racism is not (always or necessarily) racism then what it actually is becomes the crucial question.

In chapter eight of this book *Geneviève Verberk* and *Peer Scheepers* address these questions. Ethnic minorities in the Netherlands and Dutch students were both interviewed about their experience of subtle and blatant racism expressed by the Dutch. The study revealed that the blatant racist syndrome consisted of feelings of superiority, negative stereotypes and the discounting of positive exceptions to stereotyped minority behaviour. The more complex subtle racist syndrome manifested itself in a paternalistic concern for minorities, exaggeration of cultural differences, feelings of uneasiness, positive over-evaluation of superficial exotic characteristics of minorities, denial of negative feelings, and detached tolerance. Dutch 'subtle racism' thus seemed to be mundane and psychological rather than political in content. The fundamental question was whether blatant and subtle racist attitudes really are empirically distinct. This was tested on data from a nation-wide survey among Dutch adults in 1995.

The results were puzzling. It appeared that all characteristics of subtle and blatant racism formed one cluster, except for positive over-evaluation of superficial exotic characteristics of minorities and detached tolerance. The question is whether a positive reaction to exotic traits and detached tolerance alone constitute subtle racism. An argument in favour of a subtle racist interpretation was that these two positive and apparently innocent reactions correlated positively with blatant racism. Thus the authors generously gave the subtle racism concept the benefit of the doubt and tested the relationship of both forms of racism with education. In descriptive terms the outcome was enlightening. While less highly educated people were more likely to agree with blatant as well as subtle racist statements than those more highly educated, who rejected both, there was a middle-level educational category prominent in the subtle, but not the blatant, racism category. This suggests that subtle racism does exist as a distinct reaction towards ethnic minorities. Therefore it was relevant to determine whether this (curvilinear) effect of education persists if other factors affecting blatant and subtle racism are considered simultaneously. These other factors regarded attitudes and background variables.

Education may change the expression of prejudice

It appeared that a higher level of education diminishes the endorsement of blatant as well as subtle racist views by reducing the tendency towards authoritarianism and to perceive minorities as a threat, and by increasing political tolerance. This confirms the intrinsic effects of more education on attitudes and values and the extrinsic effect of perceived competition; findings confirmed by the other authors. However, there was one difference, a direct net effect of education was evident for subtle racism but not for blatant racism. This (small) direct effect of education on subtle racism might indicate that either more highly educated people are more cautious in expressing blatant racism, or that they genuinely appreciate ethnic minorities (given the content of the scale). However the likelihood of the latter is diminished by the finding that subtle racism was related to authoritarianism, political intolerance and perceived threat.

But there were other differences. Perceived threat had a much stronger effect on blatant than on subtle racism and the rejection of affirmative action was determined by perceived threat and subtle racism but not by blatant racism. In other words, less highly educated people are more blatantly racist and they seem to be against affirmative action because they perceive ethnic minorities as a competitive threat. In contrast, people who have finished intermediate levels of education have more subtle racist views and, to the extent that they have these views, they are also less supportive of affirmative action. Yet, this specific effect of subtle racism is not great itself if the widespread opposition to affirmative action in the Netherlands is taken into account.

Lessons on education

This overview of the findings presented here clarifies several things. First, prejudice and racism manifest themselves in similar ways in different countries and the factors determining and reinforcing these feelings and reactions are similar. This suggests that issues of prejudice and racism are essentially of the same nature across the European Union, Poland and the United States. This is remarkable because it means that the conclusions made are applicable not only to typical Western-European immigration countries, but also to a former communist country and to a country with inter-group relations of a more distinctly racial nature.

Second, education does indeed have a crucial effect on prejudice and racism. It appears that the more highly developed cognitive skills and competencies gained during the educational process enables people to positively appraise the situation of migrants and minorities. Moreover, a higher level of education appears to correct conventional, authoritarian and localised frames of reference in which migrants and minorities are given no space. Education also transmits values contributing to the acceptance of minorities as equal citizens and teaches people to apply values, otherwise abstractly held, to issues of ethnic and racial tolerance.

Third, education affects prejudice and racism for external reasons. It offers people an entry-ticket to the labour market and reduces the fear of competition from migrants and minorities. However, this effect might be temporary one, liable to wear off once migrants enter the higher levels of the educational system and begin to compete with the more highly educated.

Finally, there are limitations to the positive effects of education. Education may be ineffective when values and dispositions denying equality to migrants have been deeply engraved in pre-school years, immunising pupils against the positive effects of education. Furthermore the effect of education may also lead to little more than restraint in the expression of prejudice rather than to a veritable change in the perception of minorities. The effect of education may also be counteracted by political beliefs. Diagram 1.1 summarises all the effects.

Education is many things. Besides the number of years and the level achieved, its characteristics include the content of the curriculum, the school climate, and the manner of instruction. Which of these additional aspects also contribute to the final positive effect of education on tolerance is difficult to say. There is no evidence that special courses on migrants, minorities and racism really contribute to the positive effect of education. One could imagine that courses about the conditions, operation, and procedures of democracy, about the history and values underpinning democracy and practical training leading to respect for the opinions of others could be more effective ways to counteract prejudice. And so, perhaps political science, law or argumentation theory might be more effective for combating prejudice than lecturing on minorities and the multicultural society.

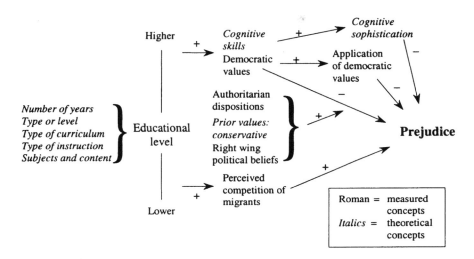

Diagram 1.1   Model of the possible effects of education on prejudice

References

Adorno, T., Frenkel-Brunswik, E., Levinson, D. and Sanford, R. (1950), *The Authoritarian Personality*, New York, Harper & Row.
Allport, G. (1954), *The Nature of Prejudice*, Cambridge MA, Addison Wesley.
Crosby, F. (1994), 'Understanding Affirmative Action', *Basic and Applied Social Psychology*, 15, pp. 13–41.
Dovidio, J. (1993), 'The Subtlety of Racism', *Training and Development*, 47, pp. 50–56.
Ekehammar, B., Nilsson, I. and Sidanius, J. (1987), 'Education and Ideology: Basic Aspects of Education Related to Adolescents' Sociopolitical Attitudes', *Political Psychology*, vol. 8, no. 3, pp. 395–410.
Hagendoorn, L. (1995), 'Inter-Group Biases in Multiple Group Systems: the Perception of Ethnic hierarchies ', *European Review of Social Psychology*, 6, pp. 199–228.
Hyman, H. and Wright, C. (1979), *Education's Lasting Influence on Values*, Chicago, University of Chicago Press
Kleinpenning, G. and Hagendoorn, L. (1993), 'Forms of Racism and the Cumulative Dimension of Ethnic Attitudes', *Social Psychology Quarterly*, 56, pp. 21–36.
Mattyssen, M., Meeus, W. and Van Wel, F. (1986) *Beelden van Jeugd* [Images of Adolescents], Groningen, Wolters Noordhof.
Nunn, C., Crockett, H. and Williams, J. (1978), *Tolerance for Non-Conformity: a National Survey of Americans' Changing Commitment to Civil Liberties*, San Francisco, Jossey-Bass.

Oakes, P., Haslam, A. and Turner, J. (1994), *Stereotyping and Social Reality*, Oxford, Blackwell.
Simpson, M. (1972), 'Authoritarianism and Education: a Comparative Approach', *Sociometry*, 35, pp. 223–234.
Sniderman, P. and Tetlock, P. (1986), 'Symbolic Racism: Problems of Motive Attribution in Political Analysis', *Journal of Social Issues*, 42, pp. 129–150.
Sniderman, P., Tetlock, P., Glaser, J., Green, D. and Hout, M. (1989), 'Principled Tolerance and the American Mass Public', *British Journal of Political Science* 19, pp. 25–45.
Turner, J., Hogg, M., Oakes, P., Reicher, S. and Wetherell, M. (1987), *Rediscovering the Social Group: a Self-Categorization Theory*, Oxford, Blackwell.
Vogt, W. (1997), *Tolerance and Education*, London, Sage.

2 Education and Prejudice against Immigrants

PIERANGELO PERI

Prejudice and schooling

That there is a link between prejudice and educational level has been demonstrated, in various countries since WWII, by empirical surveys exploring the presence and dynamics of ethnic and racial prejudice (Hyman & Sheatsley, 1964; Marx, 1967; Middletown, 1976; Quinley & Glock, 1979; Selznick & Steimberg, 1969; Bagley & Verma, 1979; Wagner & Schonbach, 1984; Beswick & Hill, 1972; Hampel & Krupp, 1977). Thus, that a higher level of education is associated with a lower level of prejudice is widely acknowledged. However, it should be pointed out that Stember's (1961) analysis of US research on prejudice and schooling and later studies directly influenced by it, found that, in some cases, the relationship was tenuous, for reasons often to do with the measurements used to represent prejudice (see Duckitt, 1992, p. 183). When analysing the relation between racism and education using empirical data, certain theoretical and methodological factors should be taken into account, such as the concept of prejudice used and its application in measurement scales to give a valid and reliable representation of the concept. This, together with sample variability and the sociocultural contexts in which the research is conducted, may help explain the differences found in the relationship between prejudice and education. I shall not discuss the development of the debate on this relationship here because not only is it well known but several satisfactory reviews of the topic are available (for example, Duckitt, 1992). Rather, I wish to discuss the significance and nature of this relationship, using data from a 1994 Italian survey on ethnic and racial prejudice, 'Regional and Ethnic Prejudice in Italy'.[1]

Prejudice as a category

Any attempt to explain the relationship between prejudice and schooling requires an examination of the concept prejudice, its nature and its origin. It should be borne in mind that the concept prejudice is open to numerous interpretations and definitions. The social sciences—sociology and social psychology, in particular—have made extensive use of the term when describing and interpreting relations and conflicts among groups. Indeed, Milner (1981) pointed out that there are as many definitions in the literature as there are studies of the problem. The term prejudice is frequently used as a synonym for stereotype, a concept especially favoured by cognitive psychology.

The etymology of the term (from Latin *praejudicum*, a judgement formed a priori), however, does not necessarily imply a negative value judgement. We may start from the premise that an a priori judgement is formulated about something that is or is not known well enough to form a definitive positive or negative judgement. Reality, like the structure of social relationships, is highly complex, and individuals as social actors perform their roles and interpret reality on the basis of cognitive categories already given to them. When knowledge is lacking, when the situation is difficult to control or when it is difficult or impossible to use complex interpretative categories, there is no alternative but to rely on cognitive categories which, although simple and crude, nevertheless provide guidance on how to react to a particular situation, how to assess it and how to adjust one's behaviour. The level of simplicity may range from crude dichotomies (good/bad, honest/dishonest, hostile/friendly, etc.) to more sophisticated judgements (where the prejudice is considered susceptible to proof). Whatever the case may be, these are all generalisations which are improperly extended to persons or groups. They are often not objectively verified but socially constructed. Nevertheless, they determine and guide, at least initially, attitudes and behaviour; they activate and legitimate hostility, intolerance, discrimination, and racism.

This immediately raises the problem of sources of prejudice. One must ask what these simplifications are based on, rather than investigate the events or facts that evoke them (an interesting topic but one only relevant to particular types of prejudice). The answer is in line with the standard tenets of the social sciences. Prejudice originates from socialisation within a particular culture or group that transmits its norms, values and reference models to younger generations. Thus, individuals internalise the prejudices and stereotypes of the culture to which they belong. These prejudices and stereotypes provide useful first-level guidance on how to behave in social situations. In other words, prejudice is socially constructed by a group, membership of which is transmitted to new members of the group by socialisation. It provides preliminary orientation regarding behaviour and values yet to be modified by the individual's ability to acquire a critical attitude and the intellectual ability to manipulate complex categories. In other words, it depends on the individual's inability to draw on a 'cognitive complexity' (MacNeil, 1974) permitting sophisticated analysis of problems and the differentiation of the rigid simplifications inherent in stereotypical images. If the opportunities to develop these capacities did not occur, the only option is to fall back on the base input, which is deemed legitimate because it is rooted in the group's version of common sense. These attitudes, which determine interpretation and thus behaviour, are then applied to new phenomena, causing them to be represented with the concepts, values and stereotypes common to the group. Added to this, there are effects of interpersonal communication and of judgements and prejudices relevant to the specific social setting. In the absence of opportunities or the ability to verify opinions—or more simply in the absence of a critical capacity—the assessments, attitudes and sentiments of the group to which the individual belongs are borrowed and deemed legitimate merely because they are widespread and widely endorsed. A 'factual proof', either based on direct personal experience or experiences of significant others, may finally validate these improper and unjust generalisations. Thus one's own or someone else's experience (usually negative) with one or more members of another group is simplistically extended to all members of that group.

At this point, one might ask whether a society or a group can or could ever be immune to prejudice. So far, the answer seems to be 'no'. Because, as said, when prejudice is defined as a form of preliminary orientation it appears to be a necessary conceptual category when dealing with a complex reality in the absence of sufficient knowledge. When added to the frequent refusal of individuals to alter their prejudiced attitudes even in the face of objective proof, the difficulty encountered in subjecting the concept prejudice to critical analysis underscores the difficulties faced in combating the phenomena. This is confirmed by the finding that when reality and personal experience contradict the prejudice, they are often dismissed as an exception, leaving the prejudice intact. Linguistically, this attitude translates into expressions like 'although...it is...' or '...is...but...'.

Earlier I pointed out that prejudice may be either positive or negative. However, although they play a part in guiding individual behaviour, positive prejudices in social discourse or communication are rarely considered. The greater emphasis placed on things to be wary of, or to protect oneself against, than on those to be viewed favourably, has caused the term 'prejudice' to be associated only with negative attitudes, both in everyday and academic discourse.

Prejudice and formal education

Assuming this approach to the dynamics of prejudice is valid, then the search for an explanation for the relationship between prejudice and schooling becomes relatively straightforward. The interpretative key is the extent to which exposure to the educational process produces:

- knowledge and information
- cognitive sophistication, and the capacity to manipulate complex conceptual categories
- tolerance of, and openness towards, democratic principles and liberal values.

As I stated earlier, reliance on prejudice and stereotypical images becomes inevitable when a person lacks sufficient knowledge about the phenomenon at hand. One of the principal purposes of formal education is to increase knowledge. It does so by bringing the individual into contact with problems and worlds often very distant from his or her everyday reality, helping to create a knowledge base on which s/he can draw when required to construe new realities. Knowledge thus raises a barrier against recourse to erroneous images based on presumed characteristics (Milner, 1981), against misinformation (Kelman & Pettigrew, 1959), and against erroneous attributions. In the specific case of ethnic and racial prejudice, it has been shown (Stephen & Stephen, 1984) that access to information on minorities and ethnic groups substantially reduces prejudice. Ignorance, therefore, is the enemy, and the more prolonged the exposure to the educational process, the wider the spectrum of knowledge and information becomes. Considering that upper secondary education coincides with a life-phase in which an individual develops a 'style' with which to address and analyse reality, one understands why education leaves an indelible imprint.

I have also stressed that prolonged formal education develops the capacity to sift and integrate information flows from the educational institution and the outside world. This capacity is augmented by the exercise of intellectual activity which allows the person to reach a level of cognitive complexity at which s/he is not reliant on forms of simplification which foster a stereotypical view of reality. As Duckitt (1992) reports, this point has been forcefully made by a number of studies (Gardiner, 1972; Sidanius, 1985; Tetlock, 1983; Wagner & Schonbach, 1984) which have shown that a high level of cognitive complexity is accompanied by a low level of prejudice. The capacity to manipulate complex concepts and categories undoubtedly protects individuals against the passive acceptance of traditional social norms and a particular group or society's prejudices. In other words, independence of judgement is augmented by the practice learnt during the educational process of subjecting the stimuli deriving from the social setting to rational verification.

Nor should we forget that educational systems also perform an important and manifest function of social reproduction by transmitting norms, values, models of behaviour, patterns of thought and action deemed necessary and appropriate in a given society. In countries with a democratic political structure, one of the tasks of the educational system is the transmission of those principles of social solidarity, tolerance, freedom, equality and democracy. It follows that, the longer an individual remains in the educational system, the more s/he will be exposed to these principles and so the greater will be her/his cognitive flexibility, adherence to democratic principles and acceptance of and tolerance of diversity (Glock et al., 1975; Selznick & Steimberg, 1969). In other words, this constitutes a more marked rejection of traditional social values whose degree of mental closure, conservatism and authoritarianism conflicts with the principles of tolerance that the educational system of a democratic society should impart. It should be pointed out that, in a society such as Italy's, characterised by a social fabric rich in ideological positions and with a well attended state-run school system, prolonged exposure to the educational system also implies interaction with an ideologically diversified teaching body representative of the many facets of society.

Prejudice, education and realistic conflict theory

By focusing attention on competitive conflict among interest groups, Sherif's (1967) realistic conflict theory formed a fundamental contribution to the study of prejudice. Briefly, those occupying a weak position in their group and who feel themselves threatened by their socio-economic peers in another group tend to adopt a prejudiced attitude towards that group. A typical example of this is the conflict that arises between 'locals' who perform low skilled jobs and the immigrants who seek to enter the labour market by gaining such jobs. To use Parkin's (1979) expression, this is a 'closure' mechanism, whereby a superordinate group seeks to prevent its prerogatives and privileges being usurped by a subordinate group. The case of immigrants is an obvious example, but the same mechanism may operate between groups in a long established superordinate/subordinate relationship (such as ethnic majority/minorities) within a particular society.

Here too, the link with the educational level is critical. Although education does not always produce upward social mobility, it at least guarantees the conservation of status by rendering individuals less vulnerable to competition by members of an outgroup. Thus, education has a twofold effect, it provides the knowledge base, critical capacity and cognitive sophistication required to avoid resorting to negative stereotypes, and it reduces the likelihood that a conflict of interest will arise with members of a subordinate group.

The Italian survey data

So far I have drawn on theories and hypotheses indicating a link between prejudice and the level of education. I shall now show where these are borne out by the empirical data from the 1994 Italian survey. The measure of prejudice used is based on agreement or disagreement with five alleged negative characteristics of non-EU immigrants, and to five attributions of responsibility for social problems.

The correlation coefficient between the measure of prejudice and educational level (the latter represented by a linear variable calculated by the number of years of formal education) is –.37. This is above the average for the majority of empirical studies which measure this correlation at about .30 (Duckitt 1992, p. 183). This is certainly due to the sensitivity of the variable used to measure prejudice. It captures both the stereotypical prejudice present in the Italian population and the perception that the non-EU immigrants are the source of the social problems.

Using three simple path analysis models that measure the causal relation between education and prejudice when mediated by a third variable, I will now empirically verify some of the hypotheses outlined earlier regarding the effect of the level of education on prejudice. The third variable in the three models is respectively: (a) conformism, (b) traditional values, and (c) professional status.

As I have explained, formal education may produce greater independence of thought and thus less social conformism, in turn affecting the level of prejudice. Similarly, longer exposure to formal education may reduce adherence to those traditional values that signal intolerance and conservatism and may influence the formation of prejudice. It was also pointed out that education reduces conflict and competition among groups, by granting access to higher occupational positions.

Examining these simple causal models—each of which introduces just one intervening variable in the relation between education and prejudice—shows that each of these variables has some weight. This very elementary analysis yields some important information, but it fails to evaluate the influence of the effects of education on the formation of prejudice. It is therefore necessary to devise a more sophisticated model, but here problems of a conceptual nature arise. It is well known that one of the main problems of path analysis arises when the researcher must define the order of the variables, or the causal structure of the phenomenon to be explained. Here, the problem occurred when a causal sequence needed to be defined for the variables conformism, traditional values and professional status; variables which reflect those elements of formal education that influence the formation of prejudice. In the language of causal modelling, a procedure based on total effects decomposition was used, which estimates the direct effect of education on prejudice and the indirect effect operating through the three intervening variables. The model thus assumes the form given in Diagram 2.1.

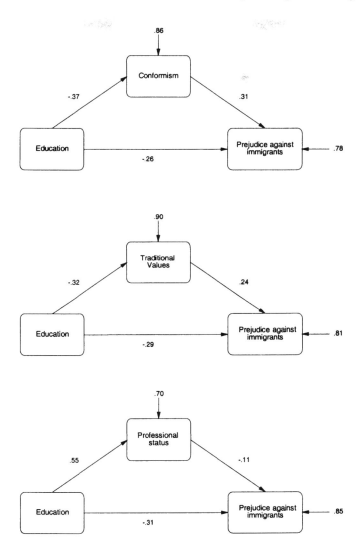

Diagram 2.1 Causal relation between education and prejudice mediated by 'conformism', 'traditional values' and 'professional status'

28 *Education and Racism*

Diagram 2.2 **Form of causal model between education and prejudice mediated by 'conformism', 'traditional values' and 'professional status'**

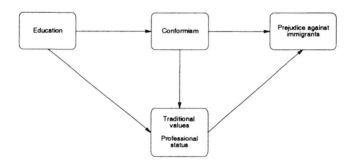

Diagram 2.3 **The 'best' model**

The diagram presents a scheme for generating causal models. How the model is used to provide upper and lower bounds for (indirect) causal effects is explained in the text.

If we decompose the effects, we find that:

E – C – P	.25 * –.37 =	.0925
E – C – (TV, PS) – P	.06 * –.37 =	.0222
		–.1147

E = education, C = conformism, P = prejudice, TV = traditional values, PS = professional status

Education and Prejudice against Immigrants 29

The result of this analysis is that, out of a total effect of education on prejudice of −.37 (which corresponds to the correlation coefficient), we have a direct effect of −.18 and, due to the intervening variables, an indirect effect of −.19. Therefore, close to half of the effect of education on prejudice operates through the intervening variables, identified earlier as the result of education. In view of the theoretical difficulty of establishing a causal order for the intervening variables, all six of the possible models were estimated. It became plain that the weight of the individual variables inevitably reflects the order in which they are introduced into the model. Because the aim of the analysis was to understand the weight of the relations internal to the group of intervening variables, two of the models are presented below: the 'best' and the 'worst' at explaining the indirect effect (= −.19) operating through the variable conformism. We can estimate how much of it *does not* operate through conformism by means of a model which instead passes through the path: E − (TV, PS) − P yields −.075. This can be calculated by taking the difference −.1147 −.19 = −.075

The result of the path E − C − P = .0575, demonstrates that this is the worst of the explanatory models. Based on these results, it is clear that the intervening variables used in the model explain approximately half the total effect of education on prejudice. The 'best' model explains about two-thirds of this, and the 'worst' about one-third. This strategy of analysis was chosen to circumvent the difficulty of ordering the variables, identified as the outcome of education, into a theoretically validated sequence. However successful the strategy, it is clear

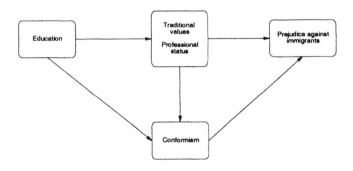

Diagram 2.4   The 'worst' model

The diagram presents a scheme for generating causal models. How the model is used to provide upper and lower bounds for (indirect) causal effects is explained in the text.

that education exerts a major influence on the formation of prejudice, both *directly*—education is here considered to include knowledge and information—and *indirectly* by affecting the formation of attitudes and values and, not least, by enabling the achievement of occupational positions less vulnerable to competition from the members of another group.

Note

1   The survery, 'Regional and Ethnic Prejudice in Italy', was carried out by Paul Sniderman, Pierangelo Peri, Thomas Piazza and Antonio Schizzerotto, as a collaboration between the Department of Sociology and Social Research of the University of Trento, the Department of Political Science of the University of Stanford, and the Survey Research Center of the University of California, Berkeley. The questionnaire was administered by phone to a sample of 2001 Italian adults representative of the Italian population in April–May 1994, using a CATI system (CASES, produced by CSM at the University of Berkeley).

References

Bagley, C. and Verma, G. (1979), *Racial Prejudice, the Individual and Society*, Westmead, England, Saxon House.
Bagley, C., Verma, G., Mallik, K. and Young, L. (1979), *Personality, Self-esteem and Prejudice*, Westmead, England, Saxon House.
Beswick, D.G. and Hills, M.D. (1972), 'A Survey of Ethocentrism in Australia', *Australian Journal of Psychology*, 24, pp. 153–163.
Duckitt, J. (1992), *The Social Psychology of Prejudice*, New York, Praegor Publishers.
Gardiner, G. (1972), 'Complexity, Training and Prejudice Reduction', *Journal of Applied Social Psychology*, 2, pp. 326–342.
Glock, C., Wuthnow, R., Piliavin, J. and Spenser, M. (1975), *Adolescent Prejudice*, New York, Harper & Row.
Hampel, R. and Krupp B. (1977), 'The Cultural and Political Framework of Prejudice in South Africa and Great Britain', *Journal of Social Psychology*, 103, pp. 193–202.
Hyman, H.H. and Scheatsley, P.B. (1954), 'The Authoritarian Personality—A Methodological Critique', in R. Christie and M. Jahoda (eds), *Studies in the Scope and Method of "the Autoritarian Personality"*, (pp. 50–122), Glencoe, Illinois, Free Press.
Kellman, H. and Pettigrew, T. (1959), 'How to Understand Prejudice', *Commentary*, 28, pp. 436–441.
MacNeil, L.W. (1974), 'Cognitive Complexity: A Brief Synthesis of Theoretical Approaches and a Concept Attainment Task Analogue to Cognitive Structure', *Psychological Report*, 34, pp. 3–11.
Marx, G.T. (1967), *Protest and Prejudice*, New York, Harper & Row.
Middletown, R. (1976), 'Regional Differences in Prejudice', *American Sociological Review*, 41, pp. 94–117.
Milner, D. (1981), 'Racial Prejudice', in J. Turner and H. Giles (eds), *Intergroup Behavior*, (pp.102–143), Oxford, Blackwell.

Parkin, F. (1979), *Marxism and Class Theory: A Bourgeois Critique*, New York, Columbia University Press.
Quinley, H.E. and Glock, C.Y. (1979), *Anti-Semitism in America*, New York, Free Press.
Selznick, G. and Steimberg, S. (1969), *The Tenacity of Prejudice, Anti-Semitism in Contemporary America*, New York, Harper & Row.
Sherif, M. (1967), *Group Conflict and Cooperation*, London, Routledge & Kegan Paul.
Sidanius, J. (1985), 'Cognitive Functioning and Sociopolitical Ideology Revised', *Political Psychology*, 6, pp. 637–662.
Stember, C.H. (1961), *Education and Attitude Change*, New York, Institute of Human Relations Press.
Stephan, W.G. and Stephan, C.W. (1984), 'The Role of Ignorance in Intergroup Relations', in N. Milner and M.B. Brewer (eds), *Groups in Contact: The Psychology of Desegregation*, (pp. 229–255), New York, Academic Press.
Tetlock, P.E. (1983), 'Cognitive style and political ideology', *Journal of Personality and Social Psychology*, 45, pp. 118–126.
Wagner, U. and Schonbach, P. (1984), 'Links between educational status and prejudice: Ethnic attitudes in West Germany', in N. Miller and M.B. Brewer (eds), *Groups in Contact: the Psychology of Desegregation* (pp. 29–52), New York, Academic Press.

3 The Effect of Education on the Expression of Negative Views towards Immigrants in France: The Influence of the Republican Model Put to the Test

FLORENCE HAEGEL

Studying the relation between the attitude towards immigrants and the level of education in France, implies first of all the measuring of two elements that are decisive for the understanding of the specific context of which these two variables form a part. To begin with, there is the special political importance of the role of immigration in French society. For more than 15 years immigration has been a central topic in public debate. Apart from being a subject of everyday conversation (CRPS Report,[1] 1997), it gains much media attention, stimulates public action, and appears regularly on the government's agenda. Above all, however, the question of the attitude towards immigrants is linked to that of the vote in favour of the National Front. Although this association is an obvious one, a vote in favour of the National Front cannot be considered as a reliable indicator of prejudice against ethnic minorities. First, negative feelings towards immigrants are far from restricted to the National Front electorate. In early 1997, 59 per cent of those surveyed in the CEVIPOF survey[2†] indicated that they felt there were too many immigrants in France, while the National Front won only 15 per cent of the votes during the general elections of June 1997. This suggests that xenophobia can not be confined to the supporters of Jean-Marie Le Pen. Second, whereas there is no doubt about the anti-immigrant factor in the National Front vote, electoral behaviour turns out to be far more complex. The analyses conducted by Nonna Mayer (Mayer, 1997) of the 1988, 1995 and 1997 CEVIPOF surveys,[3] show that although there is a clear link between the vote for the National Front and a degree of ethnocentrism (logistic regression coefficient of .6452), it also correlates strongly with an attitude of mistrust towards politics (coefficient of .6193). Thus, the National Front vote can not be classified as the political expression of xenophobia alone.

The second element specific to the French context, is the distinctive historical trajectory of national integration that progressively developed into the ideological model referred to as the republican model. Historically, this model has been primarily disseminated through the school system. Hence the frequent focus of historical studies on the role played by the school in the construction of national identity and the formation of a particular conception of citizenship (Déloye, 1994). These studies revealed that the republican model is based on the principles of equality (advancement by merit), secularism and a model of national integration founded on universalist ideals. These values influenced the formation of the national French identity. The coercive flip side of this model is the rejection of religious, regional or ethnic differences. Even before foreign minorities were required to assimilate, the school system had already assimilated the regional minorities and transformed Bretons, Alsatians, and Basques into French (Berger, 1975).

Even though the political and electoral expression of negative prejudice towards immigrants may be a crucial matter, it will not be dealt with here because, as mentioned, it is preferable to separate the questions. However, the republican model and its major mode of dissemination will be taken into account. Despite their incompleteness, the CEVIPOF polls do provide the ingredients necessary to gain a better idea of the effect of education on the attitudes towards immigrants in France. Nevertheless, because at the time of writing firm evidence was not available, the following points dealt with are more speculative than demonstrative.

Evaluation of the negative attitudes towards immigrants in France

Paradoxically, for a country where the social and political impact of xenophobia is so evident, France does not have regular and more elaborate quantitative surveys on this subject. Certain exceptions deserve to be mentioned, the studies of Gérard Lemaine and Jeanne Ben Birka (Lemaine, Ben Birka, 1989, 1994) that examine the biological roots of racism (descent, identity, contact etc.). The surveys regularly conducted by the polling institute CSA for the Human Rights Advisory Committee (Cayrol, 1997) measure the extent of ethnic prejudice using other indicators—respondents' evaluation of the level of racism in French society as well as self-evaluation of their own racist feelings or acts. The aim of these surveys is to discover the perception the French have of the place of immigrants in society, and to test the popularity of different means with which to fight the phenomena of racism.

The studies of Nonna Mayer are based on a series of electoral pollings conducted in 1988, 1995 and 1997 by CEVIPOF. Although only a few questions deal with the perception of immigrants, they allow the development of an ethnocentrism scale. Therefore, the 1997 SOFRES post-general election poll offered the chance to evaluate and interpret the ethnocentric attitudes in France (Mayer, 1997). The scale was constructed as follows:

- Some races are less intelligent than others.
- Nowadays it doesn't feel like home any more.
- There are too many immigrants in France.
- North African immigrants living in France will be French like the others one day.
- The feeling of being exclusively French: (exact question: Do you feel exclusively French, more French than European or as European as French?)

This scale (alpha = .72) captures the extent of the ethnocentric attitude in France because half of the sampling can be qualified as ethnocentric with a mark on the scale above the average (average mark = 5.8). However, more recent results indicate a decrease in xenophobia (Mayer 1997). At the time of writing it was not known whether this result indicates a trend or if it was due to heightened public activity in support of migrants at the time of the poll.

Table 3.1 The various items of the 1997 CEVIPOF survey (%)

Items	fully agree	partly agree	partly disagree	fully disagree	don't know
There are too many immigrants in France	31	28	19	20	2
Wearing of the Islamic headscarf in school should be allowed	3	7	15	73	2
Some races are less intelligent than others	8	10	13	67	2
Nowadays it doesn't feel like home anymore	26	19	21	33	1
North African immigrants living in France will be French like the others one day	8	28	25	39	–

Problems of measurement

Measuring the attitude towards immigrants

We will not concern ourselves with the various arguments surrounding the definition of racism, ethnocentrism, xenophobia (for an overview see Taguieff,

1997). Nevertheless, we cannot ignore the necessity of a clear definition of what we are measuring. Moreover, the relative shortage of data in France should not be allowed to lead to the use of inadequate indicators. Nonna Mayer avoids this pitfall by using the data supplied by the CEVIPOF surveys, and so the ethnocentrism scale already mentioned. In this scale, certain items refer to one of the dimensions of ethnocentrism, the valorisation of the ingroup (the feeling of being first and foremost French). Other items deal with racism in the biological and hierarchical sense (In France these connotations are still present in the word 'race'). The response to the item 'North African immigrants living in France will be French like the others one day' proved difficult to interpret. The amount of help respondents needed to fill out the questionnaires could be interpreted in at least two ways. Were the respondents disagreeing with the question because for them North African immigrants already are 'French like the others' in so much as they already are French nationals. Here, disagreement with the assertion stems from a literal interpretation of the republican model—to hold French nationality is to be French, all other interpretations are unacceptable. Or were they disagreeing because for them becoming French 'like the others' is not what integration is all about. Consequently, this disapproval is based on a multicultural conception. Last but not least, disagreement could be an expression of hostility towards these minorities. To avoid the ambiguity of this we decided to use the question about the presence of immigrants in France. Further, we see it as indicative of a negative attitude towards immigrants and, unlike the other questions on the ethnocentrism scale, it has been asked in all three CEVIPOF surveys.

Measuring the education variable

The two education level variables most commonly used are the age at completion of studies, and the level of the highest obtained diploma, mostly regrouped in five positions (Boy, 1997). The first variable was not used in CEVIPOF's last survey. Therefore, in this study the education variable will be differentiated by diploma. All those with no diploma were placed at the bottom of the scale. At the bottom are those who completed primary school, followed in turn by those who completed a higher level of primary school (primair supérieur), those who gained a vocational training certificate (CAP: certificat d'aptitude professionnelle) and the holders of a technical school certificate (BEP: brevet d'études professionnelle). However, this order is slightly misleading because the holders of a CAP leave school aged thirteen, which is earlier than those who finished their BEPC (brevet d'études du premier cycle), an exam taken at the age of fifteen (comparable to the British

GCSE certificate). In many respects, such as the question about the attitude towards immigrants, the answers of those with a CAP are more likely to mirror those of someone holding a primary school certificate. Similarly, those holding a BAC (baccalauréat), for which the age of completion is theoretically eighteen, are normally placed in the same category even though there is a big difference between persons holding a *general* BAC, and those with a *technical* BAC. A number of years spent in vocational training cannot be compared to the same spent in general secondary education. When the number of years enrolled in the school system is taken as a measure for the level of education, one forgets that education is not an ordinal variable and that its effect varies according to its content.

Factors influencing a negative attitude towards immigrants

If we try to rank the factors influencing a negative attitude towards immigrants, the level of education appears definitely to be the determining variable.

Table 3.2 Social factors influencing a negative attitude towards immigrants

Social factor	Coefficient
Age	.10**
Social category	.02**
Education	−.50***
Religion	−.12***
Professional status	−.10***
Gender	.01**

Logistic regression analysis; dependent variable = agrees totally with 'There are too many immigrants in France.' An '*' = coefficient with little significance. Based on the 1997 SOFRES survey (N=3010), with some comparison to the 1988 survey.

Age, controlling for the level of education, does have a small effect on the xenophobic attitude. Those over 50 years of age, no matter what their education level is, are more likely to express negative opinions about immigrants. The factor religion also has an effect of its own. In general, those who assert they are non-religious are less xenophobic. However, those who identify themselves as practising Catholics are also less xenophobic, suggesting that an adherence to Catholic values implies a less xenophobic attitude. Professional status also has a slight impact on the level of intolerance towards immigrants, the unemployed are more hostile than those in other categories. In general, gender and social category do not have a significant effect.

Table 3.3   The role of religion

Religious factor	Coefficient
Regular Catholic churchgoer	−.07
Irregular Catholic churchgoer	.26
Non-churchgoing Catholic	.28
Other religion	−.10*
Un-religious	−.3.5

An '*' = coefficient with little significance; logistic regression analysis: dependent variable = agrees totally with with 'There are too many immigrants in France.' Based on the 1997 SOFRES survey (N=3010), with some comparison to the 1988 survey.

Even if difficult to explain, the direct effect of education on the expression of racial prejudice is a long established fact (Selznick and Steinberg, 1969) Until now, two main strands of thought dominate, one optimistic interpretation stresses the direct impact of the level of education on the degree of tolerance, thus predicting a better future by the mere mechanical act of increasing everyone's level of education. In this view the benefits of education originate from the interactive effects of the cognitive and normative aspects. Many, such as Selznick and Steinberg (1969) insist that the acquisition of cognitive abilities (the ability to think abstractly, and to a degree of complexity etc.) play a role in the decrease of xenophobia. According to this model, the impact of education can also be attributed to the school system's role as a major agent of socialisation. As part of a value system, it diffuses these values by means of a normative learning process.

A more pessimistic interpretation questions if this tolerance is real. More highly educated people are not fundamentally more tolerant rather, having mastered the prevailing codes of democratic society, they are simply better than those with a lower level of education at conforming to these during a survey. Racism still exists, but takes on 'new' (Sniderman et al., 1991), 'modern' (Pettigrew, 1993), 'symbolic' (McConahay and Hough, 1976) or 'concealed' forms (Pettigrew, 1989). Because we do not have data enabling us to understand this form of racism, we cannot enter this debate. Since the highest educated are the least likely to express xenophobic opinions, it is not possible to know whether statements of this kind correspond with a deep and stable predisposition, or if they are just an attitude adopted as necessary. Consequently it would be more accurate to take into account that our analyses are only based on expressions—opinions given during a survey—rather than on an individual's predisposition.

Level of education and political preference

National integration has historically been the ideological foundation of the French Republic. For a long time, the official message regarding ethnic minorities could be summarised as follows: persons of foreign origin who become French (by naturalisation) or those born in France (*droit de sol*) are French. As such they are citizens in every respect, and the Republic does not recognise any difference, be it regional, ethnic or religious. The most direct route to integration is to obtain citizenship, followed by social advancement through the school.[4] The importance attached to the role of the school in the inculcation of political values is crucial. The reason why the school has long been the subject of competition between the Catholic church and the republican state, is that both institutions believed that control of the education system was the key to determining the value system (Tournier, 1997).

In order to explain the effect of education on xenophobia through the influence that the school has on the acquisition of tolerance, it is necessary to take into account the diversity within the school system, as well as the various other educational institutions. Apart from exerting an influence through the content of the education, the school is, for example, a meeting place for immigrant students. But first, the role of the school system in the inculcation of tolerance towards immigrants needs to be put into perspective because of the competition from other agents of socialisation.

The school does not have the monopoly in educational matters nor political socialisation in general. Certain studies have come to the conclusion that the family is the main socialising agent, and that the school's political content is only likely to be integrated if it first complies with that of the family (Percheron, 1993). Consequently, when trying to measure the effect of education we need to broaden our common sense definition to include education at school and in the family. Because of the absence of appropriate indicators with which to measure the combined effect of the influence of the family and the level of education on attitudes towards immigrants, we had to use a scale of political preference that also measured the political preferences of the mother and father.

This index is based on two questions about the parents' political orientation: 'would you say that your mother/father is (or was) more left wing, more right wing or neither left wing nor right wing?' A left wing political persuasion presupposes that at least one of the parents qualified him or herself as left wing, whilst the other must not be right wing. Meaning that, he or she can be left wing, neither left wing nor right wing or not identified. A right wing political persuasion is similarly determined.

Table 3.4   Full or partial agreement with 'There are too many immigrants in France' (%)

Educational level	Left wing	Right wing	Neither left nor right wing
Lower than BAC	67	73	71
Higher than BAC	31	51	45

Based on the 1997 SOFRES survey (N=3010), with some comparison to the 1988 survey.

The most remarkable result is that the political preference scale only provides negligible variations for those with lower levels of education: people with left wing leanings and a lower level of education are barely any less xenophobic than those with right wing political beliefs. However, independent of political preference, the higher the level of education the lower the likelihood of a negative attitude towards immigrants. The effect of education is particularly clear amongst persons from left wing families. This phenomenon can be explained in two different but not exclusive ways. One can surmise that the increased cognitive abilities gained from a higher level of education assists individuals from left wing families in recognising opinions that conform or contradict with the family's values. The strong decrease in anti-immigrant attitudes amongst those who are both left wing and highly educated can be attributed to the congruence between the messages to which they have been exposed. Thus the lower degree of tolerance of persons with a left wing political conviction and a lower education level could be related the absence of the benefit of this double exposure.

The generation effect

One could surmise, from the connection found between the level of education and the degree of hostility towards immigrants, that the populace's ever increasing level of education should lead to greater levels of tolerance with each generation. However, in order to understand these changes, it must be kept in mind that the effect of education might not be the same over time, in so much as the values transmitted through the school will not be the same for each generation. One should also be aware that this generation effect combines with that of time.

We do not have any data series taken over a sufficient period of time to capture the evolution of this effect. The CEVIPOF data only allows for an analysis per cohort over a period of approximately ten years. Examining this data, we find that overall the degree of hostility towards immigrants remains stable amongst those with lower levels of education, and shows a decrease amongst those with higher levels. These changes show an increasing polarisation related to the level of education. This suggests that aside from the decisive role education has always had in explaining xenophobic attitudes, its effect will only increase.

Amongst those with less education, the age effect is non-existent, in other words, the young are not more tolerant than the more elderly. As long as time effects seem decisive, we have to be careful with the interpretation of certain results. In 1995, a similar analysis exposed the rise of negative attitudes towards immigrants amongst the youngest of the less highly educated cohorts. (Grunberg & Schweisguth, 1997a). Two years later, within a general context of slightly diminishing anti-immigrant attitudes, this phenomenon had disappeared. Amongst the youngest cohorts of this less highly educated group, one can even notice the opposite, a development of an increase in tolerance towards immigrants. These contradictory conclusions within a two year interval could indicate that the youngest and least educated are particularly sensitive to the effect of time and the tenor of media coverage, in addition to public demonstrations in favour of immigrants.

An age effect can be distinguished for those with higher levels of education. There seems to be a rupture between the pre- and postwar cohorts, with the decrease in negative attitudes towards immigrants, in general, being attributed to the postwar generations. Within this generational unit it is important to note that the youngest are not more tolerant than the older members. The hypothesis that tolerance will automatically increase with each generation has to be reconsidered in France and the United States (Dowden & Robinson, 1993).

The generational rupture does not specifically concern the xenophobic aspect, but can also be found in various values in the area of religion and sexual freedom (Drouin, 1995). We can hypothesise that the context and the content of the socialisation regarding attitudes towards migrants of the postwar and pre-war generations are not the same. As mentioned before, the univocity of the republican model is far from being evident because the discourse on national integration has always been ambivalent. This ambivalence arises because the discourse of national integration is one of assimilation and authority, whereas the universalism propagated by the republican ideology can be associated with nationalism and colonialism (Todorov, 1989). Here the republican model paints France (country of Enlightenment and the Revolution) as the pre-eminent incarnation of universal values, a position that entails the national duty to pass these values on to colonised nations. The oldest cohorts were educated within this colonial context. The school imparted the colonial ideology and a non-egalitarian view of inter-ethnic relations, while post-war generations have been socialised in the midst or in the aftermath of the decolonisation process.

Table 3.5 Those holding a diploma lower than a BAC who fully agree that there are too many immigrants in France (%)

Year of birth	1988	1997
1971–77	–	34
1964–70	40	42
1943–63	42	41
1929–42	46	47
1908–28	45	41
1907 and before	43	*
	43	42

See note to Table 3.6.

Table 3.6 Those holding a diploma higher than a BAC who fully agree that there are too many immigrants in France (%)

Year of birth	1988	1997
1971–77	–	13
1964–70	13	13
1943–63	14	14
1929–42	35	23
1908–28	34	35
1907 and before	*	*
	19	16

Based on the 1997 SOFRES survey (N=3010), with some comparison to the 1988 survey. The surveys were administered to a population aged 18 and over. The 1988 survey did not include those born after 1970. Analysis is per cohort. An '*' = insignificant numbers of people.

Education level, authoritarian attitude and insecurity about one's future

Historically, the inculcation of republican norms and values—the apprenticeship for the role of citizenship—presupposed disciplinary action aimed at the elimination of difference. That the authoritarian aspect is inherent in the republican pedagogic vision is to be seen in its Durkheimian conception of education as a concern of the state and authority (Durkheim, 1989). Since Durkheim, pedagogical methods have altered slightly, and more importantly, what is expected from the school has changed completely. The view of the school as the site at which discipline should be instilled is decreasing in currency. Grunberg and Schweisguth (1997a) attribute the diminishing importance of authoritarian values in school to a joint effect of age and education level. That authoritarian values are related to intolerance has long been established and, since Adorno, Frenkel-Brunswick, Levinson, and Sanford's (1950) study, the connection between authoritarian and ethnocentric attitudes has been regularly confirmed, especially in France (Mayer, 1993, 1997).

In general, we know that adherence to authoritarian values is stronger amongst the less highly educated. Nevertheless, one can note that people with a higher level of education appear to have a more coherent value system. Therefore, the correlation between a hostile attitude towards immigrants and the adherence to authoritarian values is particularly strong within this category. This is the outcome of a logistic regression analysis comparing the hierarchy of certain ideological factors (authoritarianism, political persuasion) and psychological factors (insecurity about the future) according to the level of education. The ideological factors turn out to be particularly dominant amongst the more highly educated. For them the degree of intolerance is strongly related to an adherence to authoritarian values and belonging to the political right wing. In other words, people with a higher level of education express negative opinions towards immigrants less often. However, when they do, they demonstrate an ideological consistency.

The authoritarianism indicator is constructed from two questions, 'When you think about school, could you tell me with which of these two opinions you agree most? School should above all teach a sense of discipline and effort; school should above all form people with a sharp and critical mind.', 'We should reintroduce the death penalty.' The question concerning the insecurity about one's future is formulated as: 'When you think about the future of your personal and professional life, would you say you are confident or insecure?'

Table 3.7 Relationship between a negative attitude towards immigrants and authoritarianism, political preference and insecurity about the future

	Lower level of education	Higher level of education
Authoritarianism	B = .62***	B = .97***
Political preference	B = .17***	B = .34***
Insecurity about one's future	B = .27***	B = .009**

Logistic regression analysis. Based on the 1997 SOFRES survey (N=3010), with some comparison to the 1988 SOFRES. An '*' = coefficient with little significance.

Because tolerance towards immigrants amongst people with a lower level of education rests on a less coherent ideological system comprising authoritarian values and right wing political leanings, how they perceive their personal and professional future has a greater influence on their attitude to immigrants than amongst the more highly educated. Apart from being the decisive variable for the explanation of the expression of xenophobic opinions, the level of education seems to play an increasingly important role in France. This is evident in the particularly strong polarisation within the younger generation. Although difficult to interpret, education seems to have an increasingly determining effect on the overall value system, extending beyond a xenophobic attitude. Several observations are based on a cognitive interpretation. The variations that have been found between the different types of education—vocational and general—could indicate that the content, its degree of abstraction and the type of subjects taught are elements that should be taken into account. Yet, the difference between vocational and general education does not only depend on the sort of knowledge acquired. It also rests on sociological differences like school population, type of teacher and institution.

It is clear in any case that we can not restrict the effect of education to the cognitive aspect only. Differences between generations with the same level of education and especially the rupture between the pre- and postwar generations do indeed indicate that having a certain level of education provides no guarantee of immunisation against xenophobia, and that the content and the context of education form decisive parameters. In brief, the impact of education also depends on the normative aspect. In the case of France, the school has long been considered decisive in the reproduction and transmission of a value system. However, the hypothesis that the more one studies, the stronger the adherence to the republican model and the more positive one's opinion about immigrants, seems rather simplistic. It clashes with the ambivalence of the French model of national integration, and also with the competition that the school faces from other value transmitting agents, amongst others the family. Although education overall reduces the expression of xenophobic opinions, it has a stronger immunising effect on people with left wing beliefs than on those of a right wing persuasion. A higher level of education correlates with a lower score in expressing xenophobic opinions, but we do not know if this can be explained by an adhesion to a value system or simply by knowing and recognising and expressing the constituent norms of this system while being surveyed. For a minority of people, a high level of education is no antidote for the expression of hostile feelings towards immigrants. They even demonstrate a strong ideological coherence and, amongst them xenophobia is strongly related to authoritarian values and a right wing political conviction. For people with a lower level of education, the expression of xenophobic opinions is also connected with an adhesion to authoritarian values, but this link is not as strong as the role played by factors related to the perception of the world, such as an insecurity about the future.

Notes

1 CRPS stands for Centre de recherches politiques de la Sorbonne. The translation of the title of the report is 'Final report of the survey on attitude towards immigration and foreign people living in France'.

2 1997 CEVIPOF/SOFRES survey, sample taken May 26 and 31, by phone, selected using the quota method, total sample of 3010 voters representative of the French population, aged eighteen and older. SOFRES stands for Société française d'études et de sondages.

† CEVIPOF, which stands for the Centre d'étude de la vie politique française, is a center of la Fondation nationale des sciences politiques associated to the CNRS (Centre national de la recherche scientifique.

3 May 1988 CEVIPOF survey administered by SOFRES‡, nation wide sample of 4032 people representative of the French population aged 18 and over, selected using the quota method and stratified by region and urban size. May 1995 CEVIPOF/SOFRES survey, taken after the second round of the presidential election, conducted on a nation wide sample of 4078 people representative of the French population age 18 and over, selected with the quota method.

‡ SOFRES stands for Société française d'études et de sondages.

4 The notion of the 'republican school' refers to the school as it was founded by the Third Republic.

References

Adorno, T. W., Frenkel-Brunswick, E., Levinson, D.J. and Sanford, N.R. (1950), *The Authoritarian Personality*, New York, Harper & Row.
Berger, S. (1975), *Les paysans contre la politique. L'organisation rurale en Bretagne 1911–1974*, Paris, Seuil.
Boy, D. (1997), 'Les indicateurs de capital culturel', in Dupoirier, E. and Parodi, J.-L. (eds), *Les indicateurs sociopolitiques aujourd'hui*, Paris, L'Harmattan.
Cayrol, R. (1997), 'Les indicateurs du racisme et de la xénophobie' in Dupoirier, E. and Parodi, J.-L. (eds), *Les indicateurs sociopolitiques aujourd'hui*, Paris, L'Harmattan.
CRPS (1997), *Rapport final de l'enquête sur les attitudes à l'égard de l'immigration et de la présence étrangère en France*, Université de Paris I, département de science politique de la Sorbonne.
Déloye, Y. (1994), *Ecole et citoyenneté. L'individualisme republicain de Jules Ferry à Vichy: controverses*, Paris, Presses de la Fondation nationale des sciences politiques.
Dowden, S. and Robinson, J.P. (1993), 'Age and Cohort Differences in American Racial Attitudes. The Generation Replacement Hypothesis Revisited', in P. Sniderman, P. Tetlock, and E. Carmines (eds), *Prejudice, Politics and the American Dilemma*, Stanford, California, Stanford University Press.
Drouin, V. (1995), 'Enquêtes sur les générations et la politique 1958–1995', Paris, L'Harmattan.
Durkheim, E. (1989), *Education et sociologie*, Paris, PUF.
Grunberg, G. Schweisguth, E. (1997a), 'Recompositions idéologiques', in D. Boy and N. Mayer (eds), *L'électeur a ses raisons*, Paris, Presses de Science Po.
Lemaine, G. and Ben Birka J. (1989), 'Identity and Physical Appearance', *Revue internationale de psychologie sociale*, July–September.
Lemaine, G. and Ben Birka J. (1994), 'Le rejet de l'autre: pureté, descendance, valeurs, Ethnicisation des rapports sociaux', in M. Fourier and G. Vermès (eds), *Racismes, nationalismes, ethnicismes et culturalismes*, Paris, ENS-editions Fontenay/Saint-Cloud, Editions L'Harmattan.
McConahay, J.B. and Hough, J.C. (1976), 'Symbolic Racism', *Journal of Social Issues*, vol. 32, no. 2, pp. 23–45.
Mayer, N. (1993), 'Ehnocentrism, Racism and Intolerance', in D. Boy and N. Mayer (eds), *The French Voter Decides*, Ann Arbor, University of Michigan Press.
Mayer, N. (1997), 'Le rejet de l'autre', *Chroniques électorales*, Paris, Presses de Science-po.
Percheron, A. (1993), 'La socialisation politique', Paris, Armand Colin.
Pettigrew, T.F. (1989), 'The Nature of Modern Racism in the United States', *Revue internationale de psychologie sociale*, juillet–septembre.
Pettigrew, T.F. and Meertens, R.W. (1993), 'Le racisme voilé: dimensions et mesure', in M.Wieworka (ed) *Racisme et modernité*, Paris, La Découverte.
Selznick, G. Steinberg, S. (1969), *The Tenacity of Prejudice*, New York, Evanston, London, Harper & Row.
Sniderman, P. et al. (1991), 'The New Racism', *American Journal of Political Science*, no. 352 May, pp. 423–47.
Taguieff, P.-A. (1997), *Le racisme*, Paris, Flamarion.
Todorov, T. (1989), *Nous et les autres*, Paris, Seuil.
Tournier, V. (1997), 'Ecole publique, école privée: le clivage oublié. Le rôle des facteurs politiques et religieux dans le choix de l'école et les effets du contexte scolaire sur la socialisation politique des lycéens français', *Revue française de science politique*, no. 475 October, pp. 560–588.

4 'Everyday' Racism in Belgium: An Overview of the Research and an Interpretation of its Link with Education

HANS DE WITTE

Racism research in Belgium

This chapter consists of two parts. The first *descriptive* part sketches an overview of research on racism in Belgium and serves as an introduction to the second. The second *explanatory* part examines this research in detail, focusing on the question, does the level of education have a significant relationship to racism and, if so, how can this relationship be interpreted. The descriptive part begins with a historical overview of racism research in Belgium, which is followed by an examination of the methods of measurement most commonly used. This leads to a more concrete definition of the concept *racism*. I conclude with an overview of the results of racism research, paying attention both to whether forms of racism and its expression have altered over time, and to the level of racism in Belgium, compared to other EU member states.

Chronology

Systematic research into the Belgian population's attitude towards foreigners was scarce until the late 1980s.[1] Apart from occasional opinion polls on this subject (for an overview De Baets, 1989 & 1994), the only serious examination of a representative sample of the Flemish-speaking population was conducted by the Centrum voor Bevolkings- en Gezinsstudieën (Centre for Population and Family Studies) in 1973 and 1980 (Dooghe & Vanderleyden, 1974; Dooghe, 1981). Because these inquiries formed part of a larger survey, only three aspects relevant to the study of racism could be examined: knowledge about foreigners, attitude towards this population group (evaluation of ten items on a scale of 5 points) and the extent to which interviewees felt a preference for or an aversion to several nationalities. The ethnic hierarchy constructed from the last question indicated that interviewees showed a greater preference for inhabitants of neighbouring countries than for those of more distant European countries, with Turks and North-Africans being placed last.

Based on a 1989 representative sample of about 1600 respondents from Flanders, Brussels and Wallonia, The research *Onbekend of onbemind? Een sociologisch onderzoek naar de houding van de Belgen tegenover migranten* (Unfamiliar or unpopular? A sociological study on the attitudes of Belgians about migrants) (Billiet, Carton & Huys 1990), can be considered the starting point of more systematic academic research. The survey collected information on a wide range of themes, asking questions about population groups considered to be foreign, about knowledge of these foreigners, and about contacts and experiences, both positive and negative, of foreigners. The attitude of the interviewees towards foreigners was assessed, by means of an extensive semantic differential measurement, evaluating their responses to six population groups. In addition to this, interviewees attitudes to foreigners, their opinion on the rights to which foreigners were entitled and the measures the government could, or should, take, were evaluated using Likert scales. This survey was supplemented by a postal survey, which gathered information on a number of explanatory variables, and with surveys of young people (respectively Billiet et al., 1992; De Witte, 1996b). From this 'mother survey', an extensive list of items was adopted, which have since been added to by, among other things, ISPO's (Interuniversitair Steunpunt Politieke-Opinieonderzoek (Interuniversity Centre for Political Opinion Research)) post-national-election-surveys (for example Carton & Huys, 1993).

European Union surveys about Belgium form another source of data. The 1988 and 1997 *Eurobarometer* compiled a relatively large amount of data on the attitudes of the population towards migrants. The 1981 and 1990 *European Values Study* collected data on the Belgian population's perception of foreigners, by focusing on the social distance issue of the extent to which people are willing to accept foreigners as neighbours (Kerkhofs & Rezsohazy, 1984; Kerkhofs et al., 1992; Ashford & Timms, 1992).

Measuring racism

From the above overview of racism studies in Belgium it can be concluded that although racism was measured in several ways, one method dominated: the rating of a list of items using a five point Likert scale. In these lists, the category 'foreigners' was often clarified by referring specifically to Turks and

Moroccans because it was found that Belgians referred mostly to those ethnic groups when questioned about foreigners (Billiet et al., 1990, pp. 51–53). The list of items presented was analysed using factor analysis (usually confirmatory), following which those items referring to the same factor were combined into one scale. In previous research three concepts (and therefore Likert scales) were developed: a *general* scale to measure a negative attitude towards migrants, a scale for *biological* racism and a scale measuring a *positive attitude* towards the own ethnic group (see for example Billiet & De Witte, 1991).

The general scale was used by most of the research outlined above. It measures what can be characterised as *everyday* racism (De Witte, 1993a). Everyday racism refers to the least ideologically founded form of racism that, perhaps for this very reason, is the most widespread among the population. At first glance, this everyday racism comprises a range of popular opinions that can be grouped together because they all express a *negative* attitude towards foreigners. Central to this negative attitude is the idea that foreigners' *cultural* habits deviate too greatly, or that they represent *economic* competition. Typical cultural items are 'Foreigners are a threat to our culture and habits.' and 'Migrants should adjust their lifestyle more to that of Belgians.' Typical economic items are 'Migrant workers are a threat to the employment of Belgians.' and 'Migrant workers come here to profit from social security.' The research conducted used different types of scales which, to a large extent, overlap. The different items selected can always be combined into strongly reliable scales (e.g. alpha = .90 with seven items (Billiet, 1993b)). In some analyses two scales were made using items from the complete scale (Billiet, 1993a & 1996): one scale comprising items relating to the economic threat migrants supposedly pose, the second combining several items relating to cultural stereotypes (such as descriptions of migrants as 'aggressive', 'lazy' and 'rude').

As well as this everyday racism, a scale for *biological* racism is often compiled (for example Billiet & De Witte, 1991 & 1995; Billiet 1993a & 1996). This more explicitly ideologically founded form of racism refers to the belief in the hereditary inequality of races, whereby the 'white race' is considered superior on biological grounds. Typical items are 'Generally speaking, the white race is superior to other races.' and 'We have to keep our race pure and must avoid mixing with other races.' Combinations of these items also provide reliable scales (e.g. alpha = .81 with three items (Billiet & De Witte, 1991) or .86 with four items (Billiet & De Witte, 1995)).

Following Dutch research (Eisinga & Scheepers, 1989), Belgian research finally also paid attention to the attitudes towards the ingroup, which in Flemish research refers to the evaluation of 'your own ethnic group' or the 'Flemish' (Billiet et al., 1990 & 1992). Typical items are 'I am proud of my own ethnic group.' and 'Generally speaking, our country is better than most other countries.' The reliability of these scales is usually lower (e.g. alpha = .63 with three items (Billiet & De Witte, 1991). When combined with the aspect everyday racism this positive attitude towards the ingroup is known as *ethnocentrism* (Sumner, 1906).

The above overview shows that, at the time of writing, Belgian research has paid no attention to 'new' forms of racism, such as *cultural* racism (for a comparison to everyday and biological racism, see for example De Witte, 1993a) or the difference between *blatant* and *subtle* racism (Pettigrew & Meertens, 1995; see also Verberk & Scheepers in this volume). This chapter will focus on those research results relating to everyday racism, as most studies concentrate on this. Ethnocentrism will only be discussed indirectly.

Results of racism research in Belgium

How many Belgians are racist? The attitude of Belgians towards migrants can be illustrated in different ways. This chapter will limit its attention to two complementary ways: the description of a few frequency divisions and the results of a latent class analysis.

The simplest way to map a racist attitude is by studying the answer patterns with regard to several typical items. Table 4.1 contains results regarding everyday racism, obtained from a representative sample of the Flemish population in 1989 (Billiet et al., 1990; Billiet & De Witte, 1991). Factor analysis showed the uni-dimensionality of these items. They were combined into a scale, varying between zero (maximum rejection of the scale content) and ten (maximum agreement with the scale content), in which five is neutral. This scale proved to be sufficiently reliable (alpha = .79).

Table 4.1   Rating of items concerning everyday racism (%)

Items	Agreement[a]
1. Guest workers come to our country to exploit our social security system	57.4
2. Belgium shouldn't have brought in guest workers	45.0
3. Foreign workers endanger the employment of Belgians	41.8
4. In some neighbourhoods, the government is doing more for immigrants than for the Belgians who live there	32.1
5. The religion of the Muslims is a threat to the culture of the West	32.1
6. In general, immigrants are not to be trusted	25.3

[a] Combination of 'rather agree' and 'totally agree'
Source: Billiet & De Witte, 1991, p. 31.

Table 4.1 shows that those interviewed are divided among themselves with regard to their attitudes towards everyday racism. The average scale score is 5.2, which is almost the same as the neutral centre of the scale. This neutral score can be attributed to the large diversity among those interviewed. About half of them score higher than five on the scale and they therefore agree (to a lesser or greater degree) with the scale content. The other half disagree (to a lesser or greater degree) with the scale content. This diversity also becomes evident from evaluating the separate items. Items referring to economic themes (social security, threat to employment) are more likely to be approved. Statements with a more cultural content are more likely to be rejected. However, this may be attributable to the rather radical formulation of the selected items. Follow-up studies in which no less than 85 per cent of those interviewed agree to the statement 'Migrants should make a greater effort to adjust to the Belgian way of life.' strongly suggest that cultural resentments do exist (Carton et al., 1993).

The established diversity among those interviewed suggested the use of a multivariate technique that allows for the classification of the respondents in relatively homogeneous groups. Billiet (1993b) analysed data from 1989 using latent class analysis. However, he limited himself to answers relating to five of the six items from Table 4.1 (the item about Islamic religion was not included). This allowed the respondents to be divided into three groups. Approximately 38 per cent of those interviewed showed a positive attitude towards migrants: they rejected the various statements of everyday racism. A smaller group, 18 per cent, adopted a consistent negative attitude: they strongly agreed with the five analysed statements. A relatively large group of 44 per cent adopted an ambivalent attitude: they thought that migrants formed an economic threat to a certain extent, but rejected other negative statements. The results of this latent class analysis complement the frequency divisions discussed above, they show that, as well as ambivalent, positive and negative groups can also be distinguished among the population.

Various types regarding the attitude towards ethnic groups Taking into account other forms of racism can further refine classification of the population with regard to their attitude towards foreigners. In the prior section,'measuring racism', it was pointed out that besides everyday racism, biological racism was also studied, and that attention was paid to the attitude towards the ethnic group to which the respondents themselves belonged. Research shows that these three attitudes are strongly correlated (correlations between .50 and .65 see Billiet & De Witte, 1991, p. 33). Scalogram analysis was used to examine whether these attitudes are cumulative, thereby making it possible to distinguish types (De Witte & Billiet, 1990 & 1993). To this end the three scales were dichotomised. Respondents scoring higher than the neutral point (5) were considered agreers. The others were considered disagreers. The results of this analysis were included in Table 4.2.

Table 4.2 Distribution and content of the four 'ethnic types'[c]

Ethnic type	Positive attitude towards 'own' people	Scales[a] Negative attitude towards immigrants	(Biological) racism	%
1. 'Cosmopolitans'	–	–	–	17.7
2. 'Nationalists'	+	–	–	28.8
3. 'Etnocentrists'	+	+	–	24.7
4. 'Racists'	+	+	+	18.6
0. Indefinite type[b]				10.2
TOTAL				100.0

[a] A '+' = a score above the midpoint of the scale (>5); =agrees with scale's the content. A '–' = a score equal to or below this midpoint (≤5); = rejects the content. [b] Missing values or anomalous response patterns. [c] Coefficient of reproducibility = .95; coefficient of scalability = .86
Source: De Witte & Billiet, 1993.

Table 4.2 shows that the three analysed scales constitute a nearly perfect Guttman scale (see note 'c' to Table 4.2). Hence a positive attitude towards your own ethnic group constitutes the necessary, but inadequate, condition for the development of racism. Biological racism is at the same time, cumulative on everyday racism. In so doing four types are created. The *cosmopolitans* reject the content of the three scales. They feel little or no affinity with their 'own' ethnic group, they have a positive attitude towards migrants and they reject biological racism. This group constitutes almost 18 per cent of the respondents. The *nationalists* have a positive attitude towards their own people, and reject both types of racism. They constitute nearly 29 per cent of those interviewed. The *ethnocentrists*, approximately 25 per cent of the respondents, combine a positive attitude towards their own group with a negative one towards foreigners (everyday racism). However, they also reject biological racism, making them ethnocentrists in Sumner's sense (Sumner, 1906). The final group, the *racists*, comprising close to 19 per cent, go a step further than the ethnocentrists, by combining their ethnocentric attitude with biological racism. About 10 per cent of the respondents cannot be classified because they have missing scores on one of the scales or because their answer pattern deviates from the expected cumulative structure.

A comparison in time and space

Electoral research shows that everyday racism constitutes the most decisive factor influencing the vote for an extreme right wing party (for an overview De Witte, 1996a). The electoral success of extreme right wing parties in Belgium since 1991 begs the question of whether the level of everyday racism has risen over recent decades. In order to verify this, Billiet (1993b) compared the size (and structure) of the three groups distinguishable using latent class analysis in 1989 and in 1992. Having done so he concluded that the level of everyday racism had not increased during this period: the same groups (of the same size) were discernable in both years. Analogous to this is Loosveldt's comparison of the level of everyday racism among twenty to twentyone-year-olds in 1991, 1992, and 1994 (Loosveldt, 1995). He too found no change in attitude. In his extensive overview of the various opinion polls that were held in Belgium, De Baets concludes that the level of everyday racism has possibly even decreased since 1970 (De Baets, 1994). He pinpoints the turning point around the decolonisation of the, then Belgian, Congo in 1960. The conclusion that everyday racism has not increased, suggests that the data in Tables 1 and 2 represent a fair reflection of the attitude of the present population, even though it was collected nearly ten years ago.

Belgium has two dominant language communities (see also De Witte & Verbeeck, 1998). Extensive research (for example Billiet et al., 1990) has found no significant differences between the two communities' attitudes towards foreigners. A re-analysis of the 1988 *Eurobarometer* data supports this finding (Dekker & Van Praag, 1990b). The data from the 1990 *European Values Study* suggests that the Flemish speaking community is slightly less willing to accept foreigners as neighbours than the French speaking community, but the difference is not very large (Delooz & Kerkhofs, 1992, p. 239). At least on the issue of foreigners, Belgians are remarkably unanimous.

However, comparisons made within the European Union consistently show that the level of everyday racism in Belgium is higher than in other EU countries. Dekker and Van Praag (1990a & 1990b) analysed the data on racism and intolerance from the 1988 *Eurobarometer* survey. In this survey ten statements about foreigners were combined into a xenophobia scale (Dekker & Van Praag, 1990b). In Belgium, an average of 56 per cent of the respondents agreed with this scale, almost matching the figure in Table 4.1. In other countries this figure varied between 30 per cent (the Netherlands) and 47 per cent (Denmark). Compared to respondents from other countries, Belgians were more likely to assert that people of another nationality took advantage of social provisions, and to hold them responsible for increasing unemployment, crime and feelings of insecurity. Belgians were also less likely to support a policy of integration (Dekker & Van Praag, 1990a, p. 25). Likewise, more global analyses of the data show that the percentage holding a negative attitude towards foreigners, is larger in Belgium than in the other EU countries (Dekker & Van Praag, 1990a, pp. 37–38; *Eurobarometer*, 1989, pp. 90–94). The data from the *European Values Study* shows similar differences, Belgians were less inclined to accept Muslims or immigrants as neighbours (Ashford & Timms, 1992, pp. 13–14). Comparisons made between Flanders (Belgium) and the Netherlands also show a wide variance in the level of everyday racism between these two groups (Billiet et al., 1996; Raaijmakers & De Witte, 1995).

It is not so easy to *explain* this striking difference between Belgium and the rest of the EU. However, several explanations for the difference between Flanders and the Netherlands exist (De Witte, 1998). Billiet, Eisinga and Scheepers (1992, p. 313) point to the differences between the *implemented minorities policy* of the countries concerned. The Dutch minorities policy, aimed at addressing the discrimination towards foreigners, has been in place longer than the Belgian policy. Following Vos (1993 & 1994), *Flemish nationalist discourse* may also have played an indirect role, as even the more moderate Flemish nationalists (such as the political party *Volksunie* (Peoples' Union)) are 'ethnic nationalists' not 'state nationalists'. Hence one is accepted into the '(Flemish) ethnic community' if one speaks the Flemish language and/ or if one is of Flemish parents. Such 'exclusive' nationalism is by definition ethnocentric, excluding others by emphasizing the 'ethnic character' (Vos, 1993, pp. 148–149 & 1994, pp. 147–150). The difference of the extent of secularisation in both countries may also play a part (Raaijmakers & De Witte, 1995, p. 70). This explanation departs from the view that negative attitudes towards foreigners form part of a wider complex of cultural conservatism (Middendorp, 1991; De Witte, 1990). Those who emphasise cultural conservatism reject foreigners to a certain degree, because foreigners deviate from cultural traditions in society, e.g. by having a different life style and customs. Such cultural conservatism is historically linked to Roman Catholicism, partly because of the emphasis that this faith places on obeying orders from 'above'. Research supports this presumption of a strong link between allegiance to the Christian faith and cultural conservatism (Felling & Peters, 1991, pp. 251–253; De Witte et al., 1994, pp. 97–99). Becker and Vink's (1991) assertion that secularisation goes hand in hand with the weakening of cultural conservatism, suggests that the greater level of secularisation in the Netherlands than in the Flemish region (Flanders) could be responsible for the lower level of ethnocentrism in the Netherlands. The extent to which these factors also explain the difference between Belgium and the other countries of the European Union is, however, unclear for the time being.

Explanations for 'everyday' racism

A clear line of development can be seen in Belgian analyses of possible explanations for everyday racism. Prior to 1990 the emphasis was on the (univariate) breaking up of collected data into background characteristics such as sex, age and level of education. After 1990 multivariate methods of analysis were used, allowing the autonomous impact of each variable to be determined after discarding the effect of the other variables. Initially, in this multivariate series of analyses, research was limited to the analysis of background characteristics (for a description of this development Billiet 1993b, p. 152). Later, more complex models were developed using background characteristics as well as attitudinal variables. First, conclusions related to these characteristics will be discussed. Then more complex models will be describedconcluding with an elaboration of the importance of the level of education and of the way in which the impact of this variable can be interpreted.

Background characteristics influencing everyday racism

Surveys indicate that everyday racism is, along with other factors, influenced by age and the level of education of the respondents: the younger or more highly educated the respondent, the less likely they are to have racist attitudes (De Baets, 1994, pp. 185–187). By adding political preference to these variables some studies found that supporters of the then (conservative) liberal party (PVV: *Partij voor Vrijheid en Vooruitgand* (Party for Freedom and Progress)) were the most negative about integration of foreigners (Dooghe, 1981). However, because these relations are univariate, it is not possible to say anything about the relative importance of the various variables.

In *Onbekend of onbemind?* similar univariate relations were determined with, for example, age and level of education (Billiet et al., 1990). The extent to which the variables level of education, age, family income and migrants in the neighbourhood of the respondent, exerted autonomous influence on the attitude towards migrants was analysed using log linear analysis. The strongest (autonomous) effect emanated from the level of education, followed by that of age, family income and the interaction between neighbourhood and age. Less highly educated people, elderly people (>45), those with a lower family income, and elderly people living in a migrant neighbourhood, were found to have a more negative attitude towards migrants. The presence of migrants in the neighbourhood is, strictly speaking, not a background characteristic of the individual, and will thus be ignored from here on.

Further analysis of the same data using Lisrel to control for the effect of education and age on each other, also shows that level of education is the main predictor of everyday racism (Billiet, 1996, p. 20). The typology of 'agreers' and 'disagreers'to their in- and outgroup (see discussion of Table 4.2 above), was also strongly influenced by their level of education (Billiet & De Witte, 1991). Log linear analysis demonstrated that the level of education exerts an autonomous influence as to which type an individual belongs. Here, a lower level of education was also found to have a net effect on belonging to the type racist.

The pivotal role of the level of education as a predictor of everyday racism is not limited to the data mentioned above, nor to Belgium. In their secondary analysis of the 1988 *Eurobarometer*, Dekker and Van Praag (1990b) examined the differences in evaluation of their xenophobia scale as to sex, age, degree of urbanisation, level of education and social class of those interviewed. The level of education emerged as the strongest explanatory variable in *all* countries. After multivariate analysis, it was found that this variable could be used to explain between half and three quarters of the total variance explained. Here too, as with the Belgian research discussed above, age always came second.

More complex models of explanation

Slowly but surely, these rather rudimentary multivariate analyses were refined with the addition of various intermediate variables to the explanatory models. Much of this work was influenced by the work of the Dutch researchers Scheepers and Eisinga (see Billiet, 1993a, p. 60). Three variables play a central part in these more complex models: anomie, authoritarianism and cultural localism. The relation between these three intermediate variables and the negative attitude towards migrants is constantly interpreted in terms of the social (contra-) identification theory of Scheepers and Eisinga (Felling & Peters, 1991). This extension of the social identity theory of Tajfel (1982) departs from the idea that individuals pursue a positive social identity. This can be achieved via two processes: social identification with an ingroup, thereby selectively emphasizing positively valued characteristics of the group to which one belongs, and by contra-identification with an outgroup, thereby selectively emphasizing negatively valued characteristics of this group. As will be elaborated further, this broadening of the explanatory frameworks for everyday racism can be used to help us interpret the possible impact of the level of education on everyday racism.

In the study *Onbekend of onbemind?* a central role had already been given to the variable *anomie*. This variable, taken from Srole (1956), refers among other things, to feelings of social powerlessness, meaninglessness and social isolation. Using this somewhat diffuse variable, a rather vast range of feelings of social discomfort are measured. The conclusion that feelings of anomie are strongly related to indicators of everyday racism is an all too familiar concept in racism research (Srole, 1956; Hagendoorn & Janssen, 1983, pp. 140–148; Scheepers et al., 1989). The addition of this variable to a model of background characteristics therefore produces a strongly autonomous effect of anomie on everyday racism. (Billiet et al., 1990, pp. 172–176). From this analysis anomie arises as the main predictor, considerably reducing the impact of the level of education, even though this variable still exerts a net effect. The explanation for the effect of anomie derives from Eisinga and Scheepers' social (contra-) identification theory (Billiet, 1993a & 1993b). Anomic individuals experience a dislocation from society. In other words, they are looking for a social identity that can be derived from identification with their own group and from contra-identification with an outgroup: foreigners. Their reaction against migrants allows them to construct a positive social identity to compensate for their feelings of a lack of social solidarity.

A second survey which collected data from the same respondents, added the variables authoritarianism and cultural localism, among others, to the anomie variable (Billiet et al., 1992 & 1996). Authoritarianism (Adorno et al., 1950) refers to a related complex of nine sub-syndromes, of which conventionalism, authoritarian aggression and authoritarian submission are the most important (Meloen, 1991, p. 119). Cultural localism (the orientation towards the values and norms of the local community, see Lehman, 1986, in Billiet et al., 1996), was added in order to interpret the relation between adherence to the Christian faith and ethnocentrism (see Eisinga & Scheepers, 1989). Diagram 4.1 contains a summary of the results. The data was collected during 1989 and 1991. Diagram 4.1 does not contain the complete model of Billiet, Eisinga and Scheepers (1992 & 1996); only the variables relevant to the framework of this chapter were included.

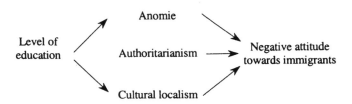

Diagram 4.1 First model explaining 'everyday' racism

Source: Billiet et al., 1992 and 1996.

The results of this more extensive model lead to several conclusions. First, everyday racism is determined by three variables. The most important of which, authoritarianism, has the strongest influence with a standardised effect parameter of .32. Cultural localism and anomie are more or less equally important with respective standardised effect parameters of .15 and .11. The addition of other variables to anomie considerably decreases its explanatory power. Second, the level of education no longer appears to exert any direct influence on everyday racism, completely circumventing these variables, and can therefore be interpreted without these variables (see below). The lack of a direct relation between level of education and authoritarianism is striking, all the more so for its deviation from the international literature (for example Eisinga & Scheepers, 1989). Billiet, Eisinga and Scheepers (1992, p. 317) suggest that the strong impact of the occupational group *'executive'* on authoritarianism may have absorbed the impact of the level of education. They also revert to Eisinga and Scheepers' social contra-identification theory to interpretate these relations. Authoritarianism, like anomie, triggers a process of social identification, whereby identification with authorities, characterising authoritarian individuals, is broadened to encompass social identification with your own group (see conventionalism below) and contra-identification with outgroups (see Eisinga & Scheepers, 1989, pp. 65–66). Cultural localists also identify with their ingroup, here the local community, thereby triggering a similar process.

During further development of this model the dependent variable everyday racism was broadened and supplemented (Billiet, 1993a & 1996). Four dependent variables were used: the attitude towards your 'own ethnic group', a negative attitude towards migrants based on cultural stereotypes (from here on: stereotypes), a rejective attitude towards migrants because they are considered an economic threat (from here on: feelings of threat), and biological racism. The explanatory powers of the three intermediate variables differs for each of the dependent variables studied. Anomie is the most important predictor of feelings of threat. Authoritarianism is the most important predictor of biological racism. The stereotypes are influenced more or less to the same extent by anomie and authoritarianism. Cultural localism exerts only a slight influence on the stereotypes. Anomie was found to have an impact on authoritarianism (see also Scheepers et al., 1992). An authoritarian attitude can after all compensate for the feelings of powerlessness and meaninglessness that are typical of an anomic individual.

In a final model a measurement for everyday racism was analysed on the basis of data collected by the *Interuniversitair Steunpunt Politieke-Opinieonderzoek* (ISPO: Interuniversity Centre For Political Opinion Research) in 1992 (Billiet, 1993b). However, the variables, anomie and cultural localism, were not included in the questionnaire, whereas authoritarianism, utilitarian individualism and political powerlessness on the other hand, were made used. These last two variables can be considered aspects of anomie. Political powerlessness is one of the essential components of anomie (Srole, 1956). Utilitarian individualism (Elchardus & Heyvaert 1990, pp. 155–161) expresses a cynical and misanthropic portrayal of mankind, and is closely linked to the aspects normlessness, meaninglessness, social isolation and powerlessness, of the concept anomie. Some examples of this would be: 'Because you always have to compromise when dealing with others, it is best not to mix with other people too much.' and 'The only things that count are power and money, the rest is just talk.' The main results of this model were summarised in Diagram 4.2. This diagram also contains a selection from the more extensive model; only those variables relevant to this chapter were included.

Diagram 4.2 shows that the three intermediate variables have an impact on the negative attitude towards migrants. Utilitarian individualism (standardised effect parameter: .27) plays a slightly more important role than authoritarianism (standardised effect parameter: .22) or political powerlessness (standardised effect parameter: .16). All three of these intermediate variables

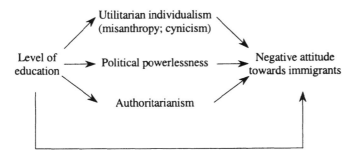

Diagram 4.2   Second model explaining 'everyday' racism

Source: Billiet, 1993b.

are influenced by the respondents' level of education. This mainly applies to the variables political powerlessness and utilitarian individualism (respective standardised effect parameters: –.30 and –.25). This time, in accordance with the international literature, the level of education also has a direct influence on the level of authoritarianism, even though this coefficient is rather weak (standardised effect parameter: –.10). It is, however, striking that here the three intermediate variables do not provide a complete explanation for the association between the level of education and everyday racism. The level of education still has a direct influence on these attitudes (standardised effect parameter: −.12). As concluded in earlier research (Scheepers et al., 1992; Billiet, 1993a), the variable political powerlessness, as an aspect of the concept anomie, also exerts an influence on the level of authoritarianism.

In search of an explanation for the importance of the level of education

The research discussed above shows that the level of education also plays an important role in explaining everyday racism in Belgium. What is striking is that the exact reasons for the strength of its explanatory role have barely been examined; the process by which the level of education influences the level of everyday racism, represents the black box of (Belgian) racism research. The studies discussed do offer various post hoc interpretations but these are rarely if ever tested empirically. This chapter will conclude by exploring possible explanations for the impact of education on the level of racism. First, the question of whether the impact of education is an empirical artifact will be examined. Second, possible explanations, derived from the above models, will be listed. And, finally, some comments regarding the way in which the level of education is generally measured, thereby arguing in favour of a more differentiated measurement in future research.

An empirical artifact?

Discussions on the results of survey research results frequently draw attention to the possibility that the relationship between the respondents' level of education and their level of racism could be no more than an empirical artifact; an effect of the chosen methodological approach. Two such arguments are the *tendency to say 'yes'* and the phenomenon of social desirability.

The tendency to say 'yes', also known as the acquiescent response bias, refers to the hypothesis that some respondents are always inclined to answer in the affirmative to the items offered (for example see Schönbach et al., 1981, pp. 130–138). It is contended that an unbalanced scale—a scale containing only racist statements, instead of both racist and non-racist ones—will cause repondents with this tendency to score higher and so be classified as racist, than if the scale were balanced. This has been used to explain the relatively high scores of less highly educated people, since the less highly educated are assumed to exhibit the acquiescent response bias to a larger extent. However, Schönbach, Gollwitzer, Stiepel and Wagner's (1981) thorough examination found nothing to support this. Further, in a re-analysis of the 1989 data Billiet (1996) found that although the acquiescent response bias correlated negatively with the level of education, suggesting that less highly educated people *were* more likely to say 'yes', the correlation with the variable everyday racism was limited (.07). Even after controlling for this tendency, and for the age of the respondents, the level of education still influenced the negative attitude towards migrants. The difference between the coefficients before and after controlling was also slight (−.267 and −.242 respectively). The role of the tendency to say 'yes' in establishing the relation between the level of education and everyday racism is, therefore, as good as negligible.

A second, frequently given, explanation—*social desirability*—refers to the respondents' inclination to *positively* adjust their answers in an interview. Social desirability is also used to explain the different responses of respondents with higher or lower levels of education (for example Dekker & Van Praag, 1990b, pp. 37–38). It is assumed that more highly educated people will be more inclined to present themselves in a more flattering light because they are more sensitive to the norms on this issue. Results of survey research, however, do not support this view. Wagner and Zick (1995), for example, conclude that the level of education also correlates with a measurement for subtle racism; a measurement partly developed to avoid socially desirable answers. Billiet, Carton and Huys (1990, p. 178) analysed the relation between the level of education and the extent to which people wished to deny migrants certain rights. The more concrete content of this scale and the manner in which the questions were asked, is likely to have reduced the incidence of socially desirable answers. The level of education was nevertheless related to the granting of rights, even though this relation was somewhat weaker than with the scale for everyday racism.

The survey results discussed provide only indirect evidence to contradict a social desirability effect. Wagner and Zick (1995) compared the attitudes of more- and less- highly educated people from the same age group in an experimental setting. One group filled out their questionnaires under bogus pipeline conditions—test subjects are persuaded that the computer, to which they give their answers, is able to discern a lie and so determine their real attitude. The control group experienced no such intervention. In the control group the familiar difference in evaluation of foreigners emerged: less highly educated people displayed a slightly more negative attitude. All those in the bogus pipeline group scored higher on the same racism measurement than their peers in the control group, demonstrating that, in the control group, both educational groups had adjusted their answers to be more socially desirable. However, contrary to expectations, those with lower levels of education were found to be slightly more sensitive to the social desirability effect than those with higher levels of education. In the bogus pipeline group, the difference between the two educational groups was more pronounced than in the control group.

In search of an explanation for the effect of education

It can be concluded that the established differences between those with higher levels of education and those with lower levels of education cannot be attributed (or only to a very limited extent) to methodological artifacts, such as an answer tendency or social desirability. This established difference might therefore be a real difference, but how should this difference be interpreted and which processes cause a higher level of education to reduce the level of everyday racism?

Comparison of the models Diagrams 4.1 and 4.2 may serve as a guideline when interpreting the influence of the level of education. The most striking difference between both models is the conclusion that the influence of the level of education in the first model (Diagram 4.1) completely circumvents the three included intermediate variables. This does not appear to be the case in the second model (Diagram 4.2) in which the level of education continues to exert a direct influence on everyday racism after controlling for the analysed attitudes. For the sake of this complete explanatory power it may be preferable to take the first model as a basis for our analysis.[2] It is also a richer model, providing more to go on with because it contains the variable cultural localism, lacking in the second model. Furthermore, in the second model the variable anomie was limited to two partial aspects of this concept, thus producing a poorer concept of anomie.

Each variable in the first model may symbolise one (or several) partial aspect(s) of the process by which the level of education influences everyday racism. The link between anomie and everyday racism may, for instance, be better understood by more explicitly linking everyday racism with each partial aspect of the concept anomie. Srole distinguishes five aspects related to the concept anomie: political and social powerlessness, normlessness and meaninglessness, social isolation and general feelings of social deterioration (Srole, 1956).

Individuals who feel *powerless* to influence their environment may try to gain control of their lives by rejecting migrants, as the individual may identify migrants as a cause of his or her problems. However, a higher level of education may also reduce feelings of powerlessness, as a higher education offers insight into the complexity of and connections between social processes (Rotter, 1966). This gives an individual the feeling of having more control over his or her life, thereby reducing the need for contra-identification with ethnic minorities.

Individuals who find themselves in a *meaningless* situation, may also try to give *meaning* to their lives by rejecting foreigners. This also relates to the theory of social contra-identification mentioned above. A higher level of education may give meaning to life, as education also transfers *values*, thereby explicitly offering (alternative) frameworks for a meaningful life (Dewaele, 1982).

Social isolation can, likewise, be neutralised by a reaction against foreigners. However, a higher level of education gives access to a more extensive, and more varied and open, social network (Flap & Tazelaar, 1988, pp. 55–57). This qualitatively and quantitatively richer social network also reduces the need for a contra-identification with ethnic minorities, since it reduces social isolation.

The relation between the perception of *socio-economic deterioration* and everyday racism can also be interpreted in terms of the scapegoat mechanism: migrants are held responsible for that which an individual feels they themselves are denied (feelings of relative deprivation). A higher level of education is the key to a higher occupational position, from and for which the acquired cultural capital allows access to higher social circles (for example De Graaf & Luijkx, 1995), thereby decreasing considerably the possibility of socio-economic deterioration.

To help us unravel the process by which a higher level of education reduces racism, the various partial aspects of the concept *authoritarianism* should also be made explicit. The three central aspects of authoritarianism have already been mentioned above. However, Adorno and his colleagues distinguish nine characteristics, together comprising the authoritarian personality syndrome (Adorno et al., 1950).

Strict conformation to conventional norms, *conventionalism*, also implies a rejection of migrants because, to a certain extent, they deviate from these cultural conventions (De Witte, 1990). A higher education increases knowledge about the customs of other 'foreign' ethinc groups and also offers a larger collection of behaviour models which can be drawn upon. This may reduce rigidity and place the uniqueness of cultural conventions into perspective, causing other codes of conduct to appear possible: difference may become less unfamiliar.

The aspect *authoritarian submission* refers to the complete and uncritical submission to moral authorities. This aspect is related to the previous one. Conventionalism may be characterised as 'horizontal' conformism (acceptance of the norms and traditions prevalent in society), while authoritarian submission may be considered an (extreme) form of 'vertical' conformism (obedience to those in positions of authority; see Tax, 1982, pp. 84–88 & De Witte, 1993b). Research by Kohn and Schooler (Kohn, 1977; Kohn &

Schooler, 1983) shows that a higher level of education weakens conformity, by preparing an individual for a higher occupational position for which a focus on self-determination is an essential prerequisite. After all, only individuals with this value orientation meet the demands for such a position. Hence, Kohn and colleagues argue that certain orientations towards values are by necessity transferred via the level of education. Conformism, and therefore authoritarian submission, is considered dysfunctional for more highly educated people.

The aspects *authoritarian aggression, cynicism and destructivism* and *power and toughness* can be discussed together, because they seem to refer to the same phenomenon. A central theme is the identification with strong powerful people, along with a negative portrayal of humankind, accompanied by a (violent) rejection of those who violate norms. That a higher level of education allows the acceptance of more than one set of norms, has already been discussed above. Therefore violation of these norms should not be so strongly rejected. Preoccupation with power and aggression may also be weakened by insight into the complexity and multi-causality of social phenomena, and of the behavior of others, offered by higher levels of education. Also Kohn's research can, again, offer a point of departure. An authoritative or aggressive approach to problems should not seem applicable when confronted with a complex situation, caused by several factors, demanding consultation and creativity. Such a situation is often encountered in the higher professional occupations filled by those with higher levels of education.

The aspects *anti-intraception, projection* and *sexual preoccupation* may also be discussed together. Authoritarian persons resist introspection, and they are inclined to attribute negatively assessed impulses, such as violations of sexual norms, to outgroups, such as foreigners. The diversity of information offered during long-term education stimulates the ability to reflect and in so doing may increase the capacity for self-analysis. The development of a better insight into one's own motivations may heighten the capacity to empathise with the situation and motivations of others. This may in itself lead to the understanding of and insight into the process leading to projection (Kaldenbach, 1986), a capacity which is also developed further by a higher level of education (Jackman & Muha, 1984).

Finally, the aspect *stereotype* is also a characteristic of an authoritarian individual. A higher level of education counteracts the use of such simple schemes and rough dichotomies by virtue of the need to process large amounts of complex information, which, by definition, rules out a reliance on such simplified representations (Schönbach et al., 1981).

Closely connected to this is the process hidden behind the variable cultural localism. Localists focus on the familiar, smaller, local environment and they are, among other things, less mobile in a cultural and cognitive sense: they are less receptive to new ideas (Eisinga & Scheepers, 1989, pp. 166–167). In other words, they are characterised by a *more* limited social and intellectual horizon which predisposes them to cultural conservatism and to a rejective attitude towards foreigners, who, for example, deviate from the local traditional lifestyle (see above). Going to school broadens this more limited horizon (Gabennesch, 1972). It does so by providing new perspectives with which to interpret reality, while also bringing people into contact with new, and therefore deviating, viewpoints and models of behaviour, leading to the understanding that one's viewpoint is only one of many.

The above summary allows the conclusion to be drawn that a higher level of education may exert an influence through *four central processes*. The first process involves the reduction of a negative attitude towards foreigners through the transfer of *information*: knowledge and models of behaviour. The broader and more diverse information offered by a higher level of education also provides an insight into the complexity and multi-causality of society and of individual behaviour. This increases feelings of control and contributes to an individual's increased capacity to assess and empathise.

Several researchers highlight *cognitive capacity*, the second process, as one of the most crucial factors (e.g. Schönbach et al., 1981; Bobo & Licari, 1989; Sidanius & Lau, 1989; Wagner & Zick, 1995). Notwithstanding the considerable variance in the terminology used—some talk about 'cognitive flexibility', others about 'intellectual complexity', 'associative flexibility' or 'cognitive sophistication'—they all refer to the capacity to process large amounts of information and to differentiate. Which, by definition differentiates the attitudes towards foreigners and relativises the uniqueness of traditions and norms. Research shows that such cognitive capacities explain a substantial part of the variance between level of education and racism or related measurements (for example Schönbach et al., 1981; Bobo & Licari, 1989; Sidanius & Lau, 1989). Implying that the reductive effect of the level of education operates to a considerable extent through this variable.

The third process through which the level of education may exert an influence, deals with the transfer of *values*. After all, value orientations and frameworks for giving meaning to life are transferred along with the content of the lessons. Belgium's Catholic schools often emphasise evangelical values such as humanism, justice, solidarity and charity. These values are central to the *socio-cultural* Christianity characteristic of the collective identity of catholic social organisations in Belgium since the 1960s (Billiet, 1995). An emphasis on such values may restrain the development of ethnocentrism and racism, because these values are contrary to the underlying values of racism, and may also counteract the seeking of meaning via contra-identification with foreigners, mentioned earlier.

A final core process has to do with the *resources* gained from and developed by education. This refers partly to the common assertion that individuals with a higher occupational position do not, or should not, develop a negative attitude towards migrants because migrants do not constitute a socio-economic threat to them (for example Billiet et al., 1990, p. 177). A higher level of education may have an indirect influence on everyday racism because it removes either the necessity or the desirability to develop a hostile view of migrants. The cultural capital acquired is pivotal to gaining a higher occupational position (Dronkers & De Graaf, 1995), and is accompanied by a focus on self-determination and a socioculturally progressive attitude (Kohn & Schooler, 1983; De Witte, 1990). This favourable socio-economic position causes contra-identification with foreigners to be not only unnecessary but also *contrary* to the values and attitudes characteristic of those occupying a higher occupational position. A second resource, economic capital, also contributes to the ease with which a higher occupational position is gained (Dronkers & De Graaf, 1995). A third resource, developed and reinforced by having undergone higher levels of education is the social capital of individuals—their social network (Flap, 1987). The more extensive and varied the social network, the less likely it is that social isolation leading to contra-identification with migrants will occur. In addition, a more extensive network also plays a part in obtaining and strengthening a better socio-economic position (Flap & Tazelaar, 1988), which in and of itself reduces the development of feelings of deprivation.

A final remark on the education variable

For the purposes of this chapter, the education variable was interpreted *vertically*, with the level of education often equating to no more than the number of years spent at school. The presence of the four main processes listed, were attributed to having spent more years at school. A longer school career leads to more *information* (knowledge and models of behaviour), to a stronger development and better training of *cognitive capacities*, to a longer socialisation period instilling particular *values* and to the establishment of a larger collection of *resources* that (indirectly) contribute to reducing racism.

Ekehammar and colleagues (1987) correctly indicate that behind this quantitative dimension, there is also a hidden qualitative dimension (for a similar discussion Van de Werfhorst et al., 1997). Leaving these dimensions undifferentiated can cause problems of interpretation leading to false conclusions. Young people who stayed in school until the age of eighteen may, after all, have attended different kinds of schooling. The four processes made explicit above do not necessarily work in the same way within all possible forms of education on offer. Hence it is useful to define a *horizontal* dimension with a more *qualitative* character: the *type* of education, next to the vertical dimension (years spent in education). Within this horizontal dimension two aspects can be distinguished: the extent to which the education is general versus vocational—*educational direction*—and the *field of study*.

An initial difference is related to the *general* versus the *vocational* character of the education. Ekehammar and colleagues (1987) conclude that there are significant differences in racism between pupils from both types of education, even though both groups have attended school for the same duration (same amount of education in years). Something similar is concluded in Belgian research (Gevaert, 1993). Belgium has three types of education. Apart from general and vocational education there is also an intermediate form, technical education. Because education is compulsory until the age of eighteen, eighteen-year-olds may finish their secondary education in one of these three types of education. From the Belgian research it becomes clear that everyday racism among seventeen to eighteen-year-olds is lower among pupils attending general education, and higher among those attending vocational education. Pupils attending technical education fall in between these groups. These differences are similar to those established in the Netherlands regarding pupils from the same age group (Raaijmakers, 1993). They are not surprising and may be interpreted in the same way as the differences regarding the amount of education. After all, compared to vocational education, general education also offers a greater and more varied amount of knowledge and models of behaviour. Furthermore, such education pays more attention to cognitive development. General education is considered preparatory; pupils generally move on to higher education and so a higher professional occupation. Thus the influence of the horizontal dimension of the level of education is analogous to that of the vertical dimension's influence on the acquisition of resources. Specific to this dimension, however, is the socialisation of values. It has been demonstrated that in vocational schools a more conformist climate prevails (Dewaele, 1982), while such schools also place a greater emphasis on discipline (Michiels, 1990). Such conformist values are strongly related to a rejective attitude towards foreigners, which can be formulated more broadly as a rejective attitude towards groups deviating from the traditional norms. This makes it likely that socialisation in schools with such a climate may also facilitate the transfer of everyday racism.

The second aspect of the horizontal dimension refers to the *field of study*. Within each type of education a number of widely divergent directions can be distinguished, each of which may be able to influence aspects such as everyday racism in a specific way. Ekehammar and colleagues (1987) distinguish three directions in their research: humanities (including social sciences), economics and technology. These directions can be distinguished both within a general education and within a vocational one. Ekehammar et al. found the highest racism score among technology students and the lowest among humanities students, irrespective of the general or vocational character of their training. The Belgian researcher Rosseel also finds strong attitudinal between pupils (or students) from human-oriented versus object-oriented studies (Rosseel, 1985). There is probably no evidence that the development of students' cognitive capacities is dependent on the selected field of study. All types of education probably offer the possibility to put these intellectual skills into practice. The field of study is, therefore, most likely to influence aspects such as everyday racism via the three remaining processes mentioned above. First of all, the specific content learned may play a role. After all, in more technical oriented education less information is given about the functioning of society and of individuals. Thus possibly providing less opportunity to develop an understanding that individual and social problems stem from a multitude of reasons, all of which are related in a complex way. The transfer of a specific pattern of ideas and values may also accompany the field of study. After all, in each school a characteristic school climate and culture prevails. It seems plausible that these aspects are also related to the field of study. However, here a problem of interpretation arises. Diagnosed differences between pupils from various fields of study may be caused by both self-selection (young people with specific attitudes select a specific education) and by socialisation (during their education young people develop to a larger extent attitudes characteristic of their field of study and its prevalent climate). The longitudinal research of Guimond and Palmer (1990) supports the idea that a socialisation effect emanates from following a specific field of study. They compared students from, among other things, the social sciences and engineering when they began their studies and then again one year later. Social science students developed an external causal attribution for poverty and unemployment during their studies, while in case of engineering students the causal attribution remained rather internal. It seems plausible to assume that such socialisation does not remain limited to these attributions, but may also be broadened to the learning of other attitudes, such as everyday racism. Finally, the field of study also influences the accumulation of resources. This way Van de Werfhorst and colleagues (1997) distinguished nine fields of study from the extent to which these supply cultural and economic resources. These last resources influence students' future job opportunities: not every type of graduate finds a job quickly. The feelings of relative deprivation resulting from this situation may also influence the evaluation of foreigners (see above).

Finally, in this contribution *the level* of racism was central, always refering to the score on a scale measuring everyday racism. Each of the three types of education outlined immediately above influence this score: those with a lower level of education, individuals attending vocational education, and individuals attending schooling in a rather object-related field of study, all score higher on such a racism scale. However, the type education undergone also influences the *consistency* of the attitudes of an individual (Bishop, 1976). A higher education (and a more general one) leads to more information about politics and to a stronger development of the cognitive capacities. This allows for a more solid cognitive structuring of attitudes, that could also be more strongly integrated in the political-ideological conceptual frameworks available in society. Correlations between separate racism items are, therefore, higher in case of people with a higher level of education (Vollebergh & Raaijmakers, 1991, pp. 71–74). The same can be concluded for correlations between such scales. Belgian findings on the effect of the type of education are similar (Kindermans, 1993, p. 68). The correlation between authoritarianism and everyday racism amounted to .47*** among pupils attending general education. Among pupils attending technical education it amounted to *only* .24***, while this correlation was simply not significant among pupils attending vocational education (r = .09). In a longitudinal analysis Vollebergh and Raaijmakers (1991, pp. 73–74) even conclude that the intra-personal stability of such scales (here: authoritarianism) is greater for more highly educated people than for less highly educated people. These conclusions suggest that more attention should be paid to the aspect consistency of attitudes in future research.

Conclusion

This chapter began with a short outline of the current state of racism research in Belgium. After listing the explanatory frameworks used in this research, possible explanations were examined for the link between education and the level of everyday racism. This relation cannot be attributed to a methodological artifact, as was seen in the overview of the tendency to say 'yes', or social desirability. In explaining this relation four processes were mapped, through which the type of education attended may have an influence on the level of racism: the transfer of information (knowledge and models of behaviour), the development of cognitive capacities, the transfer of values and the provision of resources influencing future job opportunities. It was assumed that these processes constitute intermediaries with regard to the impact of education on everyday racism.

This brings us to suggestions for further research. The assumption that education basically operates *via* these four intermediate processes, has to be tested by future research. Such research is necessary because the way in which education influences racism scores is still insufficiently understood. This process still represents the black box of racism research. Only the effect of the cognitive capacity aspect was verified. However, a comparison of this variable with other possible sources of explanation is, for the time being, lacking. Future research should also pay attention to a yet more differentiated application of the variable 'education', whereby the effect of the horizontal and vertical dimensions should be analysed separately. Finally, the variable racism should also be further differentiated. New applications of this concept, such as subtle versus blatant racism, have not yet been analysed in Belgium.

Notes

1 In this chapter, the concepts 'foreigners', 'migrants' and 'people of another nationality' will be used interchangeably because research shows that these concepts are used interchangeably by the Belgian population (Billiet et al., 1990, pp. 51–53). This research reveals that Belgians commonly refer to Turks and Moroccans, when discussing 'foreigners' or 'migrants'.

2 In Diagram 4.1, authoritarianism was not directly influenced by the level of education. Research since then (Billiet, 1993a & 1996), however, revealed that the level of education has an indirect impact on authoritarianism, via anomie. This indirect impact of the level of education on authoritarianism enables us to include the concept 'authoritarianism' in our discussion and interpretation of the effects of the educational level.

References

Adorno, T., Frenkel-Brunswik, E., Levinson, D. and Sanford, R. (1950), *The Authoritarian Personality*, New York, Harper & Row.

Ashford, S. and Timms, N. (1992), *What Europe Thinks. A Study Of Western European Values*, Aldershot, Dartmouth.

Becker, J. and Vink, R. (1991), *Secularisatie in Nederland 1966–1991: de verandering van opvattingen en enkele gedragingen*, Rijswijk, Sociaal en Cultureel Planbureau.

Billiet, J. (1993a), *Ondanks beperkt zicht. Studies over waarden, ontzuiling en politieke veranderingen in Vlaanderen*, Leuven/Brussel, Sociologisch Onderzoeksinstituut/ VUBPress.

Billiet, J. (1993b), Stabiliteit en verandering in de attitude tegenover 'vreemdelingen', in M. Swyngedouw, J. Billiet, A. Carton and R. Beerten (eds), *Kiezen is verliezen. Onderzoek naar de politieke opvattingen van Vlamingen*, (pp. 147–162), Leuven, Acco.

Billiet, J. (1995), Church Involvement, Individualism, and Ethnic Prejudice among Flemish Roman Catholics: New Evidence of a Moderating Effect, *Journal for the Scientific Study of Religion*, vol. 34, no. 2, pp. 224–233.

Billiet, J. (1996), Theoretical Dimensions and Measurement Models of Attitudes towards Ethnic Minorities, *Bulletin 1996/23*, Leuven, ISPO.
Billiet, J., Carton, A. and Huys, R. (1990), *Onbekend of onbemind? Een sociologisch onderzoek naar de houding van de Belgen tegenover migranten*, KU Leuven, Departement Sociologie.
Billiet, J. and De Witte, H. (1991), Naar racisme neigende houdingen in Vlaanderen: typologie en maatschappelijke achtergronden, *Cultuur en Migratie*, Themanummer 'racisme', no. 1, pp. 25–62.
Billiet, J. and De Witte, H. (1995), Attitudinal Dispositions to vote for a 'new' extreme right-wing party: the case of 'Vlaams Blok', *European Journal of Political Research*, 27, no. 2, pp. 181–202.
Billiet, J., Eisinga, R. and Scheepers, P. (1992), Etnocentrisme in de Lage Landen. Opinies over 'eigen' en 'ander' volk in Nederland en Vlaanderen, *Sociologische Gids*, vol. 39, nos. 5/6, pp. 300–323.
Billiet, J., Eisinga, R. and Scheepers, R. (1996), Ethnocentrism in the Low Countries: a Comparative Perspective, *New Community*, vol. 22, no. 3, pp. 401–416.
Bishop, G. (1976), The Effect of Education on Ideological Consistency, *Public Opinion Quarterly*, 40, pp. 337–348.
Bobo, L. and Licari, F. (1989), Education and Political Tolerance. Testing the Effects of Cognitive Sophistication and Target Group Affect, *Public Opinion Quarterly*, vol. 53, no. 3, pp. 285–308.
Carton, A., Swyngedouw, M., Billiet, J. and Beerten, R. (1993), *Source Book of the Voters' Study in Connection with the 1991 General Election*, Leuven, Sociologisch Onderzoeksinstituut/ISPO.
De Baets, A. (1989), Het beeld van de migrant bij de publieke opinie in Vlaanderen volgens opiniepeilingen uit de periode 1973–1988, *Cultuur en Migratie*, no. 2, pp. 31–61.
De Baets, A. (1994), *De figuranten van de geschiedenis. Hoe het verleden van andere culturen wordt verbeeld en in herinnering gebracht*, Berchem, Epo, p. 254
De Graaf, P. and Luijkx, R. (1995), Paden naar succes: geboorte of diploma's? in J. Dronkers and W. Ultee (red), *Verschuivende ongelijkheid in Nederland. Sociale gelaagdheid en mobiliteit*, Assen, Van Gorcum, pp. 31–45.
Dekker, P. and van Praag, C. (1990a), *Opvattingen over allochtonen in landen van de Europese Gemeenschap*, Rijswijk, Sociaal Cultureel Planbureau.
Dekker, P. and van Praag, C. (1990b), Xenofobie in West-Europa, *Migrantenstudies*, no. 4, pp. 37–57.
Delooz, P. and Kerkhofs, J. (1992), Ethiek. Op zoek naar een haalbaar evenwicht, in Kerkhofs et al. (eds), *De versnelde ommekeer. De waarden van Vlamingen, Walen en Brusselaars in de jaren negentig*, (pp. 221–272), Tielt, lannoo.
Dewaele, A. (1982), *De onderwijssituatie van de verschillende sociale groepen in Vlaanderen. Een literatuurstudie met bijzondere aandacht voor de arbeidersgroep*, Leuven, HIVA-KULeuven.
De Witte, H. (1990), *Conformisme, radicalisme en machteloosheid. Een onderzoek naar de sociaal-culturele en sociaal-economische opvattingen van arbeiders in Vlaanderen*, Leuven, HIVA-KU Leuven.
De Witte, H. (1993a), Een overzicht van (sociaal-)psychologische verklaringen voor 'alledaags' racisme, *Infomig. Nieuwsbrief Steunpunt Migranten*, no. 1, pp. 7–10.
De Witte, H. (1993b), Verschillen in conservatisme tussen arbeiders en bedienden. Een interpretatie vanuit het concept persoonlijke controle, *Gedrag en Organisatie. Tijdschrift voor sociale-, arbeids- en organisatiepsychologie*, vol. 6, no. 2, pp. 57–78.
De Witte, H. (1996a), On the 'Two Faces' of Right-Wing Extremism in Belgium, *Res Publica*, vol. 38, no. 2, pp. 397–411.

De Witte, H. (1996b), Ethnocentrism and Racism among Flemish Youth in Belgium, paper presented at the international conference '*Youth at Risk*', session 'Ethnification of Social Conflicts. Racism and the Environment of Ethnic Youngsters', 20–22 September 1996, Noorderwijkerhout, the Netherlands.

De Witte, H. (1998), 'Torenhoge verschillen in de Lage Landen. Over het verschil in succes tussen de Centrumstroming en het Vlaams Blok', in J. van Holsteyn and C. Mudde (eds), *Extreem-rechts in Nederland*, (pp. 157–173), Den Haag, Sdu uitgevers.

De Witte, H. and Billiet, J. (1990), 'Een volk, een leider? Extreem-rechtse opvattingen en stemgedrag in Vlaanderen', paper presented at the NVPP-symposium '*Rechts-extremisme: zeepbel of tijdbom*', 23 November 1990, Amsterdam.

De Witte, H. and Billiet, J. (1993), 'A Typology of Multicultural Attitudes', presentation at the Congress '*Christian Universities and European Culture*', Session '*Cultural Deprivation*', 10–13 November 1993.

De Witte, H., Billiet, J. and Scheepers, P. (1994), 'Hoe zwart is Vlaanderen? Een exploratief onderzoek naar uiterst-rechtse denkbeelden' in *Vlaanderen in 1991*, [special edition] *Res Publica*, vol. 36, no. 1, pp. 85–102.

De Witte, H. and Verbeeck, G. (in press), 'Belgium: a Divided Unity', in L. Hagendoorn, G. Çsepeli, H. Dekker and R. Farnen (eds.), *European Nations and Nationalism: Theoretical and Historical Perspectives*, Aldershot, Ashgate.

Dooghe, G. (1981), 'De gastarbeiders', in G. Dooghe et al. (eds), *Feiten en meningen over actuele problemen*, (pp. 17–57), Antwerpen/Amsterdam, De Sikkel/De Nederlandse Boekhandel.

Dooghe, G. and Vanderleyden, L. (1974), *Bevolking en publieke opinie*, Kappelen, De Sikkel/De Nederlandse Boekhandel.

Dronkers, J. and de Graaf, P. (1995), 'Ouders en het onderwijs van hun kinderen', in J. Dronkers and W. Ultee (eds), *Verschuivende ongelijkheid in Nederland. Sociale gelaagdheid en mobiliteit*, (pp. 46–66), Assen, Van Gorcum.

Eisinga, R. and Scheepers, P. (1989), *Etnocentrisme in Nederland*, Nijmegen, ITS.

Ekehammar, B., Nilsson, I. and Sidanius, J. (1987), 'Education and Ideology: Basic Aspects of Education Related to Adolescents' Sociopolitical Attitudes, *Political Psychology*, vol. 8, no. 3, pp. 395–410.

Elchardus, M. and Heyvaert, P. (1990), *Soepel, flexibel en ongebonden. Een vergelijking van twee laat-moderne generaties*, Brussel, VUBPress.

Eurobarometer (1989), *Racisme en onverdraagzaamheid*, Brussel, Council of Europe.

Felling, A., Peters, J. and Scheepers, P. (1986), *Theoretische modellen ter verklaring van etnocentrisme*, Nijmegen, ITS.

Felling, A. and Peters, J. (1991), 'Culturele pluriformiteit in Nederland. Verschillen in cultuurpatroon tussen sociale categorieën en ideologische groeperingen', in A. Felling and J. Peters (eds), *Cultuur en sociale wetenschappen. Beschouwingen en empirische studies*, Nijmegen, ITS.

Flap, H. (1987), 'De theorie van het sociale kapitaal', *Antropologische Verkenningen*, vol. 6, no. 1, pp. 14–27.

Flap, H. and Tazelaar, F. (1988), 'De rol van informele sociale netwerken op de arbeidsmarkt: flexibilisering en uitsluiting', in Flap, H. and Arts, W. (eds), *De flexibele arbeidsmarkt. Theorie en praktijk*, [special edition] *Mens & Maatschappij*, vol. 63, pp. 48–64.

Gabennesch, H. (1972), Authoritarianism as World View, *American Journal of Sociology*, 77, pp. 857–875.

Gevaert, A. (1993), *Etnocentrisme bij scholieren. Een onderzoek naar de geslachtsverschillen inzake de houding ten opzichte van migranten*, unpublished report of Psychology Department, Leuven, KU Leuven.

Guimond, S. and Palmer, D. (1990), 'Type of Academic Training and Causal Attributions for Social Problems', *European Journal of Social Psychology*, 20, pp. 61–75.
Hagendoorn, L. and Janssen, J. (1983), *Rechts-omkeer. Rechtsextreme opvattingen bij leerlingen van middelbare scholen*, Baarn, Amboboeken.
Jackman, M. and Muha, M. (1984), 'Education and Intergroup Attitudes: Moral Enlightenment, Superficial Democratic Commitment, or Ideological Refinement?', *American Sociological Review*, 49, pp. 751–769.
Kaldenbach, H. (1986), *Diskriminatie: hoe reageer je erop?* Haarlem, Uitgeverij De Toorts.
Kerkhofs, J. and Rezsohazy, R. (eds)(1984), *De stille ommekeer. Oude en nieuwe waarden in het België van de jaren tachtig*, Tielt, Lannoo.
Kerkhofs, J., Dobbelaere, K., Voyé, L. and Bawin-Legros, B. (eds) (1992), *De versnelde ommekeer. De waarden van Vlamingen, Walen en Brusselaars in de jaren negentig*, Tielt, Lannoo.
Kindermans, S. (1993), *Etnocentrisme bij scholieren. Een onderzoek naar de invloed van autoritarisme*, Niet gepubliceerde eindverhandeling Departement Psychologie, Leuven, KU Leuven.
Kohn, M. (1977), *Class and Conformity: a Study in Values. With a Reassessement, 1977*, 2nd edn, Chicago, University of Chicago Press.
Kohn, M. and Schooler, C. (1983), *Work And Personality: an Inquiry into the Impact of Social Stratification*, New Jersey, Ablex publishing corporation.
Loosveldt, G. (1995), 'Jongeren en beelden over migranten', *Tijdschrift voor sociologie*, vol. 16, no. 1, pp. 51–61.
Meloen, J. (1991), 'De autoritarisme-concepten van Adorno et al. en Altemeyer vergeleken: theoretische analyse en empirische test', in Scheepers, P. and Eisinga, R. (eds), *Onderdanig en intolerant. Lacunes en controverses in autoritarisme-studies*, (pp. 103–126), Nijmegen, ITS.
Michiels, K. (1990), *Scholen en leerlingen en de vernieuwing in het BSO*, Leuven, HIVA-KULeuven, 140.
Middendorp, C. (1991), *Ideology in Dutch Politics. the Democratic System Reconsidered 1970–1985*, Assen/Maastricht, Van Gorcum.
Pettigrew, T. and Meertens, R. (1995), 'Subtle and Blatant Prejudice in Western Europe', *European Journal of Social Psychology*, 25, pp. 57–75.
Raaijmakers, Q. (1993), Opvattingen over politiek en maatschappij, in W. Meeus and H. 't Hart (eds), *Jongeren in Nederland. Een nationaal survey naar ontwikkeling in de adolescentie en naar intergenerationele overdracht*, (pp. 106–132), Amersfoort, Academische Uitgeverij.
Raaijmakers, Q. and De Witte, H. (1995), 'Traditionele opvattingen en rechts-extreme partijvoorkeuren bij Vlaamse en Nederlandse scholieren', *Jeugd en Samenleving*, vol. 25, nos. 1/2, pp. 62–73.
Roof, W. (1974), 'Religious Orthodoxy and Minority Prejudice: Causal Relationship or Reflection of Localistic World View?' *American Journal of Sociology*, 80, pp. 643–664.
Rosseel, E. (1985), *Ruiters en ridders van de lege dageraad. Evoluties in de arbeidsethiek van de jeugd.* Brussel, Vrije Universiteit Brussel.
Rotter, J. (1966), 'Generalized Expectancies of Internal Versus External Control of Reinforcement, *Psychological Monographs*, 80, whole no. 609(1).
Scheepers, P., Felling, A. and Peters, J. (1989), Etnocentrisme in Nederland: theoretische bijdragen empirisch getoetst, *Sociologische Gids*, 1, pp. 31–47.
Scheepers, P., Felling, A. and Peters, J. (1992), 'Anomie, Authoritarianism and Ethnocentrism: Update of a Classic Theme and an Empirical Test', *Politics and the Individual*, vol. 2, no. 1, pp. 43–59.

Schönbach, P., Gollwitzer, P., Stiepel, G. and Wagner, U. (1981), *Education and Intergroup Attitudes*, European monographs in social psychology no. 22, London, Academic Press.

Sidanius, J. and Lau, R. (1989), Political Sophistication and Political Deviance: a Matter of Context, *Political Psychology*, vol. 10, no. 1, pp. 85–109.

Srole, L. (1956), 'Social Integration and Certain Corrolaries. An Exploratory Study', *American Sociological Review*, 21, pp. 709–768.

Sumner, W. (1906), *Folkways*, Boston, Ginn.

Tajfel, H. (1982), *Social Identity and Intergroup Relations*, Cambridge, Cambridge University Press.

Tax, B. (1982), *Waarden, mentaliteit en beroep. Een onderzoek ten behoeve van een sociaal-culturele interpretatie van sociaal-economisch milieu*, Lisse, Swets and Zeitlinger.

Van de Werfhorst, H., Kraaykamp, G. and de Graaf, N. (1997), 'Opleidingsrichting en leefstijl. Het belang van opleidingshulpbronnen versus beroepskenmerken voor leefstijlkeuzes', *Mens & Maatschappij*, 72, no. 4), 335–351.

Vollebergh, W. and Raaijmakers, Q. (1991), 'Intergenerationele overdracht van autoritarisme', in Scheepers, P. and Eisinga, R. (eds), *Onderdanig en intolerant. Lacunes en controverses in autoritarisme-studies*, (pp. 61–77) Nijmegen, ITS.

Vos, L. (1993), 'De rechts-radicale traditie in het Vlaams-nationalisme', *Wetenschappelijke Tijdingen*, (3), 129–149.

Vos, L. (1994), 'De nationale identiteit in België: een historisch overzicht', in Detrez, R. and Blommaert, J. (eds), *Nationalisme. Kritische opstellen*, (pp. 120–150) Berchem, EPO.

Wagner, U. and Zick, A. (1995), 'The Relation of Formal Education to Ethnic Prejudice: its Reliability, Validity and Explanation', *European Journal of Social Psychology*, 25, pp. 41–56.

5 The Impact of Education on Racism in Poland Compared with Other European Countries

ALEKSANDRA JASINSKA-KANIA

Introduction

The Polish *Encyclopaedia* (1996, p. 460) defines *racism* as:

> a complex of viewpoints based on the pseudoscientific thesis of the inequality of the human races...Arguments set forth in support of these viewpoints...are not convincing...Racism was adopted in Hitler's Germany as a basis for the Nazi ideology used during WWII as a theoretical justification for genocide, particularly of the Jews. Nowadays a different form of racism is more common. This form does not differentiate between white groups but proclaims the superiority of 'white' over 'coloured' races, especially black. According to this viewpoint blacks are, evolutionarily, a backward race, unable to responsibly use the achievements of civilization...From a scientific point of view, racism represents unfounded beliefs...unethical and clearly contradictory to generally accepted moral principles...Racism has been condemned by many international bodies such as the UNO in their 1948 'Declaration of Human Rights'...[1]

Clearly racism is perceived as incompatible with any criteria of political correctness in Poland. Thus, it is not surprising that, when surveyed, the majority of the population rejects racist statements. However, the concept race is unclear, particularly in Poland, a country that has had a relatively homogeneous ethnic population since WWII.

I will use the results of the 1988 'Poles and Others' survey[2] to discuss what Polish people understand by the term race. I will also present some results of an analysis of determinants of Poles' attitudes towards various national and ethnic groups based on opinion polls conducted in the 1990s (Jasinska-Kania, 1991). Then I will examine comparative measures of racism and ethnic intolerance in Poland and other European countries used in the *European Values Study* (*EVS*).[3] Finally, based on the results of the 1990 *EVS*,

I will analyse the influence of education and other socio-demographic variables, as well as various socio-psychological and political attitudes on the willingness to accept people of another race and ethnic groups as neighbours in Poland in comparison with other European countries.

The meaning of *race* in Poland

In the 1988 survey 'Poles and Others' a 1000 representative sample of the adult population were asked: 'There are people of different races living in the world; do you think that the following people (Arabs, blacks, British, Chinese, Germans, Italians, Jews, and Slovaks) belong to the same race as Poles?'. The distribution of answers is presented in Table 5.1.

Table 5.1 Perception of different groups as belonging to the same race as Poles (%)

Groups of people	'rather no'	'rather yes'	'don't know'
Blacks	89	6	5
Chinese	88	7	5
Arabs	80	10	10
Jews	47	42	11
Italians	24	69	7
Germans	24	72	4
English	22	72	6
Slovaks	7	89	4

Source: Nowicka, 1994, p. 187. (N=906)

A large majority of Poles identified blacks (89 per cent), Chinese (88 per cent), and Arabs (80 per cent) as belonging to races different from their own. Opinions were divided over Jews. Forty-seven per cent thought Jews belong to another race, but 42 per cent included them in the same race as Poles, and 11 per cent could not answer the question. Twenty-four per cent excluded Italians, and Germans from their own race and 22 per cent excluded British. Yet, some 70 per cent did not exclude these groups. Seven per cent classed Slovaks as belonging to another race, but the vast majority (89 per cent) felt they belonged to the same race. These responses indicate that Poles connect the concept of race largely with skin colour and related physical characteristics, as seen in the figures for blacks and Chinese, but also with the perception of cultural and religious distance. The responses show that in spite of Arabs' and Jews' similar physical characteristics, Arabs are more frequently excluded from the Polish racial community than are Jews. That almost half the respondents indicated Jews as belonging to another race can be interpreted as an effect of memories of the past. A smaller percentage of Poles linked race to various national and ethnic characteristics (Nowicka, 1990).

Neither the respondents' age nor education influenced their perception of the racial distinctiveness of blacks, Chinese and Arabs from Poles. A higher level of education increases the likelihood that the use of race as a basis for differentiation will be limited to descriptions of distinctive physical traits. It also increases the likelihood of tolerance and diminished social distance towards other national and ethnic groups. The higher the respondents' level of education, the more likely they are to include Jews, Slovaks, Italians, British, and Germans in the same racial group as Poles. But the effect of level of education is not uni-linear. The type of education has a separate effect on the perception of racial differences. The respondents with vocational training were more likely than those with general secondary education to perceive Germans, British, Italians, and Jews as belonging to the same race as Poles, whereas respondents with general secondary education were more inclined to emphasise national and cultural distinctions between various groups.

Table 5.2 Education and perception of different groups as belonging to the same race as Poles (%)

Education	Blacks	Chinese	Arabs	Jews	Italians	Germans	British	Slovaks
Elementary incomplete	3.8	7.6	9.4	37.7	62.3	66.0	69.9	79.3
Elementary complete	8.7	9.3	11.6	40.6	66.0	66.9	65.4	84.8
Vocational or secondary incomplete	5.7	4.9	9.4	42.7	73.6	80.0	78.9	93.5
Secondary general	2.8	3.3	8.8	39.8	66.3	69.6	71.3	92.3
Tertiary (college and higher)	6.4	4.7	8.5	53.2	80.9	69.4	91.5	93.7

Source: Nowicka 1990, p.169. (N=907)

The survey consisted of questions designed to measure social distance towards the already mentioned groups of people: readiness to identify the child of a Polish mother and father belonging to one of the above mentioned groups as Polish; willingness to accept a blood transfusion from a member of these groups; and expressing tolerance towards these groups of people in various social contexts, such as potential neighbours and marital partners. The pattern of responses to all these questions was similar. The ranking of outgroups in a hierarchy of social distance was, for the most part, the same. The greatest social distance was maintained towards blacks, followed by Arabs, then Chinese, with Jews ranked in the middle. A much smaller and diminishing social distance was expressed towards, respectively, Italians, Germans, English, and Slovaks (Nowicka, 1994). Age and education of respondents had a significant effect on all measures of social distance, younger and more highly educated people were more willing to accept social contacts with outgroups.

The questionnaire included questions designed to measure blatant racist attitudes. Respondents were asked: 'Do you think there are better and worse races in the world?.' More than two-thirds (68 per cent) denied the existence of such racial differences; 15 per cent believed in the superiority of some races; 17 per cent did not know how to answer the question. Belief in racial inequality increased with the age of the respondents and decreased in parallel with the level of education. Responses to this question correlated only with the rejection of a black person as a potential blood donor or marital partner. Fifty-seven per cent of those believing in racial inequality mention blacks as an inferior race, followed by Arabs (15 per cent), and then Chinese and Jews (4 per cent). Three per cent mentioned the 'white race' as superior. The reasons for racial inferiority of blacks, given in answers to the open question directed only to the respondents who believed in racial inequality, focused on economic characteristics: laziness, inefficiency, lack of discipline and poor organisation, poverty, and low standards of living. Perceived cultural characteristics, such as savagery and primitive and strange customs were also mentioned. However, eight per cent of 'racists' view these inferior characteristics as being the result of external factors such as racial discrimination, exploitation, and even geographical factors. Asked whether people of different races can live harmoniously in one country, 74 per cent of the respondents answered either 'definitely yes' (23 per cent) or 'rather yes' (51 per cent), while 17 per cent indicated 'rather not' and two per cent 'definitely not' and seven per cent 'did not know.'

An analysis of the results of the surveys on Poles' attitudes towards various national and ethnic groups conducted in the 1990s (Jasinska-Kania,

1991) revealed that the list of groups towards whom negative attitudes were held included two distinct groups. Those from neighbouring countries to the west and the east, particularly those associated in the national memory with acute conflicts: Ukrainians, Russians, and Germans, and those traditionally considered totally different from Poles or simply alien: Gypsies, Arabs, Turks, and blacks. In a 1990 survey the attitudes toward groups perceived as most ethnically different from Poles were influenced above all by the respondents' place of residence. Xenophobia was stronger in rural areas and small towns than in large cities. The respondents' level of education appeared to be the most important explanatory factor for attitudes towards other nationalities, contributing to a lower level of generalised xenophobia and ethnocentrism and to a higher level of knowledge of historical and current relations between national and ethnic groups (Jasinska-Kania, 1991).

The comparative measure of racial prejudice and ethnic intolerance in Europe

The only empirical data allowing a comparison of the level of racism and xenophobia in Poland with other European countries were collected as part of the 1990 *European Values Study* (*EVS*). *EVS* Survey respondents were given identical lists of different groups of people and were asked to indicate 'Which groups of people you would not like to have as neighbours.'

Drawing on the conceptual distinction made by Sniderman, Tetlock, Glaser, Green, and Hout (1989) Nevitte (1996, p. 63), in his analysis of the 1981 and 1990 *World Values Study* data, distinguished 'situational tolerance', a willingness to maintain contacts with various groups of people in specific contexts, from 'principled tolerance', which is expressed by respondents who selected 'tolerance and respect for other people' as an important educational value.

The findings made from a comparative analysis of the *World Values Study* data suggest that the West European and North American publics increasingly acknowledge that tolerance is an important educational value. In 1981, support for principled tolerance was expressed by about half of all respondents. During the 1981–90 period this support increased by about 25 per cent; the rise was particularly sharp in West Germany, Spain, Canada, and the Netherlands, where virtually everyone selected 'tolerance and respect for other people' as one of the most important qualities to teach children. The *European Values Study* indicate that in Poland 76 per cent of respondents, a similar proportion as in the pooled European sample, mentioned tolerance as an important educational value.

The analysis conducted by Nevitte revealed that 'the apparent increases in support for the principle of tolerance brings little or no extra leverage in predicting how tolerant publics will be in specific situations' (1996, p. 67). 'When it comes to racial/immigrant tolerance, for instance, publics in advanced industrial states are about as tolerant in 1990 as they were in 1981' (Nevitte, 1996, p. 76). However, results from pooled comparative data mask significant cross-national variations: racial intolerance notably increased in Italy, France and Belgium, but declined in the Netherlands and West Germany.

The measure of racism and ethnic intolerance used in the study was rather rough but it can be interpreted as a simple indicator of what, following Hagendoorn's terminology (1993), can be called 'aversive racism' which 'expresses itself in a reluctance on the part of white people to engage in any kind of intimacy with black people and in the rejection of contact with ethnic outgroups' (Kleinpenning & Hagendoorn, 1993, p. 23). The percentage of respondents who indicated 'people of different race', immigrants and foreign workers, Jews, Hindus, and Muslims as unwanted neighbours in Eastern and Western European countries in 1990 are displayed in Tables 5.3a and 5.3b.

The data shows not only differences in the level of ethnic intolerance between particular countries, but also reveals irregular patterns of intolerance towards specific ethnic groups. Although, in most countries, Muslims are most often rejected as potential neighbours, in Belgium they are more tolerated than Jews. In the Czech and Slovak Republics, and Hungary respondents were more concerned to keep people of another race at a distance than they were Muslims. In countries where Gypsies were included in the list of ethnic groups—the Czech and Slovak Republics, Hungary, and Poland— they evoked the highest level of rejection. The percentage of respondents who would not accept immigrants and foreign workers as their neighbours were higher in Belgium, West Germany, Norway, Italy, France, Denmark, and Great Britain, than in other countries where the problems of immigration may be less pressing.

In general, the level of aversive racism in Eastern Europe was higher than in Western Europe. However, the percentage of respondents expressing social distance towards people of another race in Poland and East Germany was lower than in Portugal and Belgium (Van den Broek & de Moor 1993, p. 211).

Table 5.3a Those who do not want to have members of other ethnic groups as neighbours: Western Europe (%)

Groups	PR	BE	NO	IT	FRG	FR	ES	GB	NL	DK	NI	SE	IE
Different race	17.1	16.9	12.4	12.1	9.9	9.4	8.7	8.2	7.4	7.0	6.9	6.5	5.9
Immigrants and foreign workers	10.1	20.3	15.8	13.4	16.2	12.8	7.5	10.8	8.9	11.6	7.2	8.9	5.1
Jews	22.0	13.0	8.9	12.3	7.2	6.7	8.2	6.7	3.3	3.1	6.3	5.6	6.4
Hindus	17.4	16.9	13.9	12.3	13.0	8.0	7.8	11.4	7.0	5.8	9.2	8.8	9.6
Muslims	19.2	26.6	21.2	14.3	19.7	17.5	10.5	16.4	14.1	15.4	14.8	17.0	13.4

The 1990 *EVS* covers the following West European countries: Portugal (PR), Belgium (BE), Norway (NO), Italy (IT), West Germany, Federal Republic of (FRG), France (FR), Spain (ES), Great Britain (GB), the Netherlands (NL), Denmark (DK), Northern Ireland (NI), Sweden (SE), Republic of Ireland (IE).

Table 5.3b Those who do not want to have members of other ethnic groups as neighbours: Eastern Europe (%)

Groups	BG	SK	CZ	HU	PL	DDR	Eastern Europe	Western Europe
Different race	39.0	28.3	23.9	22.9	16.8	13.3	20.6	9.4
Immigrants and foreign workers	34.4	23.4	22.7	22.2	10.0	20.7	18.1	11.3
Jews	30.2	26.1	12.7	10.3	17.7	8.6	16.3	7.0
Gypsies[a]		70.8	73.1	59.7	36.6			
Muslims	40.8	26.1	22.4	18.3	19.6	22.2	22.7	15.1

[a] In Poland (PL), Hungary (HU), Slovak Republic (SK) and the Czech Republic (CZ), Gypsies were included in the list instead of Hindus; in Bulgaria (BG) and the former East Germany (DDR) Gypsies or Hindus were not included in the list.
Source: Van den Broek and De Moor, 1994, p. 211.

Education and other predictors of social distance toward people of another race, ethnic groups, and immigrants

The *EVS* data allows not only some cross-national comparisons but also testing for the effect of some predictors of racism and ethnic intolerance in European countries. Explanations of reluctance to accept people of another race and immigrants as neighbours can be sought in the socio-demographic characteristics of respondents as well as in their values, attitudes, and political orientations. On the basis of theoretical literature and previous empirical research one may advance hypotheses about the impact of age, gender, level of education, working status, occupational status, household income, and place of residence. Racism and ethnic intolerance have also been linked to such values, attitudes, and dispositions as general distrust, emotional instability, dissatisfaction with life and ones' financial situation, materialism, feeling of powerlessness, conformist or right wing political orientations, religiosity, moral absolutism, and rejection of economic and political liberalism.

Results of the probit analysis, conducted by Nevitte (1966) on the pooled data from the *World Values Survey*[4] conducted in 12 countries in Western Europe and North America, revealed that out of the 15 predictors entered into the analysis only four consistently predict levels of tolerance across all dimensions: those scoring high on post-materialism, interpersonal trust, and efficacy—belief that one can 'do something' about an unjust law—as well as those who score low on the conformity indicator are less likely to reject different groups of people as neighbours and tend to rate tolerance and respect for others as important values to teach children. The most powerful predictor of intolerance towards people of another race and immigrants was acceptance of the statement 'When jobs are scarce, employers should give priority to people of our own nationality over immigrants.'

The impact of various socio-demographic characteristics was not quite clear. Only age effects situational tolerance, older people tended to be less tolerant than younger ones. However, age was not found to be related to acceptance of principled tolerance.

The most striking result was that education had no significant effect on tolerance towards different racial and immigrant groups. These findings were used by Nevitte to question 'the conventional wisdom...that higher levels of formal education encourage greater tolerance'. He states: 'the data certainly suggest that education encourages publics to recognise that tolerance is an important value. But neither support for that belief, nor higher levels of formal education, appear to have a powerful or consistent impact on public beliefs about what kinds of people citizens want living next door' (Nevitte, 1996, p. 70). Similar findings from a regression analysis conducted on pooled data from 15 Western countries was reported by Van den Broek and Heunks (1993, p. 91) who concluded that the impact of education on ethnic tolerance was declining.

The Polish data collected as part of the 1990 *EVS* project shows, however, that situational tolerance was most likely to be found in those with higher levels of education, those with superior occupational status and among younger age groups (for more detailed discussion see Heyns & Jasinska-Kania, 1993).

In order to explore what determines people's reluctance to accept those of another race, immigrants, and ethnic minorities as neighbours, a logistic regression analysis was conducted on the pooled data from 14 European countries weighted for structure of population. This was repeated using only the national sample from Poland. Logistic regression analysis is a statistical technique appropriate for the dependent variables measured on the binary scales (1 = a group unwanted as a neighbour, 0 = a group not mentioned).

Age is the single socio-demographic variable, for the European population, showing a significant effect on social distance towards each of the five target groups. Younger people do not want to limit their social contacts to those of the same race or ethnicity, while older people are more afraid to have foreigners and strangers of another race and ethnicity in their neighbourhood. The impact of age on social distance can be explained by older people's general tendency toward social isolation, traditionalism, and fear that strangers will disturb established customs and ways of life. Gender has a significant impact on intolerance towards Jews and Muslims: men are more likely than women to reject them as neighbours.

Education is a significant predictor of social distance towards people of another race, immigrants or foreign workers and Jews, with lower educated respondents more often expressing unwillingness to accept these groups as neighbours. However, the impact of education on the rejection of Muslims and Hindus is statistically insignificant.

Although professional status and opportunities for work are related to education, these factors have an independent effect on tolerance towards people of another race, ethnic minorities, and immigrants. Professionals are the only occupational group in Europe significantly less likely than others to express the desire to exclude people of another race, immigrants and foreign workers, Jews, Hindus and Muslims from their neighbourhood. Middle level office workers, foremen and supervisors, are also more tolerant towards immigrants and ethnic minorities, than those from lower level occupations. Respondents with a higher professional status are significantly more willing to accept Jews and Hindus as neighbours. Agricultural workers express the greatest reluctance at having members of any of the minority groups in their neighbourhood. Farmers, particularly, wish to keep people of another race

Table 5.4 **Socio-demographic predictors of social distance towards various ethnic groups in Europe**[a]

Socio-demographic variables	People of a different race	Muslims	Immigrants and foreign workers	Hindus	Jews
Education	−.25	−	−.12	−	−.27
Age	.13	.14	.11	.11	.07
Sex	−	−.15	−	−	−.17
Working status	−	−	−	−	−
30 hours or more	−	−	−	.44	−
less than 30 hours	−	.33	−	−	.41
self employed	.59	−	−	.48	.75
retired	.39	−	−	.47	.46
housewife	−	−	−	−	−
student	−	−	−	−	−
Professional status	−	−	−	−	−
employer > 10 employees	−	−	−	−	−1.17
employer < 10 employees	−	−	−	−.60	−1.07
professional worker	−.55	−.42	−.82	−.83	−1.53
middle level office worker	−	−.25	−.33	−.63	−1.14
junior level office worker	−	−	−	−.37	−.70
foreman	−	−	−	−.56	−1.30
skilled manual worker	−	.37	−.44	−	−.33
semi-skilled manual worker	−	.34	−	−	−
unskilled manual worker	.33	−	−	.61	−.31
farmer	.61	−	.51	.49	−
agricultural worker	.78	.54	.57	−	−
military personnel	−	−	−	−	−.53
Household income	−	−	−	−.02	−
Residence	−	−	−	−.03	−.06

[a] Pooled data (weighted for size of country's population) from 14 countries: Belgium, Denmark, France, Great Britain, Italy, the Netherlands, Northern Ireland, Norway, Poland, Portugal, Republic of Ireland, Spain, Sweden, Federal Republic of Germany
Logistic regression coefficients B significant at $p < .05$
Analysis conducted by Dr. Jan Poleszczuk, Institute of Sociology, University of Warsaw.

and Hindus at a distance. Members of the armed forces are reluctant to accept immigrants or foreign workers as neighbours. Self-employed and retired individuals tend to reject people of another race, Hindus, and Jews. Finally, those with the lowest household income do not want Hindus living next door.

Place of residence also has a significant effect on the level of desired social distance expressed towards Jews and Hindus. Reluctance to accept them in a neighbourhood is stronger in villages and in small towns than in big cities. Table 5.5 summarises the results of the logistic regression analysis of the effects of variables measuring attitudes, socio-psychological dispositions, and political orientations on social distance towards various minority groups in Europe.

Of the 13 attitudinal variables used in the analysis five turned out to be significant predictors of the European public's social distance towards all target minorities. Ten predict rejection of Jews, Muslims, and Hindus, eight have an impact on discrimination against people of another race and six predict intolerance towards immigrants and foreign workers.

The majority of those Europeans who do not accept people of another race, immigrants, and ethnic minorities as their neighbours are more likely to distrust people in general and even to distrust their own family. They tend to identify more with their own locality or region than with Europe or the world as a whole. They tend to hold right wing beliefs, and are eager to endorse the opinion that people of their own nationality should be given priority over immigrants when jobs are scarce. This finding might be interpreted as an expression of the belief that ethnic minorities and immigrants compete unfairly by accepting lower standards and conditions of work than nationals are prepared to. However, those who are dissatisfied with their household's financial situation are significantly more concerned to maintain social distance towards people of another race, Muslims, Hindus, and Jews, than they are concerned to exclude immigrants from their neighbourhood. Those who are particularly intolerant towards racial and ethnic minorities are more likely to express the moral absolutist position—'there are absolutely clear guidelines about what is good and evil'—than the relativist opinion—'what is good and evil depends entirely upon the circumstances at the time.' Those respondents who identify themselves as religious are more willing to accept Jews and Hindus, but are more reluctant to have Muslims as their neighbours. Adherence to liberal-economic ideology effects the level of social distance towards Muslims on one hand and Hindus and Jews on the other, those who believe that competition is good, hard work brings a better life, and people can only accumulate wealth at the expense of others are more likely to accept Jews and Hindus but to wish to keep Muslims at a distance. Preference for freedom over equality also has an impact on rejection of Muslims, which may be a result of the stereotype that Muslims are fundamentalists, and so hostile to liberal values.

The most puzzling finding is that those individuals inclined to accept principled tolerance, selecting 'tolerance and respect to others' as an important value to teach children, are not willing to tolerate people of another race, Jews and immigrants in their neighbourhood. The only feasible interpretation for this puzzle seems that they imagine these people to be intolerant and

Table 5.5   Attitudes predicting social distance towards various ethnic groups in Europe[a]

Variables	People of a different race	Muslims	Immigrants & foreign workers	Hindus	Jews
Mistrusts people generally	.34	.37	.33	.22	.22
Mistrusts own family	.16	.16	.21	.16	.16
Mistrusts own nationality	–	–	–	–	–
Left–right political orientation	.06	.10	.09	.07	.05
Freedom over equality	–	–.21	–	–	–
Moral absolutism/relativism	–.15	–.16	–	–.22	–.18
Satisfaction with financial situation	–.03	–.02	–	–.05	–.07
Religious	–	.10	–	–.14	–.30
Tolerance as educational value	.39	–	.45	–	.28
Local/global identification	–.04	–.03	–.04	–.03	–.04
Jobs for own nationality	1.16	1.14	1.35	1.02	1.18
Equalised incomes; State ownership and responsibility	–	–	–	–	–
Competition harmful; hard work doesn't bring success; enough wealth for everyone	–	–.07	–	.08	.15

[a] Pooled data (weighted for size of country's population) from 14 countries: Belgium, Denmark, France, Great Britain, Italy, the Netherlands, Northern Ireland, Norway, Poland, Portugal, Republic of Ireland, Spain, Sweden, Federal Republic of Germany.
Logistic regression coefficients B significant at $p < .05$.
Analysis conducted by Dr. Jan Poleszczuk, Institute of Sociology, University of Warsaw.

disrespectful. Similar analyses conducted separately on the national sample data from selected European countries reveal somewhat different configurations of predictors of racism and xenophobia in each country.

In Poland education is a significant predictor of tolerance towards people of another race, immigrants and foreign workers, Gypsies and Jews, even though its effect on social distance towards Muslims is insignificant. Age effects reluctance to accept people of another race and Muslims as neighbours, but not social distance towards other target groups. Professional status is a significant predictor of intolerance towards immigrants: semi-skilled and unskilled manual workers do not want to have foreign workers in their neighbourhood; military personnel tend to exclude Muslims. Students, people working less than 30 hours and the unemployed are more likely to accept Gypsies in their neighbourhood. Poor people are less tolerant towards

Table 5.6 Socio-demographic predictors of social distance towards various ethnic groups in Poland

Socio-demographic variables	People of a different race	Muslims	Immigrants & foreign workers	Gypsies	Jews
Education	−.11	−	−.08	−.12	−.07
Age	.14	.16	−	−	−
Sex	−	−	−	−	−
Working status	−	−	−	−	−
30 hours or more	−	−	−	−	−
less than 30 hours	−	−	−	−	−
self-employed	−	−	−	−.14	−
retired	−	−	−	−	−
housewife	−	−	−	−	−
student	−	−	−	−.12	−
unemployed	−	−	−	−.09	−
Professional status	−	−	−	−	−
employer > 10 employees	−	−	−	−	−
employer < 10 employees	−	−	−	−	−
professional worker	−	−	−	−	−
middle level office worker	−	−	−	−	−
junior level office worker	−	−	−	−	−
foreman	−	−	−	−	−
skilled manual worker	−	−	−	−	−
semi-skilled manual worker	−	−	.15	−	−
unskilled manual worker	−	−	.25	−	−
farmer	−	−	−	−	−
agricultural worker	−	−	−	−	−
military personnel	−	.25	−	−	−
Household income	−	−	−	−.02	−
Residence	−	−	−	−	−.08
r^2	.08	.05	.07	.05	.07

Regression coefficients B included in the table are significant at p < .05.
Analysis conducted by Dr. Jan Poleszczuk, Institute of Sociology, University of Warsaw.

Gypsies than those who are financially better off. Anti-semitism is stronger in villages and small towns than in big cities. However, socio-demographic variables explain only a small proportion (5–8 per cent) of the variation in tolerance towards various minority groups.

A higher proportion of the variation in social distance towards minorities is explained by variables measuring values, attitudes, psychological dispositions, and political orientations (see Table 5.7). No single variable has

Table 5.7 Attitudes predicting social distance towards various ethnic groups in Poland

Variables	People of a different race	Muslims	Immigrants & foreign workers	Gypsies	Jews
Mistrusts people generally	–	–	–	.25*	–
Mistrusts own family	–	.16*	.38	–	–
Mistrusts own nationality	–	–	–	.28*	–
Left-right political orientation	–	–	.42	.32	–
Freedom over equality	–	–	–	–	–
Moral absolutism/relativism	–	–	.26	–	.29*
Satisfaction with life	–	–.33	–.35	–	–
Religious	–	–	–	–	–
Tolerance as educational value	–	–	–	–	–
Local/global identification	–.23*	–	–.39	–	–.23*
Jobs for own nationality	–	–	.22	–	–
Equalised incomes; State ownership and responsibility	–	–	.22	–	–
Competition harmful; hard work brings no success; enough wealth for everyone	–	–	–	–	–
Proud to be Polish	–	–	–	.31	–
Voluntary work for local community	–	–	–	–.31	–
r^2	.19	.32	.51	.29	.18

Regression coefficients B included in the table are significant at p < .05, except * p < .08.
Analysis conducted by Dr. Jan Poleszczuk, Institute of Sociology, University of Warsaw.

a significant effect on intolerance towards all target groups. If a wider global identification is emphasised over a local one, a greater tolerance can be expected towards immigrants, Jews, and people of another race, although less significantly so for the last two groups (p < .08). The effect is insignificant for Muslims and Gypsies. Right wing political orientation has an influence on intolerance towards immigrants and Gypsies but not towards other groups. Dissatisfaction with life in general predicts only rejection of immigrants and Muslims.

Seven of the 15 variables used in the analysis predict reluctance to have immigrants or foreign workers as neighbours: distrust, dissatisfaction with life, fear of foreigners as competitors for jobs, local versus global identification, moral relativism, right wing political leanings, and anti-liberal state oriented economic ideology. The respondents who do not want to accept immigrants in their neighbourhood are most likely to mistrust even their family, to identify more with the village or town where they live than with Europe or the world, to give priority to Polish people over immigrants in the employment market, to be dissatisfied with their life, to endorse moral relativism—contrary to the absolutist orientation of intolerant people in the pooled European sample, to identify as right wing, and to endorse anti-liberal state oriented economic ideology.

The exclusion of Gypsies from a neighbourhood is most likely to be demanded by those who do not regard doing voluntary work as important for their local community and those who lean more towards the right, as well as those who are proud to be Polish and generally do not trust people, even of their own nationality, though the significance for the latter two is low ($p < .08$). Although intolerance towards Jews is associated with moral relativism and with feelings of a local identification, the level of significance is low ($p < .08$). Muslims are more likely to be rejected as neighbours by those who are unsatisfied with their life and those who mistrust their family. The effects of most of the attitudinal variables on the reluctance to have people of another race in a neighbourhood are insignificant, with the exception of feelings of identification with ones' locality, though once again the level of significance is low.

Conclusions

The results of the analyses discussed above largely confirmed expectations of what the influence of education on the decrease of racism and xenophobia would be. In general, the analysis supports the argument that a younger age, higher levels of education and a higher occupational status, are more likely to encourage closer contacts with and a greater tolerance towards racial and ethnic minorities. As expected, racial and ethnic tolerance is also related, though not as consistently, to attitudes, values, and dispositions, such as interpersonal trust, satisfaction with financial situation, rejection of moral absolutism, left wing political orientation, liberal economic values, and global identification with the world. Education, as follows from other analyses, has an impact on formation of these attitudes and dispositions.

Contrary to the findings of Van den Broek and Heunks (1993), and later of Nevitte (1996), who in their analyses of the results of the pooled West

European and North American values survey data, found that education had no significant impact on social distance towards different racial and ethnic groups, the logistic regression analysis conducted by the Polish team showed such an effect not only in Poland but also in the pooled European sample (see Table 5.4). This difference in findings may be due to several reasons. Although the analysed data were partially overlapping, each of three analyses mentioned above also included or excluded specific countries. Another reason may be the different statistical analysis techniques used in each case. Another explanation can be sought in the weighting of the data. In countries such as Ireland, Denmark, Norway, and Sweden, with relatively small populations, high levels of education, and low levels of immigration, the impact of education on willingness to accept social contact with people of other races is most likely declining relative to the larger European nations, such as West Germany, Italy, Great Britain, France, and Spain, where levels of education are generally not so high, and immigration related problems more pressing. If the samples from the former group of countries are calculated in the same way as for the latter, which alone constitutes 75 per cent of the European population and together with Poland 85 per cent, the effect of education can be obliterated.

Nevitte is correct when stating that variations in levels of racial intolerance 'might well be attributed to contextual factors. For example, the fact that levels of racial/immigrant intolerance are typically higher in West Germany may well reflect the fact that levels of immigration have been five times higher than in most other advanced industrial states...The tolerance of some publics, in other words, has been more vigorously tested than others' (Nevitte, 1996, p. 70). However, results of our analysis indicate that not only these 'contextual factors' influence the aversive racism in Europe but also a complex of psychological and ideological orientations and attitudes that may be related to a lower level of education. A relationship demanding further exploration.

In Poland the effect of education on attitudes towards people of another race can be related to somewhat different factors. Immigration to Poland during the time of the *EVS* survey was negligible (it increased greatly during the latter half of the decade). The concept of race was meaningless for the largest and the least educated part of the population. At the same time those who were better educated knew that the term racism was not politically acceptable. It would be interesting to see whether and how these attitudes will change when contacts with people of another race become an experience of everyday life for a larger part of population.

Notes

1 Translation of the author from: *Nowa encyklopedia powszechna PWN* (New General Encyclopaedia), 1996,vol. 5, Warszawa: PWN, p. 460 (PWN = Polskie Wydawnictwo Naukowe = Polish Scientific Publisher).

2 The survey 'Poles and Others' was prepared and analysed by Ewa Nowicka, Slawomir Lodzinski and Jan Nawrocki, as a part of the research project 'National stereotypes in the Polish society' directed by Aleksandra Jasinska-Kania. Field work was implemented by the Center for Public Opinion Research (OBOP) on a 1000 representative sample population of over sixteen-year-olds. Results were published in Nowicka 1990. Unfortunately, the data is not available for a secondary analysis.

3 The European Values Systems Study Group was initiated in 1978 by Jan Kerkhofs of the Catholic University of Louvain and Ruud de Moor of Tilburg University. In 1981 the first large scale survey of values and beliefs was conducted in 10 Western European countries: Belgium, Denmark, France, the Federal Republic of Germany, Great Britain, Italy, the Netherlands, Northern Ireland, Republic of Ireland, and Spain. Comparative surveys based on the same questionnaire were also carried out in the 1980s in over 20 countries worldwide within the *World Values Survey* (*WVS*) directed by Ronald Inglehart from the University of Michigan. In 1990 the survey was repeated in the countries of Western Europe. At the same time, the *EVS* project has been joined by Poland as well as by several other countries from Eastern Europe. In Poland the study was carried out by Aleksandra Jasinska-Kania, Jadwiga Koralewicz and Mira Marody; field work implemented by the Center for Public Opinion Research (OBOP) on a 1200 representative sample population of over sixteen-year-olds. The analysed data came from Belgium, Denmark, France, Great Britain, Italy, the Netherlands, Norway, Northern Ireland, Republic of Ireland, Poland, Portugal, Spain, Sweden and West Germany.

4 *World Values Survey* (*WVS*) used a questionnaire similar to that used by the *European Values Survey* (*EVS*) but included more countries outside Europe.

References

Broek, van den, A. and Heunks, F. (1993), 'Political Culture: Patterns of Political Orientations and Behaviour', in P. Ester, L. Halman and R. de Moor (eds), *The Individualizing Society: Value Change in Europe and North America*, Tilburg, Tilburg University Press.

Broek, van den, A. and de Moor, R. (1993), 'Eastern Europe after 1989', in Ester, P., Halman, L. and de Moor, R. (eds), *The Individualizing society: Value change in Europe and North America*, Tilburg University Press.

Ester, P., Halman, L. and de Moor, R. (eds) (1994), *The Individualizing Society: Value Change in Europe and North America*, 2nd edn, Tilburg, Tilburg University Press.

Hagendoorn, L. (1993), 'Ethnic Categorization and Outgroup Exclusion: Cultural Values and Social Stereotypes in the Construction of Ethnic Hierarchies', *Ethnic and Racial Studies*, vol. 16, no. 1.

Heyns, B. and Jasinska-Kania, A. (1993), 'Values, Politics and the Ideologies of Reform: Poland in Transition', *Research on Democracy and Society*, 1, pp. 169–194.

Jasinska-Kania, A. (1991), 'The Systemic Transformation and Changes in Poles' Attitudes towards Various Nations and States', *The Polish Sociological Bulletin*, no. 4, pp. 299–312.

Kleinpenning, G. and Hagendoorn, L. (1993), 'Forms of Racism and the Cumulative Dimension of Ethnic Attitudes', *Social Psychology Quarterly*, vol. 56, no. 1, pp. 21–36.

Nevitte, N. (1996), 'Tolerance and Intolerance in Advanced Industrial States: The Cross-Time Evidence', in L. Halman and N. Nevitte (eds), *Political Values Change in Western Democracies*, Tilburg University Press.

Nowicka, E. (1990), *Swoi i obcy*, Warszawa, UW IS.

Nowicka, E. (1994), 'Social Distance towards Germans among Contemporary Poles. An Empirical Study', in R. Grathoff and A. Kloskowska (eds), *The Neighbourhood of Cultures*, Warsaw, Institute of Political Studies, Polish Academy of Sciences.

Sniderman, P., Tetlock, P.E., Glaser, J.M., Green, D.P. and Hout, M. (1989), 'Principled Tolerance and the American Mass Public', *British Journal of Political Science*, 19, pp. 25–45.

6 Explaining Individual Racial Prejudice in Contemporary Germany

JÜRGEN R. WINKLER

Introduction

Violent attacks on African and Asian migrants and Turkish residents as well as increased electoral support for the extreme right are frequently identified as evidence for the existence of growing racism and racial prejudice among Germans. Moreover, public opinion and social scientists believe that negative intergroup attitudes are increasing, most notably in eastern Germany. Thus, various attempts have been made to seek an explanation for why *eastern* Germany. Observing aggressive behaviour against members of ethnic minorities, an increasing number of scholars feel an urgent need to investigate the causes of racial attitudes.

Although the concept of racism has become one of the central categories in current international social science discourse on racial phenomena, the concept is not widely used in Germany. The attempt by the Nazi regime to racialise thoroughly the German social formation has ensured that any attempt to use the term *race* is suffused with the meaning instilled and legitimised by fascism. Until now, the popular understanding of racism implied that the human species consists of a number of distinct biological types. Therefore, many German social scientists view the use of race as illegitimate. They believe that were they to use the term it would either lend credence to the doctrine that one race is biologically superior to another or it could be used to insinuate that Germans categorise human beings into biologically determined categories and see themselves as superior to other nations.

The key discursive concepts most widely used, in the German literature on the subject and in the public domain, about immigration and foreigners are *Gastarbeiter* (guest worker) and *Ausländer* (foreigner). The attitudes against them are expressed by the ideas of *Ausländerfeindlichkeit* (foreignness), *Fremdenfeindlichkeit* (strangeness), and xenophobia. However, my use of the term *racial prejudice* differs from the one used in the public domain. Racial prejudice is simply defined as a set of unjustifiable negative attitudes towards an ethnic group and its members. These attitudes stigmatise other groups of human beings according to perceived differences. These differences are taken to denote distinctive cultural characteristics and to prevent successful integration into the ingroup. Racial attitudes are thought of as subjective, meaning-based interpretations of social experience. Negative prejudices are determined socially rather than biologically. In Germany little progress has been made in studying negative attitudes towards ethnic groups and their members, because most articles have focused on labelling rather than explaining. Labelling reveals little, for example, about the factors explaining intergroup attitudes.

This paper proposes a structural explanation of racial attitudes, presents the empirical evidence for it, explores racial prejudice and examines its causes. I assume that the level of racial prejudice depends upon five main causes that are analysed in the following sections. In the section 'Racial prejudice: measuring, development and demography', I address the question how to measure racial prejudice, distinguishing its various forms and levels. I then analyse the development of two of these over the last decade, and give a summary of the socio-demography of intergroup attitudes in contemporary Germany. Using factor analysis, I define a general measure of racial prejudice and distinguish six dimensions of negative attitudes towards ethnic minorities. Building upon previous empirical and theoretical work, several determinants of racial prejudice are discussed and analysed in the section 'Determinants of racial prejudice'. I deal first with the influence of economic and cultural variables that describe the perceived position of individuals in society. I then examine the effects of more stable personality variables on racial prejudice, and I suggest a new construct as a main determinant of racial attitudes. A brief investigation into the contact hypotheses is followed by a discussion of the role of education. In the section 'A model explaining racial prejudice' I develop a more explicit and complete model of racial prejudice, and relate racial prejudice to measures of socio-demographic variables including education, perceived socio-cultural circumstances, a more stable personality pattern, contact intensity, and perception of outgroups. This new view is offered as an alternative to existing methods of studying prejudice towards ethnic groups.

The data analysed here is based on the 1996 ALLBUS[1] survey, conducted in March, April, and June of 1996. The data comes from interviews with a random sample of 3,518 respondents representative of the voting population of the Federal Republic of Germany. Because the purpose of this paper is to explain the negative attitudes of Germans towards ethnic groups and their members, interviews with respondents who do not hold German citizenship were not considered. The set of data relevant to this study is, therefore, that of the 3,290 interviews conducted with Germans. In as much as respondents of eastern Germany are over represented, all analyses that follow are weighted. The 1996 survey focused upon intergroup attitudes. Hence, the data set includes a large set of items relating to intergroup relations that make it possible to distinguish several forms of racial prejudice as well as to examine their causes.

Racial prejudice: measuring, development and demography

Measuring racial prejudice

As I am interested in constructs rather than items themselves, before explaining racial prejudice I have to solve two problems. First, I have to identify the dimensions of racial prejudice. Second, I have to address the measurement problem, by finding a way to quantify the phenomenon before tackling the main research objective. To date, only a few attempts have been made to measure German racial prejudice nationwide. Fortunately, the 1996 ALLBUS survey includes a large set of questions designed to measure levels of antipathy towards a variety of outgroups. In the survey, these outgroups are called 'asylum seekers', 'ethnic German immigrants from Eastern Europe', 'Italians', 'Jews', 'Turks', or simply 'foreigners'. For the German population, Turks, the largest group of non-nationals, constitute the most important cultural outgroup. As other scholars have shown, they have come to symbolise foreignness.

The general survey included thirty-five items designed to test negative attitudes towards ethnic minorities. To identify groups of items that appear to define meaningful underlying latent variables, the items were factor analysed (see Table 6.1a in the Appendix to this chapter). Several methods of factor analysis produced the same structure. However, the investigation of the item set indicating negative attitudes towards ethnic groups extracted seven factors. With one exception, the variables with high loadings on one factor were then used to construct measures of different forms of racial prejudice. Two factors concerning social distance were integrated into one scale, so that six scales comprise the dependent variables in this study. Each factor is defined by the items that load most heavily on it. By referring to the content of those items, one can discern the nature of the latent variable that each factor represents. All items loading strongly on factor one concern stereotype and general prejudice. Those loading on factor two and factor four concern social distance to different outgroups. Those loading on factor three concern the question of whether outgroups should have the same right as Germans. Items loading on factor five concern anti-Semitism. Items loading on factor six concern personal discrimination, and, finally, those loading on factor seven concern immigration to Germany.

In order to measure the various forms of racial prejudice, those questions relating to prejudice towards asylum seekers, Jews, Turks, Italians, or, simply, foreigners are used. The scores created from the factor analysis all correlate .98 or higher with simple sums of the questions. Since the factor scores are almost identical to the simple sums, I use the more interpretable sums of scores as dependent variables. To create the six scales I summed the scores of all the items with high loadings and, to make comparisons easier, divided the sum by the number of items belonging to one factor. Four scales (general prejudice, social distance, anti-Semitism, and equal rights) range from one to seven. The immigration scale and the personal agreement of discrimination scale range in values from one to three. Internal consistency of scales is typically equated to Cronbach's coefficient alpha. Reliability (Cronbach's alpha) of the general prejudice scale is .85, for the social distance scale .82, for the immigration scale .70, for the anti-Semitism scale .74, for the equal rights scale .75, and for the personal discrimination scale .74. The means for the dependent variables are shown in the tables.

However, speaking about racial prejudice implies that the variables describing forms of racial prejudice bear certain similarities. Therefore, I assumed the existence of a latent factor to be causing the scores on all six separate scales. To test this hypothesis, all six racial attitude scales were again factor analysed. As expected, principal component analysis of the scales extracted one factor. This component explains 53 per cent of the variance in the six scales that measure different forms of racial prejudice. The loading of the general prejudice scale on the overall racial prejudice dimension is .83. That of the social distance scale is .76. The loadings of the anti-Semitism and the immigration scale are .67, that of the equal rights scale is .72, and for the personal discrimination scale it is .69.

To measure individuals' general tendency to express racial attitudes, the factor score for each individual is computed. This factor score is based on the scores of one respondent on the six scales and the loadings of the scales on the principal component. Diagram 6.1 helps us to understand how the scales and items are causally related to the dependent theoretical constructs used. Individuals with high scores on the general prejudice scale reject immigration

Explaining Individual Racial Prejudice in Contemporary Germany 97

and equal rights, favour discrimination and segregation, express anti-Semitism and negative stereotypes.

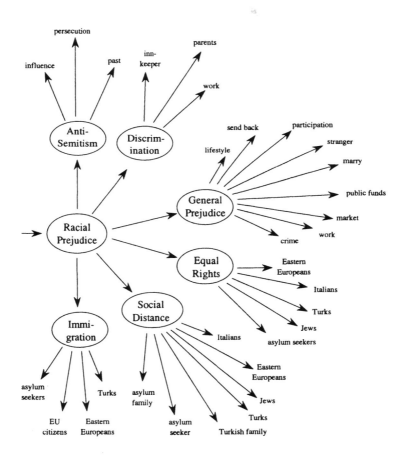

Diagram 6.1   Causal relation of scales and items to the dependent theoretical constructs

The first dimension of racial prejudice is called general prejudice and stereotypes. Items expressing beliefs about the personal attributes of foreigners living in Germany load highest on this factor. Forty-five per cent of the variance in the items is explained by this component. The percentages confirm that racial prejudices undoubtedly exist in German society (see Table 6.2a in the Appendix to this chapter). While criminological statistics show that the crime rate amongst foreigners is nearly the same as amongst Germans, 40 per cent of Germans believe that members of outgroups are more criminally inclined than Germans. Even more Germans believe that outgroups are a problem for the economy and the welfare state. Almost one third feels a foreigner in their own country because of the presence of ethnic groups. There is not doubt that these percentages indicate a high resistance to ethnic minorities.

Anti-Semitism is form of racial prejudice of long standing in Germany. Hatred of Jews stemmed not only from their allegedly excessive political influence and their supposedly un-Christian affinity with money, but also from their strong identification with their own culture and religion. Today, we tend to distinguish between two forms of anti-Semitism: traditional anti-Semitism and secondary anti-Semitism. Traditional anti-Semitism is expressed in statements such as 'Jews have too much influence in the world'. Four out of ten Germans agree with this statement. Secondary anti-Semitism refers to the German past, and is expressed in sentences such as 'Jews are partly to blame for their own persecution'. A total of 16.5 per cent of Germans agree with this statement. The anti-Semitism factor explains 66 per cent of the variance in the three items (see Table 6.3a in the Appendix to this chapter).

Another important dimension of racial attitudes is social distance. To measure social distance, two kinds of questions were included in the general survey. Both kinds of items are based on the relationship of individuals with members of different outgroups. First, respondents were asked what they think about Italians, Turks, Jews, and asylum seekers in their neighbourhood. Second, the respondents were asked how they would react if a family member were to marry a member of an ethnic minority, to which the majority of Germans indicated that they would not wish for asylum seekers to marry into their families (see Table 6.4a in the Appendix to this chapter). Nearly every second German does not like asylum seekers in their neighbourhood. The social distance factor explains 72 per cent of the variance in the items.

The next three constructs refer to negative behaviour towards outgroups. In contemporary Germany, two issues address institutional discrimination against ethnic minorities. The first is, should ethnic minorities living in Germany be granted rights, the second concerns whether the border should be closed to immigrants. Individuals were asked if foreigners living in Germany should receive a status equal to that of Germans. Again, the percentage of Germans who, for example, reject any equal rights for foreigners is very high. The immigration component explains 52 per cent of the variance of the items (see Table 6.5a in the Appendix to this chapter). The equal rights component explains 67 per cent of the variance in the items (see Table 6.6a in the Appendix to this chapter), and the personal discrimination component explains 66 per cent of the variance in the items (see Appendix, Table 6.7a).

The development of racial prejudice

As the figures show, the existence of widespread racism in present day Germany is beyond doubt. However, a question is whether the level of negative attitudes towards outgroups has risen in the last decade (Jaschke, 1994; Heitmeyer, 1987; Hargreaves & Leaman, 1995; Wieviorka, 1994). Most German scholars argue that the perceived increase in racial prejudice is the result of poor economic conditions combined with a dramatic increase in violent behaviour against members of ethnic groups during the first half of the 1990s. For this, there is evidence enough. However, a review of existing literature reveals that no longitudinal study of the stability or otherwise of racial attitudes has been carried out. A longitudinal examination of changes in racial attitudes requires the assessment of each individual's racial prejudice at several different points in time. The only available evidence consists of very few cross-sectional comparisons of aggregated racial attitudes. However, contrary to popular opinion, the few existing empirical studies found a decrease rather than an increase in expressed racial prejudice between 1980 and 1994 (Hill, 1993; Wiegand, 1992; Eckert, Willems & Würtz, 1996). As far as anti-Semitism is concerned, all empirical studies have concluded that anti-Semitism declined in the post-1945 period (Bergmann & Erb, 1991; 1996). Therefore, social scientists had been convinced of a continued improvement in the climate of German racial attitudes. The decrease in racial prejudice since the 1950s corresponded to the often stated changing political culture (Dalton, 1993). According to Bergmann and Erb (1991; 1996) and many others, the changing racial attitudes are strongly associated with education and age.

Comparable data is required to build an accurate picture of the development of racial attitudes. Besides data on anti-Semitism, the social sciences, unfortunately, had almost no interest in studying racial attitudes over time. In the period 1980 to 1996, only the general survey included four items useful for comparative research. All four items belong to the general prejudice scale. Respondents were asked if foreigners should adapt their lifestyle to that of Germans, whether they should be sent home if jobs are scarce, if political participation of foreigners should be forbidden and if foreigners should seek a partner among their own ethnic group.

To answer the question whether racial prejudice has decreased or increased over the last decade, I undertook a secondary analysis of this data. I counted the negative answers (see answers four, five and six on the seven-point scale) and computed the average scores. The results are presented in Table 6.1. In the period from 1980 to 1994, negative attitudes towards racial groups decreased. For example, in 1980 64.8 per cent said that foreigners should adjust their lifestyles more whereas in 1990 the figure was 50.9 per cent. A closer look at the aggregated responses reveals that the rank order did not change. But, in the period 1994 to 1996, there was a dramatic increase in 'yes' answers as well as an increase of the means. Moreover, there was a dramatic increase in expressed negative attitudes towards ethnic minorities in eastern Germany. Any explanation of the development of expressed racial prejudice in Germany has to explain why racial attitudes in the period prior to 1994 decreased rather than increased, and why they then increased from 1994 onwards. I will return to this point in the discussion at the end.

Table 6.1   Racial attitudes in Germany: 1980–1996

Item	1980	1984	1988	1990	1994	1996	Region
They should adapt their lifestyle to German circumstances.	64.8	60.1	56.7	50.9	49.7	59.3	west-%
					50.2	61.2	east-%
	5.0	4.8	4.7	4.4	4.4	4.9	west-M
					4.5	5.0	east-M
If work is scarce, foreigners should be sent back.	52.1	41.6	35.7	30.0	22.6	25.1	west-%
					31.4	41.0	east-%
	4.4	4.0	3.7	3.4	3.0	3.3	west-M
					3.6	4.1	east-M
Foreigner's political participation should be forbidden.	49.9	46.3	37.3	34.7	32.3	35.8	west-%
					27.8	37.4	east-%
	4.4	4.2	3.8	3.7	3.5	3.8	west-M
					3.3	4.0	east-M
They should marry someone from their own country.	43.0	33.2	32.3	23.1	18.2	19.8	west-%
					25.6	28.7	east-%
	4.0	3.4	3.4	2.8	2.6	2.7	west-M
					3.1	3.3	east-M

The response options range from 1 = 'strongly disagree' to 7 = 'strongly agree'. Higher means indicate higher scores on racial prejudice. The percentage refers to all agreeing responses, 5, 6 and 7 were included in one category. Scale construction: Likert scale.

Data is available on attitudes towards immigration for the four items of the immigration scale for 1990, 1992, and 1996. Using this data it can be seen if attitudes on immigration to Germany changed. In the first half of the 1990s, immigration was widely debated and ranked amongst the most important issues on the political agenda. In 1993 a majority in the Bundestag passed a constitutional amendment to reduce immigration to Germany. Thus, the answers say something about the effect of the mass media and of politics on public opinion. Again, I counted the respondents who stated that Germany should be closed for immigration, and computed the means of the variables. Table 6.2 shows the results. While a decline in negative attitudes on immigration in the period 1990–1992 is observable, Table 6.2 shows a slight increase for the period 1992–1996. Furthermore, Table 6.2 reveals some remarkable differences between the eastern and western parts of Germany.

Table 6.2   Negative attitudes on immigration to Germany

Against Immigration of	Year			Region
	1990	1992	1996	
Ethnic Germans from	19.5	10.0	11.5	west-%
Eastern Europe		11.3	17.7	east-%
	2.0	1.9	2.0	west-M
		2.0	2.0	east-M
Asylum Seekers	29.7	22.8	21.7	west-%
		19.1	21.1	east-%
	2.1	2.1	2.1	west-M
		2.0	2.1	east-M
Workers from the	12.6	9.0	12.1	west-%
European Union		23.6	37.8	east-%
	1.8	1.7	1.8	west-M
		2.1	2.3	east-M
Turks	33.4	28.3	32.5	west-%
		36.3	49.4	east-%
	2.2	2.2	2.2	west-M
		2.3	2.5	east-M

The response options range from 1 = 'immigration should be possible' to 3 = 'immigration should be forbidden'. Higher means indicate higher scores on negative attitudes against immigration. The percentage refers to code 3. Scale construction: Likert scale.

The demography of racial prejudice

A stream of research has focused on individual correlates of racial prejudice in attitude surveys rather than on explaining the phenomenon. The main thrust of empirical research has been to determine who expresses negative attitudes against racial minorities. The results of these studies are generally consistent.

Recent research has focused on the differences in the expression of racial prejudice between eastern and western Germany. Most studies have found a higher degree of racial prejudice in the eastern than in the western part of Germany. According to mainstream interpretations, these regional differences are the result of the poor economic climate and the high degree of anomie caused by the political revolution in the former East Germany.

In early research, Stouffer (1955) suggested that urbanism effects political tolerance and racial prejudice. According to Stouffer the diversity and heterogeneity of urban life induce heightened tolerance among city dwellers. The concentration of people with heterogeneous backgrounds and characteristics in urban areas leads, it is argued, to multiple secondary associations with others of divergent attitudes. Country dwellers, on the other hand, are more homogeneous in terms of background and characteristics, and are more engaged in relationships with others of similar values. Although the right wing parties gained a remarkable percentage of the electorate in cities like Berlin, Frankfurt, Bremerhaven, and, recently, Hamburg, in general, surveys have confirmed Stouffer's early hypothesis (see, Falter, 1994). The role of gender has been far more important than urbanism in the German debate on racial attitudes and right wing extremism. While some have argued that racial prejudice is essentially a characteristic of men, others have observed only slight or no differences between men and women (Falter, 1994; Heitmeyer, 1987; Heß, 1996).

As mentioned, several post-1945 studies on anti-Semitism have revealed a decrease in expressed negative attitudes against Jews. Explanations of this improvement focus on two demographic variables: education and age. Surveys have consistently shown that political tolerance has increased, especially amongst more highly educated young people. In part, older people revealed value priorities reflecting their socialisation in Weimar and Nazi Germany. According to existing literature dealing with attitudes towards minorities, education is one of the most important factors explaining racial prejudice (Bergmann & Erb, 1991; Weil, 1985). Due to increased rates of participation in higher education, it has been assumed that more tolerant people will in time, replace the older more intolerant people.

In addition, recent research on racial prejudice and right wing extremism has drawn attention to socio-economic background and occupation, both of which are related with education (Eckert, Willems & Würtz, 1996; Krauth & Porst, 1984; Winkler, 1996). To the best of my knowledge, all surveys undertaken in the last decade have found that individuals from lower socio-economic backgrounds express higher levels of racial prejudice. Thus, I predict that people from lower socio-economic backgrounds are more likely to express prejudice against racial minorities than those from higher socio-economic backgrounds.

The mean scores by prejudice by region, urbanism, gender, age, occupation, prestige of occupation, education and the percentage of foreigners are displayed in Table 6.8a of the Appendix. Consistent with earlier research, urban dwellers and western Germans are more racially tolerant than their non-urban and eastern German counterparts. Tolerance increases in line with the level of urbanisation. Residents of non-urban areas express a higher level of racial prejudice than their urban counterparts. The only dimension showing no link between racial prejudice and region is that of equal rights for ethnic minorities. Except for anti-Semitism, individuals from eastern Germany score higher on the remaining scales. Individuals with low-prestige occupations exhibit greater levels of intolerance than those with high-prestige occupations.

In addition, Table 6.3 reveals that education is strongly associated with attitudes towards ethnic minorities. All relations are highly significant. Education shows the strongest links overall with general racial prejudice, immigration, and anti-Semitism. Weaker associations can be seen between education, social distance, equal rights and personal discrimination

Prior research has shown that the socio-demographic variables are corrupted. Not only occupational prestige and education correlate highly, but also education and age. Thus, the bivariate empirical links do not tell the whole story. If our aim is to find out if racial prejudice is caused by socio-demograhic variables, the compositional effects have to be controlled. Hence, I regressed the different measures of ethnic prejudice on the most important socio-demographic variables. Because, for example, the title of employee reveals nothing about the status of an individual, I have used the prestige of an occupation as constructed by Wegener (1984). Table 6.3 reveals the partial effects of socio-demographic variables on the various latent factors of racial prejudice. It can be seen that racial prejudice is positively related to 5 factors: region, urbanism, age, occupation, and education. It is evident that older individuals are less tolerant than their younger counterparts despite the varying compositional attributes. Whereas age has very strong effects on general prejudice, anti-Semitism, and discrimination, its effect on immigration is much weaker, and it has almost no effect on equal rights.

Table 6.3 Regression of racial prejudice on socio-demographic variables

Demography	Dimension of Racial Prejudice						Racial Prejudice
	General Prejudice	Social Distance	Anti-Semitism	Immigration	Equal Rights	Discrimination	
Region	.112	.167	−.068	.145	(−.002)	.137	.116
	.370	.432	−.260	.148	(−.009)	.223	.284
Urbanism	−.103	−.122	−.150	−.090	−.120	−.103	−.157
	−.077	−.072	−.129	−.021	−.104	−.039	−.086
Gender	(.014)	−.066	−.086	(.003)	(−.031)	(−.034)	(−.044)
	(.040)	*−.141*	*−.272*	*(.002)*	*(−.097)*	*(−.048)*	*(−.088)*
Age	.261	.152	.218	.075	(.050)	.230	.227
	.022	*.010*	*.021*	*.002*	*(.005)*	*.010*	*.014*
Occupation	−.215	−.104	−.121	−.165	−.126	−.097	−.192
	−.010	*−.004*	*−.006*	*−.002*	*−.006*	*−.002*	*−.006*
Education	−.144	−.099	−.165	−.189	−.135	−.112	−.191
	−.177	*−.097*	*−.235*	*−.072*	*−.193*	*−.071*	*−.175*
Subordinate Group	(.018)	.106	.117	(−.024)	(.056)	(.043)	(.071)
	(.008)	*.037*	*.061*	*(−.003)*	*(.029)*	*(.010)*	*(.024)*
r^2	23%	9%	16%	17%	7%	13%	23%

First row: standardised regression coefficients. Second row: unstandardised regression coefficients () p >.01. Men are coded 0 and women 1. Eastern Germany is coded 1 and western Germany is coded 0. Occupation: magnitude prestige.

The statistically and substantively strongest socio-demographic determinants on racial prejudice are that negative attitudes towards ethnic groups decrease with increased levels of education and urbanisation, and that prejudice occurs more frequently amongst older people and those with low-prestige occupations. Most of the individual characteristics have strong effects on racial prejudice. The substantially larger r^2s for equations predicting prejudice, anti-Semitism and immigration, show that these factors are more strongly influenced by socio-demographic variables than, for example, equal rights.

It has been argued that negative attitudes against ethnic minorities increase whenever their percentage relative to the dominant group increases (see Blalock, 1967). The dominant group is said to perceive the subordinate groups as a threat to their position. The greater the relative size of the subordinate group, and the worse the economic climate, the more threatened the dominant group feels. The more threatened a group is, the more racial prejudice it will express. In an empirical analysis of racial attitudes across the European Union, Fuchs, Gerhards, and Roller (1993) have argued negative attitudes expressed towards foreigners relate to the percentage of foreigners in a country. Contrary to Fuchs et al., I have found that the size of the subordinate group has no significant influence on most dimensions of racial prejudice. While older individuals with lower levels of education and lower status occupations living in eastern Germany express the highest level of racial prejudice, younger, more highly educated individuals in higher status occupations living in western Germany express the lowest. This obvious difference demands attention and it is to it that I now turn.

Determinants of racial prejudice

Socio-cultural insecurities

The most popular explanations of racial prejudice found in existing literature and in German public opinion views racial prejudice as resulting from economic conditions and perceived threat. One hypothesis is that individuals facing bad economic conditions tend to hold negative attitudes towards the members of ethnic minorities. The economic decline in Weimar Germany for example has been consistently linked to the formation, rise and political success of the Nazi party that was indeed a racist party. This approach follows the frustration-aggression-hypothesis which predicts that a worsening in a person's economic situation increases frustration and thus leads to increased prejudice against outgroups (Dollard, Doob, Miller, Mowrer & Sears, 1939). The theoretical basis of the argument is the assumption that individuals behave as self-interested persons, producing negative attitudes towards outgroups with whom they are in competition. This hypothesis is commonly used to argue that immigration to countries with economic problems produces racial prejudice or leads to a resurgence of racism (Hargreaves & Leaman, 1995, p. 21). Blalock (1967) argues that competition for scarce resources increases with the size of the minority group relative to the dominant group. Increasing competition between groups leads to intergroup threat that results in prejudice. Following Blalock the size of the subordinate group relative to the dominant group is a major demographic cause of perceived threat. As migrants usually find themselves in direct economic competition with low-wage earners and un-skilled labourers, the observed relationship between some demographic variables and racial prejudice also seems to be explained. In addition, it is the most distinct determinant of the resurgence of racism in public opinion.

Another approach views racial prejudice as a function of the collective threat to the dominant group. Here, the main factor producing racial prejudice is the perceived circumstances of the group to which an individual belongs, rather than the individuals real or perceived economic position. Prejudice emerges when an individual believes that minority groups threaten their (dominant) group. Bad collective economic circumstances cause members of the dominant group to fear losing their economic advantage over the subordinate ethnic groups. Hence a worsening of economic circumstances among the dominant German group increases prejudice not only amongst those Germans directly affected by bad economic conditions or in direct competition with immigrants. It also increases negative racial attitudes amongst those Germans not affected.

Vanneman and Pettigrew (1972) have found that fraternal-deprivation to be a stronger predictor than individual deprivation. Following this, levels of racial prejudice and opposition to immigration should increase in times of economic recession. Thus implying that to improve the relationship between ethnic minorities and Germans, economic conditions have to be improved. Another variant of this approach connects an objective threat with racial prejudice. Bobo (1983, p. 1197) for example argues that racial prejudice is a result of a real, as opposed to a perceived, threat to the dominant group's resources. According to this view, racial prejudice increases whenever the privileges of the dominant group are challenged.

Another view has been popular during the last decade in the debates on racial prejudice in Germany. In this view the modernisation process weakens identification with social and political institutions, and leads to insecure socio-cultural orientations (anomie) evoking racial prejudice (Heitmeyer, 1987). They contend that insecure and less integrated individuals develop negative racial attitudes towards minorities. Accordingly, prejudice in the dominant group is a function of anomie and political distance rather than of perceived economic threat. According to Wieviorka (1994), all European countries are undergoing huge transformations leading to an increase in racism. He argues that individuals experiencing feelings of injustice, fear a loss of social identity, view politicians as responsible for their situation, and develop negative racial attitudes, imputing their misfortune to migrants (Wieviorka, 1994, p. 179). Few studies have attempted to find a direct relation between economic conditions, socio-cultural uncertainties and levels of racial prejudice, and the empirical findings have been contradictory.

In order to investigate the empirical relationship between the mentioned variables and negative attitudes towards ethnic groups, I first considered the level of prejudice towards ethnic groups in several subgroups of Germans. Following both the competition hypotheses and Hargreaves and Leaman (1995, p. 24), the individuals most likely to be prejudiced against minorities are expected to be those who are unemployed or who fear unemployment. Contrary to this, I found no difference between these two groups and those without such fears. The results are too weak by far to sustain the view that competition gives rise to racial prejudice. However, it is clear that unemployed persons show a slightly higher level of racial prejudice than their employed counterparts. Further, there is a closer link between those variables indicating personal economic deprivation as well as collective economic deprivation and negative attitudes against outgroups. Thus, the bivariate empirical findings support the individual economic deprivation hypothesis as well as the collective economic deprivation hypothesis (see Appendix, Table 6.9a).

Much the same picture emerges from those racial attitudes concerning what I call the socio-cultural deprivation hypothesis. First, it can be seen that individuals unsatisfied with the performance of the political system tend to have higher levels of racial prejudice. Second, empirical findings reveal that an increase in anomie goes with an increase in racial prejudice. The greater the individual's socio-cultural uncertainties, the more likely they are to express prejudice against outsiders.

Because several of these variables are corrupted, I choose a more stringent test. Table 6.4 displays the estimated effects of the variables under consideration, controlled for other variables. A perusal of the estimates reveals that four out of nine items account for more than a trivial amount of the variance: the perceived economic situation in one year, one's perceived fair share, the performance of the political system, and anomie. Racial prejudice is mainly expressed by individuals facing relative economic, social or political deprivation. Thus, racial attitudes develop as social, economic, and political discontent grows. However, if we compare the model of Table 6.4 with that of Table 6.3, which includes only demographic variables, we find that the contribution of this new model is much higher than the contribution of the model presented in the previous section.

I will now introduce a new concept that replaces the variables in Table 6.4. The idea is that these variables are caused by a common underlying factor. Relative and collective economic deprivation, the perceived performance of the political system, and anomie express forms of perceived cultural

108 Education and Racism

deficiencies. To build an economic model a concept is needed which correlates not only highly with these variables but which has almost the same explanatory power. I suggest replacing the individual variables with a single broader concept that I call *socio-cultural insecurity*.

Table 6.4 Regression of racial attitudes on socio-cultural insecurity variables

Socio-cultural Insecurity	General Prejudice	Social Distance	Anti-Semitism	Immigration	Equal Rights	Discrimination	Racial Prejudice
Unemployment	(.010)	(.025)	(−.006)	(.046)	(−.022)	(.033)	(.019)
	(.063)	(.117)	(−.042)	(.085)	(−.153)	(.102)	(.086)
Fear of un-	(−.014)	(.015)	(−.036)	(.012)	(−.004)	(.009)	(−.004)
employment	(−.065)	(.055)	(−.195)	(.018)	(−.023)	(.022)	(−.014)
CIES	(.018)	(.005)	(.009)	(−.009)	(.039)	(.011)	(.017)
	(.032)	(.007)	(.021)	(−.005)	(.082)	(.011)	(.023)
FIES	.067	.055	.113	(.032)	(.017)	.061	.078
	.142	.092	.279	(.022)	(.041)	.066	.123
CCES	.058	.054	(.030)	.092	(.036)	(.000)	.062
	.101	.073	(.061)	.049	(.072)	(.000)	.080
FCES	(.000)	(.005)	(−.007)	(.025)	.047	(−.022)	(.011)
	(.002)	(.007)	(−.013)	(.014)	.097	(−.020)	(.015)
Fair share	.144	.086	.068	.127	.065	.085	.132
	.175	.082	.096	.048	.091	.053	.119
Political system's	.106	.097	(.043)	.112	.068	.088	.118
performance	.246	.177	(.116)	.080	.182	.105	.203
Anomie	.167	.063	.123	.170	.075	.058	.150
	.109	.032	.094	.035	.057	.020	.073
r^2	12%	5%	6%	13%	4%	3%	12%

First row: standardised regression coefficients. Second row: unstandardised regression coefficients between ( ) p >.01. CIES: contemporary individual economic situation. FIES: future individual economic situation. CCES: contemporary collective economic situation. FCES: future collective economic situation.

The measurement of socio-cultural insecurity required the construction of two new variables, one for the contemporary individual economic situation (CIES), and one for the perceived contemporary collective economic circumstance (CCES). After which the variables future individual economic situation (FIES), future collective economic situation (FCES), fair share, performance of the political system, and anomie were factor analysed to determine how many factors there were underlying the items. This extracted only one factor accounting for much of the variation among the items, thus reducing the five variables to the common factor underlying them all. Then, intergroup attitudes were regressed on this new factor. Table 6.5 shows the result. Prejudice was found to increase along with individual socio-cultural insecurities and, the explanatory power of this simple model is as high as that of the model in Table 6.4. While the first model includes nine independent variables that are often used in survey studies to explain political attitudes, the new model includes only one independent variable with the same explanatory power. This empirical finding strongly supports my idea. Thus, in the following sections, I use only this new construct to predict negative attitudes against racial minorities.

If the effects of socio-economic insecurity on various forms of racial prejudice are not spurious, they should persist when the potentially corrupting influence of compositional differences is removed. The coefficients in Table 6.6 indicate that this is indeed the case. Taking into account the controlled net effects, the higher an individual's score on the socio-ecomomic insecurity scale, the greater the scores on the scales measuring forms of racial prejudice. Although the introduction of controls reduces the effect of socio-economic insecurity, it still has a very strong influence overall on racial prejudice. A perusal of the estimates also reveals some differences concerning the dimensions of racial prejudice.

Table 6.5 The effect of socio-cultural insecurity on racial attitudes

	General Prejudice	Social Distance	Anti-Semitism	Immi-gration	Equal Rights	Discrim-ination	Racial Prejudice
SCI	.335	.222	.212	.342	.196	.175	.338
	.458	.238	.333	.146	.308	.124	.345
r^2	11%	5%	5%	12%	4%	3%	11%

First row: standardised regression coefficients. Second row: unstandardised regression coefficients () p >.01. SCI: socio-cultural insecurity.

Table 6.6 **Regression of racial prejudice on socio-demographic variables and socio-cultural insecurity**

	Dimension of Racial Prejudice						Racial Prejudice
	General Prejudice	Social Distance	Anti-Semitism	Immigration	Equal Rights	Discrimination	
Region	.059	.077	−.107	.091	(−.033)	.114	.061
	.194	.336	−.407	.093	(−.126)	.194	.148
Urbanism	−.113	−.077	−.158	−.100	−.127	−.107	−.167
	−.084	−.076	−.135	−.023	−.109	−.041	−.092
Gender	(.011)	−.063	−.089	(−.000)	(−.033)	(−.035)	−.047
	(.030)	−.147	−.280	(.000)	(−.104)	(−.050)	−.096
Age	.275	.164	.227	.088	.059	.236	.241
	.023	.011	.022	.002	.006	.010	.015
Occupation	−.182	−.079	−.097	−.132	−.104	−.082	−.157
	−.008	−.003	−.005	−.002	−.005	−.002	−.005
Education	−.096	−.060	−.124	−.143	−.104	−.092	−.143
	−.120	−.065	−.187	−.054	−.149	−.059	−.131
%-subgroup	(.015)	.103	.115	(−.028)	(.054)	(.041)	(.068)
	(.007)	.037	.060	(−.004)	(.028)	(.010)	(.023)
SCI	.243	.169	.175	.246	.162	.104	.253
	.328	.180	.274	.103	.253	.073	.253
r^2	28%	12%	18%	22%	9%	14%	28%

First row: standardised regression coefficients. Second row: regression coefficients () p >.01

Structural dispositions

Many individuals find themselves in similar socio-economic situations, and yet they express very different levels of racial prejudice. Taking this into account, one becomes aware that individuals differ not only in terms of socio-cultural circumstances. There are also differences to be seen in their personality pattern, cultural values, and belief systems. Perhaps attitudes towards members of ethnic minorities are chiefly determined not by perceived socio-economic and socio-cultural circumstances, but more by stable personality variables. Attention, therefore, needs to be turned to approaches that focus on the personality formation and belief system of the bearers of racial attitudes.

The most rigorous attempt in this direction was made by Adorno et al. (1950) in their study of the authoritarian personality. They were convinced of a strong link between the expression of racial prejudice and personality traits. According to Adorno et al. individual convictions form a coherent pattern bound together by a common underlying factor. An individual's attitude was seen as an expression of deep-underlying personality traits. In addition, Adorno et al. assumed that these were formed during early childhood and were, therefore, a product of socialisation within the family. They suggested that racial prejudice is the result of a particular personality type: the authoritarian personality. An authoritarian person believes in law and order, whilst favouring values such as obedience and materialism he or she also objects to liberal values. Furthermore, such a person is characterised as excessively submissive to authority and mysticism, as anti-democratic, conservative, and holding right wing political views.

However, this classic study reduced racial prejudice to an invariable personality factor, discounting both the context in which it is expressed, and the individual's perceived socio-economic circumstances. It is these limitations imposed by the decontextualisation of racial attitudes from the social that caused other scholars to criticise the study.

However, using modified concepts of authoritarianism, recent studies to explain racism in Germany have revealed a strong link between the personal pattern and expressed attitudes against ethnic minorities (Hopf et al., 1995; Oesterreich, 1993; Lederer and Schmidt, 1995). These new studies use the idea of an authoritarian disposition to explain racial prejudice. This disposition is characterised by a need for authority, a focus on material interests, right wing orientations, and an opposition to liberal values. They assume, however, that the personality variable under consideration is modified by new experience. Unfortunately, no study has tested the effect of such a structural disposition on racial prejudice, net of the control of socio-cultural insecurities and further determinants.

Contrary to the competition hypothesis, Tajfel and Turner (1979) have argued that individuals favour ingroup over outgroup members, even when the two groups are not competing for limited resources and individuals are not frustrated. The mere fact of categorisation leads to negative attitudes towards outgroups. Besides other things, being in an ingroup leads to more favourable attitudes toward members of the ingroup, and less favourable attitudes toward members of an outgroup. Social identity theory views the mere act of categorising individuals into an ingroup and an outgroup as a result of the identification with social groups. The basic assumption is that individuals strive for a positive self-concept and derive self-esteem from their social identity as a member of an ingroup. The act of identification with an ingroup evokes social competition between ingroup and outgroups. According to Tajfel and Turner, individuals with low self-esteem do identify with and favour the ingroup more than individuals with high self-esteem. The stronger the ingroup favouritism is, the more likely it is that socio-cultural uncertainties will be the cause of prejudice against outgroups. In addition, a high identification with the ingroup leads to a feeling that ethnic minorities are intrinsically different and alien. Following social identity theory I expect a link between identification with the ingroup and the perception of differences between ingroup and outgroups. And, further, that those individuals who identify strongly with the ingroup will express high levels of prejudice.

One way to shed some light on the subject is to investigate the relationship between specific structural variables and racial prejudice. According to Adorno et al. and many others we expect, that right wing individuals, people who identify strongly with Germany and individuals who favour authoritarian above liberal values, to express a much higher level of racial prejudice than those lacking these traits.

To measure the dimension authoritarian values versus liberal values I have built a Likert scale of summed scores including eight variables comprising items such as law and order, free speech, obedience, strong leadership, and values relating to the education of children. A ten point left-right-scale was used to measure if an individual held right wing political views. Individuals who scored six or higher were coded 1, those who scored five or less were coded 0. To measure the identification with the ingroup, I used the scores of the general-national-pride-item which scores from one (not proud to be a German) to four (very proud to be a German).

The mean levels of various racial prejudice scales in the subgroups (see Appendix, Table 6.10a). There are strong bivariate effects of the authoritarian, the ingroup, and of the right wing dimension of the personality pattern on racial prejudice. Right wing individuals who score high on the authoritarian-liberal-dimension, and who express a high identification with the ingroup also reveal very high levels of racial attitudes towards ethnic minorities.

Furthermore, Table 6.7 shows that all three variables have statistically very significant effects on racial prejudice, with the strongest effect to be seen on the authoritarian scale. The exception to the rule is the equal rights scale. The explanatory power of this model is much higher than that of the socio-demographic variable model. It explains almost the same variance as the model in Table 6.6 does, which includes the socio-cultural insecurity scale and a set of demographic variables.

One can, of course, build models to explain racial prejudice including all three variables and others as independent causes of racial prejudice. However, as can be shown, opposing liberal values, national pride and identification with the dominant group are confounded. An authoritarian personality possesses a strong sense of national pride, and is right wing. Authoritarian personalities show low self-esteem, which motivates high identification with an ingroup. Therefore, the concepts of national pride and of right wing ideology could be conceptualised as dimensions of the authoritarian personality. However, I would rather suggest that the three concepts under consideration reflect an underlying second-order factor that is an expression of a more general structural disposition.

Table 6.7 The effects of structural dispositions on racial attitudes

Disposition	Dimension of Racial Prejudice						Racial Prejudice
	General Prejudice	Social Distance	Anti-Semitism	Immigration	Equal Rights	Discrimination	
Authoritarian Liberalism	.381 .103	.211 .045	.251 .079	.208 .018	.113 .036	.304 .043	.337 .068
National Pride	.188 .277	.092 .107	.142 .244	.126 .058	.136 .233	.073 .056	.174 .192
Rightwing	.133 .367	.128 .278	.151 .485	.053 .046	.129 .413	.102 .145	.159 .328
r^2	28%	10%	15%	9%	7%	14%	24%

First row: standardised regression coefficients. Second row: unstandardised regression coefficients () p >.01

To prove this hypothesis, the variables were factor analysed. Principal component analysis of the three constructs revealed one major dimension. This component explains 49 per cent of the variance of the three constructs used in the model in Table 6.7. The loading of the liberal versus authoritarian values scale on the resulting component is .78, the loading of national pride is .73, and the loading of right wing beliefs is .60. The final measure of political personality or structural disposition consists of scores computed for each respondent based on the variables in Table 6.7 and their loadings on the principal component. I used the factor scores of this second-order factor to determine the influence of this disproportional factor on racial prejudice relative to other influences.

Table 6.8 The effects of socio-cultural insecurity and structural disposition on racial prejudice

	General Prejudice	Social Distance	Anti-Semitism	Immi-gration	Equal Rights	Discrim-ination	Racial Prejudice
SCI	.340	.225	.215	.345	.198	.179	.343
	.464	.241	.339	.147	.312	.126	.350
Structural Disposition	.507	.314	.384	.292	.272	.343	.483
	.698	.339	.609	.126	.432	.244	.496
r^2	37%	15%	19%	20%	11%	15%	35%

First row: standardised regression coefficients. Second row: unstandardised regression coefficients () p >.01. SCI: socio-cultural insecurity.

So far, we have seen that socio-cultural circumstances and structural dispositions affect racial prejudice. Many individuals with high scores on the socio-cultural insecurity scale express a low level of racial prejudice. Whereas some other individuals score less on the socio-cultural insecurity scale, but express a high level of racial prejudice. However, whether racial prejudice is the result of socio-cultural variables or from personality variables is still a matter of debate. Given only the scores of socio-cultural insecurity, and structural disposition, which of these two variables is the better predictor of a person's racial prejudice? Table 6.8 reveals the impact of both variables on racial prejudice. First, we see that both variables cause all forms of racial prejudice. The higher an individual's score lies on both the socio-cultural insecurity scale and on the structural disposition scale, the greater the scores on the racial prejudice scales. Second, it can be seen that in general structural disposition has a stronger effect than socio-cultural insecurity. Notice, third, the exception. Socio-cultural circumstances influence immigration more than structural disposition. Finally, this model explains much more variance in the dependent variables than the previous models.

Contact with members of ethnic minorities

Allport (1954) and other social scientists believed that contact among ethnic groups reduces the intensity of racial prejudice. According to Rothbart and John (1993, 42) the basic idea is that antagonistic groups generate unrealistically negative expectations of one another and simultaneously avoid contact. Insofar as contact occurs, the unrealistically negative perceptions of the group members are modified by experience. In other words, hostility is reduced as a result of increasingly favourable attitudes toward individual group members, which then generalise to the group as a whole.

While several studies have shown that contact alone does not reduce negative attitudes, there is, however, a substantial body of research that has shown that contact can reduce racial prejudice, provided it takes place under particular conditions. Contact should be positively supported by political institutions, it should be of sufficient duration and closeness to allow meaningful relationships to develop, the individuals involved should be of equal status, and, the contact should be of a co-operative nature (see Brown, 1995).

Table 6.9 reveals the level of racial prejudice as a function of the type of contact with members of minorities. The intensity of racial prejudice as a function of the number of contacts is shown in Table 6.11a (see Appendix to this chapter). As we can see in Table 6.9, individuals having contact at work, in their neighbourhood or in their family, and those with friends from ethnic minorities show a lower level of racial prejudice than their counterparts do. Contact has an effect on all dimensions of racial prejudice. The means in Table 6.9 reveal that having friends from ethnic minorities reduces racial attitudes more than having contact with members of ethic minorities at work. The greatest contact effect is on stereotypes about racial groups. To my knowledge, these empirical observations are consistent with the research findings on the contact hypothesis (Amir, 1969; Zentrum für Türkeistudien, 1995). In addition, Table 6.9 reveals that the contact intensity is negatively related to all forms of racial prejudice. Again, these findings strongly support the contact hypothesis.

Besides the appropriate contact conditions for successful reduction of racial prejudice, it has also been argued that the effect of contact on racial prejudice depends also on an individual's socio-cultural situation and structural disposition. If socio-cultural circumstances worsen, one could expect, for example, that the level of racial prejudice to increase amongst persons with no contact with members of racial minorities than among persons with more frequent contact. In addition, amongst individuals with liberal structural dispositions, the intensity of contact should have a greater effect than among right-wing-authoritarian people. Therefore, left-wing-liberals with more frequent contact should display the least negative racial attitudes, and right-wing-authoritarian individuals with no contact the most. Figures 1 and 2 show that this is exactly the case. Notice that left-wing-liberals without contact with members of ethnic minorities express the same level of racial attitudes as their rightwing-authoritarian counterparts with a high level of contact.

Table 6.9 Contact and the level of racial prejudice

Dimension of Racial Prejudice	Work no	Work yes	Neighbourhood no	Neighbourhood yes	Friends no	Friends yes	Family no	Family yes
General Prejudice	4.0	3.5	4.1	3.4	4.3	3.3	3.9	3.3
Social Distance	4.2	3.8	4.2	3.8	4.3	3.7	4.1	3.7
Anti-Semitism	3.5	3.1	3.4	3.3	3.6	3.0	3.4	3.2
Immigration	2.1	2.0	2.1	2.0	2.2	1.9	2.1	2.0
Equal Rights	3.9	3.6	3.9	3.6	4.1	3.4	3.8	3.5
Discrimination	2.0	1.7	2.0	1.8	2.1	1.7	1.9	1.7
Racial Prejudice	0.2	-0.3	0.1	-0.2	0.3	-0.4	0.1	-0.4

The role of education

During the 1950s, Stouffer (1955) found that education had a major effect on levels of tolerance. Since then, other studies have also found that more highly educated individuals express less racial prejudice. A negative relationship between higher levels of educational attainment and negative attitudes towards ethnic minorities has been a stable and consistent finding in empirical research until today. However, there is considerable debate about the interpretation of the link between education and racial prejudice. Several interpretations have been proposed.

First, education can be seen as a measure of social status. Especially political sociologists of the 1950s and 1960s assumed that socio-economic status, and education in particular shape political attitudes. It was argued that the link between education and intolerance towards ethnic minorities was merely demonstrative of class interests. According to the working class authoritarian thesis, people with lower levels of education express higher levels of racial prejudice, because they belong to the working class. Lipset, (1959) and Adorno et al. (1950) argued that members of the working class tend to be authoritarian. However, in the debate concerning racial attitudes in Germany, the most common argument is that the people with lower levels of education belong to the lower classes, and that these classes tend to express racial prejudice against ethnic minorities because they are confronted with high levels of socio-cultural insecurity. In this interpretation, the association made between education and racial attitudes is the result of the perceived socio-cultural situation rather than from working class authoritarianism.

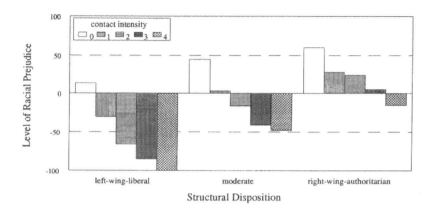

Figure 6.1 Level of racial prejudice: by structural disposition and contact intensity

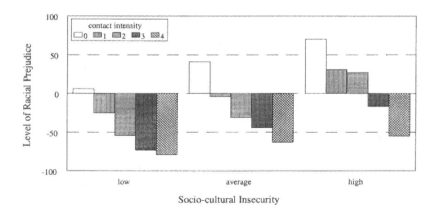

Figure 6.2 Level of racial prejudice: by socio-cultural insecurity and contact intensity

Second, in Adorno et al.'s (1950) classic study on prejudice, more highly educated people tend to be more secure and so are better able to tolerate ethnic minorities. More highly educated individuals are able to handle complex situations and are more able to process complex information. Thus, lower levels of education indicate cognitive limitations. Although these cognitive limitations result in part from early family socialisation, education alters individuals increasing their tolerance towards ethnic minorities. Accordingly, personality development and the growth of cognitive abilities cause a shift towards less negative attitudes. While Adorno et al. attribute the link between education and racial prejudice to the authoritarian personality structure of those with lower levels of education, in later scholars have put this aside (see Hyman and Wright, 1979).

Third, following Selznick and Steinberg (1969) more highly educated individuals are more tolerant because they are socialised in a less prejudiced culture than those less highly educated. Hence, in this view the link between education and racial attitudes is an effect of a transmission of values by social institutions rather than one of personality development and cognitive abilities. Accordingly, the link between education and negative attitudes towards outgroups varies across cultures, suggesting that it should only be found in countries with liberal cultural traditions. This interpretation is also supported by Weil's (1985) comparative and historical study of anti-Semitism.

Fourth, following Jackman (1973), the less frequent expression of racial attitudes by more highly educated people in surveys merely reflects a different response style. Jackman and Muha (1984) found that more highly educated individuals only expressed less intolerant attitudes in abstract principles. No difference in the level of expressed tolerance was found when individuals with high or low educational backgrounds responded to specific policies. Jackman and Muha's view that more highly educated individuals only express greater tolerance towards ethnic minorities in so far as these attitudes serve their own interests, casts doubt on the positive role of education.

It has also been argued that the relationship between education and racial attitudes is solely an artifact of the instruments used in opinion surveys, in other words that those with higher levels of education have a feeling for the 'right' answers.

However, the interpretation that more highly educated individuals only express less racial prejudice in abstract terms does not apply in the German case. Multivariate analyses reveal that education retains an important effect on all dimensions of racial prejudice even after several independent demographic factors are taken into account. Only when controlling for structural disposition, socio-cultural insecurity, perception, and contact, does the direct effect of education decrease, even though it still exerts a significant effect on racial prejudice. The net influence of education on a specific policy such as immigration is remarkable, especially considering that education has no direct effect on social distance, a factor directly related to integration.

There is little support for the view that the links between education and racial prejudice are also a result of class interests. If this hypothesis is valid, then multivariate analysis should reveal not only that occupational prestige has a major effect on levels of racial prejudice, but also a decrease in the effect of education on racial attitudes. Considering only the effects of demographic variables on attitudes against ethnic minorities, the effects found in bivariate analysis of both variables decrease. Yet both independent variables have statistically significant effects on racial prejudice in the direction hypothesised. Perhaps the empirical findings would have been different if the analysis had been carried out during the 1950s. One has to consider that since the educational revolution, a higher level of education no longer guarantees a more prestigious occupation, thus the relationship between education and social status has dissipated. Hence the status thesis no longer explains the relationship between education and racial prejudice.

As far as the link between education and racial prejudice is explained by the working class authoritarian thesis, it can be expected that the relationship between education and racial minorities will vanish if authoritarianism is controlled for. However, contrary to this, regression analyses reveal that the coefficients for education do not substantially change. Thus, these findings do not support the working class thesis.

In contrast to the working class authoritarian thesis, the socio-cultural insecurity thesis predicts that education and occupation causes socio-cultural insecurity, and that the latter causes racial prejudice. In a regression analysis, one can expect that the bivariate association between education and racial prejudice to vanish. Furthermore, the effect of socio-cultural insecurity on racial attitudes should be greater than the effect of structural disposition. As already shown, this is the case. In addition, people with lower levels of education should demonstrate greater levels of racial prejudiced caused by socio-cultural insecurity than more highly educated people. I will return to this point later.

Studies on German political culture show remarkable changes during the post-1945 period. Therefore, the argument that education socialises individuals into the dominant culture of a country implies that education and age are important factors explaining racial prejudice. In testing this hypothesis, I expected, older German people to be less tolerant towards outgroups even if education is controlled for, in addition I expected a smaller effect of education on racial prejudice among the eastern German cohorts, than among those in western Germany. If correct this suggests that education should have one of the strongest negative effects on anti-Semitism. The reason for this prediction is that official culture rejects anti-Semitism. Figure 6.3 and Table 6.10 reveal that this is indeed the case. The effect of education on racial prejudice is greater in western Germany than in eastern Germany. Finally, education also has a strong influence on anti-Semitism.

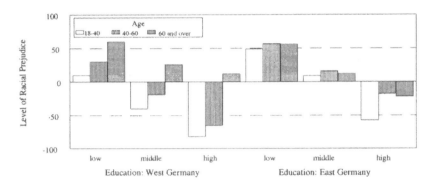

Figure 6.3 Level of racial prejudice by age and level of education

The socialisation hypothesis is also supported by other studies (Bergmann & Erb, 1991; Weil, 1985; Winkler, 1997). Students who majored in social sciences and humanities are more tolerant towards ethnic minorities than those who majored in the natural sciences. Following the socialisation hypothesis and assuming a more liberal upbringing since the 1960s, this explains some of the decrease in racial prejudice in the period since 1945. However, a stringent test of the socialisation hypothesis, requires a cross-national comparison of the relationship between education and racial attitudes. Whilst more highly educated people in non-liberal societies should posses negative attitudes towards ethnic minorities, in liberal societies they should express more positive attitudes.

The socialisation hypothesis explains why under certain conditions more highly educated people express high levels of racial prejudice whereas under other conditions they do not. The cognitive ability hypothesis cannot explain these variations, nor can it explain why younger more highly educated people are less likely to express racial attitudes than older people with the same level of education. The socialisation hypothesis can explain this.

Table 6.10 Regression of intergroup attitudes

Intergroup Attitudes	Dimension of Racial Prejudice						Racial Prejudice
	General Prejudice	Social Distance	Anti-Semitism	Immigration	Equal Rights	Discrimination	
Region	(.024)	.073	−.109	.077	−.067	.076	(−.028)
	(.084)	.198	−.430	.080	−.266	.132	(−.047)
Urbanism	−.077	−.099	−.135	−.081	−.108	−.084	−.132
	−.057	−.059	−.117	−.019	−.093	−.032	−.072
Gender	(.016)	−.071	−.073	(.001)	(−.030)	−.084	−.041
	(.044)	−.154	−.231	(.001)	(−.094)	−.032	−.083
Age	.087	(.015)	.125	(−.009)	−.068	.137	.064
	.007	(.000)	.012	(.000)	−.007	.006	.070
Occupation	−.104	(−.007)	(−.051)	−.104	(−.059)	(−.039)	−.083
	−.005	(.000)	(−.003)	−.001	(−.003)	(.000)	−.003
Education	(−.034)	(−.027)	−.093	−.106	(−.057)	(−.051)	−.081
	(−.042)	(−.026)	−.132	−.040	(−.081)	(−.032)	−.074
%-Subgroup	(.063)	.145	.119	(.007)	.092	(.076)	.115
	(.028)	.051	.061	(.000)	.048	(.018)	.038
SCI	.251	.162	.187	.250	.150	.109	.253
	.333	.172	.290	.103	.232	.075	.252
Structural disposition	.369	.208	.251	.164	.188	.203	.319
	.502	.226	.397	.069	.297	.144	.325
Contact	−.146	−.183	(−.017)	−.091	−.116	−.106	−.154
	−.165	−.165	(−.022)	−.031	−.153	−.062	−.130
Perception of ethnic minorities	.193	.235	.189	.123	.244	.166	.262
	.061	.060	.069	.012	.090	.027	.063
r^2	45%	24%	28%	28%	20%	22%	47%

First row: standardised regression coefficients. Second row: unstandardised regression coefficients () p >.01. SCI: socio-cultural insecurity. Region: West (0), East (1); Gender: men (0), women (1).

Yet, one could argue that the motivation behind the expression of racial attitudes by a more highly educated individual differs from that of those with a lower level of education, and that cognitive abilities influence these motivations. Individuals with a high socio-cultural insecurity may, if less highly educated, be driven more by affect, whereas more highly educated individuals may be more ideological driven (Sniderman, Brody & Tetlock, 1991). Following this, I propose that racial prejudice expressed by the less highly educated is determined more by their socio-cultural circumstances and by their perception of ethnic minorities. On the other hand structural disposition rather than socio-cultural insecurity may be the main determinant of the racial attitudes of the more highly educated. To prove these hypotheses, I regressed racial attitudes of both groups separately on the independent variables. The results are shown in Tables 6.11 and 6.12.

Table 6.11 Regression of intergroup attitudes (those with lower levels of education)

Intergroup Attitudes	General Prejudice	Social Distance	Anti-Semitism	Immigration	Equal Rights	Discrimination	Racial Prejudice
Region	(.040)	.112	−.143	(.095)	(−.085)	(.065)	(.024)
	(.136)	.321	−.573	(.102)	(−.348)	(.122)	(.061)
Urbanism	(−.055)	−.130	−.153	(−.058)	(−.099)	(−.071)	−.133
	(−.040)	−.079	−.131	(−.013)	(−.088)	(−.029)	−.072
Gender	(.019)	−.077	−.110	(−.011)	(−.054)	(−.050)	−.065
	(.049)	−.166	−.333	(−.009)	(−.168)	(−.071)	−.124
Age	.077	(−.004)	.086	(−.038)	(−.063)	(.076)	(.032)
	.006	(.000)	.008	(.000)	(−.006)	(.004)	(.002)
Occupation	−.111	(−.036)	(−.041)	−.114	(−.022)	(−.065)	−.093
	−.007	(−.002)	(−.003)	−.002	(−.002)	(−.002)	−.004
%-Subgroup	(.061)	.179	(.114)	(−.021)	(.083)	(.103)	.125
	(.029)	.071	(.063)	(−.003)	(.048)	(.027)	.044
SCI	.293	.184	.182	.288	.197	.107	.298
	.370	.193	.268	.114	.300	.075	.277
Structural	.331	.214	.207	.152	.143	.177	.294
disposition	.461	.248	.337	.066	.240	.136	.301
Contact	−.183	−.154	(−.036)	−.096	−.119	−.149	−.179
	−.204	−.143	(−.047)	−.033	−.160	−.092	−.147
Perception of	.223	.267	.206	.120	.265	.173	.300
ethnic minorities	.064	.064	.070	.011	.093	.028	.064
r^2	40%	23%	18%	20%	17%	15%	39%

A model explaining racial prejudice

As shown, most of the independent variables have statistically significant effects on racial prejudice in the direction hypothesised. However, although the models discussed demonstrate the direct causes of negative attitudes against racial groups and its members, they do not provide a full understand-

Explaining Individual Racial Prejudice in Contemporary Germany 123

ing of the phenomenon. To understand the development of racial attitudes and the role of the constructs used, a method is required by which the causal relationships among the variables can be conceptualised. One such method is to use path diagrams. Using this, I will propose a complex explanatory model of racial prejudice. Because the computer cannot reveal the causal relations among the variables, I have examined the accuracy of several causal models. Diagram 6.2 outlines how the used set of variables is interrelated in the final model. The dependent variable is the overall racial prejudice scale, which estimates the actual magnitude of racial prejudice for each person.

Table 6.12 Regression of intergroup attitudes (those with higher levels of education)

Intergroup Attitudes	Dimension of Racial Prejudice						Racial Prejudice
	General Prejudice	Social Distance	Anti-Semitism	Immigration	Equal Rights	Discrimination	
Region	(.014)	(.050)	(−.036)	(.053)	(−.054)	(.056)	(.020)
	(.044)	(.147)	(−.150)	(.055)	(−.219)	(.100)	(.049)
Urbanism	(−.081)	(−.024)	(−.102)	(−.119)	(−.048)	(−.053)	(−.099)
	(−.052)	(−.015)	(−.084)	(−.025)	(−.039)	(−.019)	(−.049)
Gender	(−.011)	(−.075)	(−.034)	(−.031)	(−.046)	(.002)	(−.048)
	(−.025)	(−.160)	(−.100)	(−.023)	(−.136)	(.002)	(−.085)
Age	.105	(−.014)	.143	(.020)	(−.039)	.176	(.088)
	.009	(−.001)	.015	(.000)	(−.004)	.008	(.006)
Occupation	(.059)	(−.019)	(−.068)	−.115	−.123	(.028)	(−.097)
	(.021)	(.000)	(−.003)	−.001	−.005	(.000)	(−.003)
%-Subgroup	(.059)	(.113)	(.093)	(.058)	(.102)	(−.018)	(.100)
	(.021)	(.037)	(.042)	(.007)	(.046)	(−.003)	(.027)
SCI	.205	.158	.173	.160	(.044)	(.002)	.179
	.269	.191	.287	.067	(.073)	(.001)	.180
Structural disposition	.449	.226	.278	.183	.239	.259	.391
	.515	.238	.403	.067	.347	.164	.344
Contact	−.108	−.220	(−.016)	(−.111)	(−.097)	(−.081)	−.156
	−.104	−.197	(−.020)	(−.034)	(−.120)	(−.043)	−.116
Perception of ethnic minorities	.155	.171	.163	(.067)	.174	.177	.218
	.047	.048	.062	(.007)	.067	.030	.051
r^2	38%	19%	19%	12%	12%	20%	36%

124 *Education and Racism*

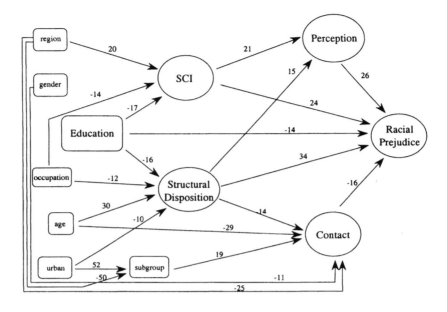

Diagram 6.2   A model explaining racial prejudice

In Diagram 6.2 I have placed two second-order factors, socio-economic insecurity and structural disposition, in the most central position. The first represents a relatively unstable, self-perceived position of individuals in society. The second represents a relatively stable personality pattern of individuals, comparable to the political self. The model also includes demographic variables as exogenous variables.

The final result of the path analysis is shown in Diagram 6.2. A straight arrow indicates a causal relationship and the direction of causality. The absence of an arrow between variables means that they are unrelated. The numbers along the paths are standardised path coefficients, each one expressing the relative strength of the causal relationship.

Diagram 6.2 indicates that five variables have relevant effects on racial prejudice, when controlled for the net compositional differences. They are education, the belief system and perceived socio-cultural circumstances, the perception of outgroups and contact with them. The diagram also reveals that socio-cultural insecurity, structural disposition, and the perceived differences between ingroup and outgroups influence racial attitudes more than the intensity of contact with members of ethnic minorities and education. Notice that the commonly neglected personality variable is the largest direct cause of racial prejudice. Both perceived-socio-economic insecurity and structural disposition are also directly related to the perception of minority groups. Right wing and insecure individuals perceive more differences between ingroups and outgroups than others.

When discussing the contact hypothesis, I mentioned that the dominant group generates negative views of ethnic minorities and therefore avoids contact (Amir 1969). It can be expected that individuals with structural dispositions who favour racial attitudes also avoid contact with members of ethnic minorities. Thus suggesting that structural disposition has a negative effect on contact, even on the net effect of the controls. As we can see from Diagram 6.2, this is indeed the case. Right-wing-individuals have less contact with members of ethnic minorities than left-wing-liberals. Other determinants of contact intensity are region, age of an individual and the relative size of subordinate groups in the communities.

What is the role of education in this model? Education causes variation in three variables. First it effects the perceived socio-cultural circumstances, second, the type of belief system, and third it has an effect on racial prejudice but it has no effect on contact intensity or on perceptions towards outgroups. While the structural disposition is a product of socialisation and education, socio-cultural insecurity is caused by the position in the social structure and education. Although the direct effect of education on negative attitudes towards ethnic minorities is small, as can be seen from the indirect effects on racial prejudice, the overall effects are very high. Yet, we have to consider that the direct effect of education on racial prejudice varies according to the model being tested.

What are the differences between less highly educated and more highly educated people? To answer this question, I conducted two additional path analyses for both groups. The results are shown in Diagram 6.3 (less highly educated people) and Diagram 6.4 (more highly educated people). If we compare the relative strength of the effects on racial prejudice, some remarkable differences appear. For example, while among the less highly educated the impact of socio-cultural insecurity and structural disposition is almost identical, among the more highly educated the relative impact of structural disposition surpasses that of socio-cultural disposition. Furthermore, among those less highly educated, the perception that the outgroup is different from the ingroup is determined to a greater extent by ingroup's perceived socio-cultural insecurities than by their structural disposition. Among more highly educated people, structural disposition is more important.

126 *Education and Racism*

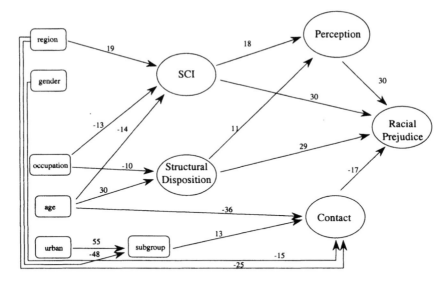

Diagram 6.3 A model explaining racial prejudice (less highly educated people)

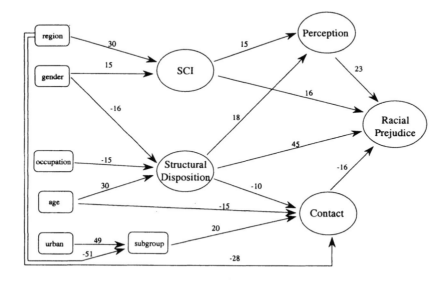

Diagram 6.4 A model explaining racial prejudice (more highly educated people)

Conclusion

The predominant research on racial prejudice based on sample surveys has focused on the relationship between demographic characteristics, economic circumstances, minority group size and prejudiced attitudes. Most studies have viewed racial prejudice as the result of individual propensities, social and economic experiences, economic crises, or authoritarianism. These rival interpretations have been viewed as contradictory and, therefore, no attempts have been made to integrate them in models explaining racial prejudice. Although these studies have added to our understanding of negative attitudes towards ethnic minorities, they have failed to produce a general model.

In contrast to the mainstream of empirical research in Germany, I suggest that more general constructs need to be used as main determinants of racial prejudice. To achieve this I propose combining several socio-cultural and socio-economic variables to a general construct called *socio-cultural insecurity*. The constructs right wing views, authoritarianism, and national pride could all be combined into a general personality construct called *structural disposition*. While the first is the main cause of short-term fluctuations in racial prejudice, the latter is mainly responsible for long-term variations. The empirical analysis carried out here has shown that these constructs are powerful analytical tools. Consistent with recent findings of significant effects of socio-cultural and personality variables on racial prejudice, I have shown that perceived socio-cultural insecurity and political personality structure impact strongly on all considered forms of intergroup attitudes, when controlled for the net of compositional effects. Beyond that, contact intensity, the perception that outgroups are different to Germans and education appear to have strong effects on the expression of racial attitudes. Education, in particular, appeared to have an important indirect impact on racial prejudice. The more highly educated have developed a more open-minded personality that impedes the development of negative racial attitudes. It was also shown that among more highly educated people structural disposition is by far the most important determinant of racial prejudice.

The explanation of individual racial prejudice given above explains why some individuals in contemporary Germany have a low level of racial prejudice whilst others have a high level. If we are interested in reducing the intensity of racial prejudice in the long run, education appears to be an important instrument. Education has a strong impact on the formation of a liberal and open-minded personality. Equipped with such a personality individuals are less susceptible to negative views about ethnic minorities, better able to manage complex situations, have easier contact with members of outgroups, and react more tolerantly under unfavourable conditions. In addition, the content of education can reduce negative racial attitudes by influencing the perception held of outgroups, especially among less highly educated people—limited as it may be the role of these actors still remains crucial. However, analyses such as the one presented here are also limited, suggesting that some things can be counteracted but others can not. The broader cultural environment and public opinion may represent a threshold for individuals' expression of negative attitudes towards outgroups. This then, seems to be more relevant for less highly educated people than for more highly educated people. The expression of negative racial attitudes among less highly educated people is motivated more by personal insecurities whilst the expression of negative racial attitudes among well-educated people is mainly determined by their stable personality traits. Therefore, the social climate is less influential for the more highly educated. Yet the social climate is the only domain where politics has a direct effect. This is where politics comes in. The government, parties, and media are central actors in forming the political agenda that shapes the social climate.

Appendix

Table 6.1a   Dimensions of racial attitudes

Items	General Prejudice	Social Distance 1	Equal Rights	Social Distance 2	Anti-Semitism	Discrimination	Immigration
• They take away work from Germans.	.73	−.21	−.14	−.03	.04	−.13	.15
• They are a burden on public funds.	.71	−.17	−.15	−.07	.08	−.10	.15
• Their presence in Germany causes problems on the labour market.	.70	−.07	−.03	−.04	.11	.03	.00
• If work is scarce, foreigners should be sent back.	.56	−.10	−.19	−.11	.09	−.27	.28
• They are more likely to commit crime than Germans.	.55	−.14	−.10	−.16	.10	−.20	.05
• We feel as if we are the foreigners, because there are so many in Germany.	.54	−.10	−.18	−.17	.21	−.17	.18
• They should adapt their lifestyle to German circumstances.	.49	.01	−.06	−.24	.16	−.08	.13
• Foreigners political participation should be forbidden.	.43	−.01	−.24	−.22	.20	−.17	.20
• They should marry someone from their own country.	.38	−.14	−.10	−.16	.12	−.30	.25

Explaining Individual Racial Prejudice in Contemporary Germany

Items	General Prejudice	Social Distance 1	Equal Rights	Social Distance 2	Anti-Semitism	Discrimination	Immigration
• How pleasant are Italians in your neighbourhood?	−.11	.76	.09	.00	.02	.13	−.07
• How pleasant are Jews in your neighbourhood?	−.12	.71	.18	.05	−.29	.06	.02
• How pleasant are Germans from Eastern Europe in your neighbourhood?	−.14	.69	.12	.15	.01	.00	−.01
• How would you feel if an Italian were to marry into your family?	−.10	.69	.09	.22	−.03	.14	−.18
• How would you feel if an ethnic German from Eastern Europe were to marry into your family?	−.11	.66	.14	.33	−.02	.03	−.15
• How would you feel if a Jew were to marry into your family?	−.11	.62	.17	.27	.34	.08	−.10
• How pleasant are Turks in your neighbourhood?	−.26	.49	.19	.47	−.05	.18	−.04
• Italians should have equal rights.	−.14	.20	.83	.08	−.05	.10	-11
• Germans from Eastern Europe should have equal rights.	−.16	.21	.78	.05	−.04	.04	−.13
• Turks should have equal rights.	−.26	.10	.76	.33	−.12	.14	−.08
• Jews should have equal rights.	−.10	.25	.70	−.04	−.35	.07	−.08
• Asylum seekers should have equal rights.	−.20	−.03	.63	.53	−.11	.07	−.05
• How would you feel if an asylum seeker were to marry into your family?	−.18	.27	.13	.79	−.16	.11	−.13
• How would you feel if a Turk were to marry into your family?	−.20	.35	.11	.70	−.15	.20	−.12
• How pleasant are asylum seekers in your neighbourhood?	−.25	.33	.16	.66	−.09	.10	.26
• Jews have too much influence in the world.	.24	−.09	−.09	−.13	.72	−.13	.02
• Today, many Jews try to obtain benefits due to persecution in the past.	.20	−.04	−.12	−.17	.72	−.04	.05
• Jews are partly to blame for their persecution.	.24	−.12	−.12	−.03	.70	−.13	.07
• I am disconcerted that Germans have committed so many crimes against Jews.	.24	−.08	−.09	−.01	.40	−.19	.13
• An innkeeper refuses to serve a foreigner.	−.13	.13	.10	−.01	−.16	.77	−.03
• Parents forbid their seventeen-year-old daughter to befriend a Turkish boy.	−.17	.08	.08	.28	−.16	.72	−.09
• An entrepreneur, who must reduce his staff, dismisses his foreign workers first.	−.30	.11	.09	.12	−.07	.71	−.10
• Immigration of workers from the European Union	.18	−.16	−.12	.06	−.01	−.03	.77
• Immigration of Turks	.21	−.07	−.11	−.16	.10	−.10	.73
• Immigration of ethnic Germans from Eastern Europe	.15	−.10	−.07	−.07	.07	−.05	.55
• Immigration of asylum seekers	.28	.01	−.08	−.32	.24	−.11	.46
EIGENVALUE	10.8	2.5	1.9	1.7	1.4	1.3	1.2
PER CENT OF VARIANCE	30.9	7.1	5.5	4.6	4.0	3.6	3.5

130 *Education and Racism*

Table 6.2a   Scale: general prejudice and stereotypes

Item		%	Mean
V50	They should adapt their lifestyle to German circumstances.	59.7	4.9
V51	If work is scarce, foreigners should be sent back.	28.4	3.5
V52	Foreigners' political participation should be forbidden.	36.1	3.8
V53	They should marry someone from their own country.	21.7	2.8
V71	We feel as if we are foreigners, because there are so many of them in Germany.	29.1	3.2
V73	They are a burden on public funds.	41.9	4.1
V75	Their presence in Germany causes problems on the labour market.	46.1	4.3
V77	They take away work from Germans.	36.3	3.9
V78	They tend to commit crime more than Germans.	40.2	4.0

The response options range from 1 = 'strongly disagree' to 7 = 'strongly agree'. Higher means indicate higher scores on general prejudice and stereotypes. The percentage refers to all agreeing responses, 5, 6 and 7 were included in one category. Scale construction: Likert scale.

Table 6.3a   Scale: anti-Semitism

Item		%	Mean
V137	Jews have too much influence in the world.	24.9	3.2
V139	Today, many Jews try to obtain benefits due to past persecution.	46.5	4.3
V140	Jews carry some of the blame for their own persecution.	16.5	2.6

The response options range from 1 = 'strongly disagree' to 7 = 'strongly agree'. Higher means indicate higher scores on anti-Semitism. The percentage refers to all agreeing responses, 5, 6 and 7 were included in one category. Scale construction: Likert scale.

Table 6.4a   Scale: social distance

Item		%	Mean
V122	How pleasant are Italians in your neighbourhood?	7.3	3.1
V123	How pleasant are ethnic Germans from Eastern Europe in your neighbourhood?	17.0	3.6
V126	How pleasant are Jews in your neighbourhood?	10.6	3.4
V124	How pleasant are asylum seekers in your neighbourhood?	48.6	4.7
V125	How pleasant are Turks in your neighbourhood?	34.8	4.2
V129	How would you feel if an asylum seeker were to marry into your family?	60.4	5.1
V130	How would you feel if a Turk were to marry into your family?	55.1	4.9

The response options range from 1 = 'very unpleasant' to 7 = 'very pleasant'. For the purpose of this study, the scores were re-coded, so that the scores range from 1 = 'very pleasant' to 7 = 'very unpleasant'. Therefore, higher means indicate higher social distance. The percentage refers to all 'unpleasant' responses, 5, 6 and 7 were included in one category. Scale construction: Likert scale.

Explaining Individual Racial Prejudice in Contemporary Germany 131

Table 6.5a Scale: attitudes towards immigration

Item		%	Mean
V31	Immigration of ethnic Germans from Eastern Europe	12.8	2.0
V32	Immigration of asylum seekers	21.5	2.1
V33	Immigration of workers from the European Union	17.5	1.9
V34	Immigration of Turks	36.0	2.3

The response options range from 1 = 'immigration should be possible' to 3 = 'immigration should be forbidden'. Higher means indicate higher scores on negative attitudes against immigration. The percentage refers to code 3. Scale construction: Likert scale.

Table 6.6a Scale: attitudes towards equal rights for racial minorities

Item		%	Mean
V132	Italians should have equal rights.	27.7	3.4
V133	Germans from Eastern Europe should have equal rights.	25.6	3.2
V134	Asylum seekers should have equal rights.	65.1	5.1
V135	Turks should have equal rights.	45.1	4.2
V136	Jews should have equal rights.	20.9	3.0

The response options range from 1 = 'strongly disagree' to 7 = 'strongly agree'. For the purpose of this study, the scores are re-coded, so that the scores range from 1 = 'strongly agree' to 7 = 'strongly disagree'. Therefore, higher means indicate higher disagreement to equal rights for ethnic minorities. The percentage refers to all 'disagree' responses, 5, 6 and 7 were included in one category. Scale construction: Likert scale.

Table 6.7a Scale: personal agreement to discrimination

Item		%	Mean
V82	An innkeeper refuses to serve a foreigner.	10.3	3.5
V83	Parents forbid their 17-year-old daughter to befriend a Turkish boy.	32.6	2.9
V84	An entrepreneur, who must reduce his staff, dismisses his foreign workers first.	27.1	3.0

The response options range from 1 = 'strongly approve' to 4 = 'strongly disapprove'. For the purpose of this study, the scores are re-coded, so that the scores range from 1 = 'strongly disapprove' to 4 = 'strongly approve'. Therefore, higher means indicate higher approval of concrete everyday discrimination. The percentage refers to all 'approve' responses, 3 and 4 were included in one category. Scale construction: Likert scale.

Table 6.8a   Demography and racial prejudice

Demography	\<Dimensions of Racial Prejudice\>						Racial Prejudice
	General Prejudice	Social Distance	Anti-Semitism	Immigration	Equal Rights	Discrimination	
Region							
West	3.7	4.0	3.4	2.0	3.8	1.9	-0.1
East	4.2	4.3	3.1	2.2	3.8	2.1	0.2
Gender							
Women	3.9	4.0	3.3	2.1	3.8	1.9	0.0
Men	3.7	4.1	3.4	2.1	3.8	1.9	0.0
Age							
18–30	3.3	3.8	2.8	1.9	3.6	1.6	-0.4
31–40	3.5	3.9	3.0	2.0	3.6	1.8	-0.2
41–50	3.6	4.0	3.3	2.0	3.7	1.9	-0.1
51–60	4.1	4.2	3.7	2.1	3.9	2.0	0.2
61–	4.5	4.4	4.0	2.2	4.1	2.2	0.5
Urbanism							
–5000	4.1	4.3	3.7	2.2	4.0	2.0	0.3
–20000	4.0	4.2	3.5	2.1	4.0	1.9	0.1
–100000	3.8	4.0	3.3	2.1	3.6	1.9	0.0
–500000	3.6	4.0	3.1	2.0	3.7	1.8	-0.1
>500000	3.5	3.8	3.1	1.9	3.5	1.7	-0.3
Occupation							
Worker	4.3	4.3	3.7	2.2	4.1	2.1	0.3
Employee	3.7	4.0	3.2	2.0	3.6	1.8	-0.1
Civil servant	3.2	3.9	3.0	1.9	3.3	1.7	-0.4
Self-employed	3.6	4.1	3.6	2.1	3.8	1.6	0.0
Prestige							
Very low	4.3	4.3	3.7	2.2	4.1	2.1	0.4
Low	4.2	4.3	3.7	2.2	4.1	2.0	0.3
High	3.7	4.0	3.3	2.0	3.7	1.8	-0.1
Very high	3.2	3.8	2.9	1.9	3.3	1.7	-0.4
Education							
Low	4.3	4.3	3.9	2.2	4.1	2.1	0.4
Middle	3.7	4.0	3.2	2.0	3.7	1.8	-0.1
High	3.0	3.7	2.6	1.8	3.2	1.6	-0.6
Percentage of Subordinate Group							
< 4%	4.1	4.2	3.2	2.2	3.8	2.0	0.2
4 – 12%	3.9	4.1	3.5	2.1	3.9	1.9	0.0
> 12%	3.5	3.9	3.2	1.9	3.6	1.8	-0.3
TOTAL	3.8	4.1	3.4	2.1	3.8	1.9	0.0

Table 6.9a   Socio-cultural insecurities and racial prejudice

Socio-cultural insecurity	General Prejudice	Social Distance	Anti-Semitism	Immigration	Equal Rights	Discrimination	Racial Prejudice
Unemployed							
No	3.8	4.1	3.4	2.1	3.8	1.9	0.0
Yes	4.3	4.3	3.6	2.2	3.9	2.1	0.3
Fear of Unemployment							
No	3.8	4.1	3.4	2.1	3.8	1.9	0.0
Yes	3.9	4.2	3.3	2.1	3.8	2.0	0.1
Economic Situation of Germany							
Excellent	3.2	3.6	3.0	1.7	3.2	1.7	-0.6
Good	3.5	3.9	3.2	1.9	3.6	1.9	-0.2
In part	3.7	4.0	3.3	2.0	3.7	1.9	-0.1
Bad	4.0	4.2	3.5	2.1	3.9	1.9	0.1
Very bad	4.5	4.3	3.9	2.3	4.3	2.1	0.5
Individual Economic Situation							
Excellent	2.9	3.8	2.8	1.8	3.2	1.6	-0.6
Good	3.7	4.0	3.2	2.0	3.6	1.9	-0.1
In part	4.0	4.2	3.5	2.1	3.9	1.9	0.1
Bad	4.2	4.3	3.6	2.2	4.1	2.0	0.3
Very bad	4.7	4.4	3.8	2.3	4.4	2.2	0.6
Future Economic Situation of Germany							
Much better	3.3	3.3	1.9	2.1	2.4	1.7	-0.7
Better	3.6	4.0	3.1	2.0	3.7	1.9	-0.2
Equal	3.8	4.0	3.4	2.0	3.7	1.9	0.0
Worse	3.8	4.1	3.4	2.1	3.8	1.9	0.0
Much worse	4.3	4.3	3.8	2.2	4.1	2.0	0.4
Future Individual Economic Situation							
Much better	3.2	3.4	2.6	1.9	3.6	1.7	-0.5
Better	3.5	3.9	2.9	2.0	3.7	1.8	-0.2
Equal	3.8	4.1	3.4	2.1	3.8	1.9	0.0
Worse	4.0	4.2	3.6	2.1	3.9	1.9	0.1
Much worse	4.4	4.4	4.2	2.3	4.2	2.1	0.5
Belief in Obtaining One's Fair Share							
More	3.2	3.9	2.9	1.9	3.3	1.7	-0.4
Right	3.6	4.0	3.3	2.0	3.7	1.8	-0.1
Less	4.1	4.3	3.6	2.2	4.0	2.0	0.2
Much less	4.6	4.4	3.7	2.3	4.2	2.2	0.5
Performance of the Political System							
Good	3.5	3.8	3.2	1.9	3.6	1.9	-0.2
Satisfied	3.7	4.0	3.3	2.0	3.7	1.8	-0.1
Bad	4.3	4.3	3.7	2.2	4.1	2.1	0.4
Very bad	4.8	4.6	4.0	2.3	4.4	2.2	0.7
Anomie							
Low	3.4	3.9	3.1	1.9	3.5	1.8	-0.3
Average	3.7	4.0	3.4	2.0	3.7	1.9	-0.1
High	4.3	4.3	3.5	2.2	4.1	2.0	0.4
Socio-Cultural Insecurity							
Low	3.4	3.8	3.0	1.9	3.4	1.8	-0.4
Average	3.8	4.0	3.4	2.0	3.8	1.9	0.0
High	4.3	4.4	3.7	2.2	4.1	2.1	0.4
TOTAL	3.8	4.1	3.4	2.1	3.8	1.9	0.0

Table 6.10a Structural dispositions and racial prejudice

Disposition	General Prejudice	Social Distance	Anti-Semitism	Immigration	Equal Rights	Discrimination	Racial Prejudice
Liberal versus Authoritarian							
Strongly liberal	3.0	3.7	2.6	1.9	3.3	1.6	-0.6
Liberal	3.5	4.0	3.2	2.0	3.7	1.8	-0.2
Moderate	3.9	4.2	3.5	2.1	4.0	2.0	0.1
Authoritarian	4.3	4.3	3.7	2.2	4.0	2.1	0.3
Strongly authoritarian	4.7	4.4	4.0	2.2	4.1	2.2	0.5
Right Wing							
No	3.5	3.9	3.1	2.0	1.8	1.8	-0.2
Yes	4.2	4.3	3.8	2.1	2.0	2.0	0.3
National Pride							
No	3.0	3.6	2.7	1.9	3.1	1.7	-0.6
Little	3.5	4.0	3.1	2.0	3.7	1.8	-0.2
Proud	4.0	4.2	3.5	2.1	3.9	1.9	0.1
Very	4.5	4.4	3.9	2.2	4.2	2.1	0.4
Structural Disposition							
Left liberal	2.7	3.5	2.4	1.9	3.0	1.5	-0.8
Liberal	3.5	4.0	3.2	2.0	3.7	1.8	-0.2
Moderate	3.9	4.2	3.5	2.1	3.9	2.0	0.1
Authoritarian	4.2	4.3	3.6	2.1	4.1	2.0	0.3
Right wing authoritarian	4.7	4.5	4.1	2.2	4.2	2.2	0.6
TOTAL	3.8	4.1	3.4	2.1	3.8	1.9	0.0

Table 6.11a Contact intensity and the level of racial prejudice

Racial Prejudice	0	1	2	3	4	r	Mean
General Prejudice	4.4	3.9	3.5	3.1	2.8	-.37	3.8
Social Distance	4.4	4.1	3.8	3.6	3.5	-.30	4.1
Anti-Semitism	3.7	3.4	3.3	3.0	2.9	-.16	3.4
Immigration	2.2	2.1	2.0	1.9	1.8	-.28	2.1
Equal Rights	4.1	3.8	3.5	3.4	3.1	.19	3.8
Discrimination	2.2	1.9	1.8	1.7	1.6	.26	1.9
Racial Prejudice	0.4	0.0	-0.2	-0.5	-0.7	-.36	0.0

Note

1 The findings in this research are drawn from the ALLBUS-Survey (Allgemeine Bevölkerungsumfrage der Sozialwissenschaften) conducted by ZUMA (Zentrum für Umfragen, Methoden und Analysen, Mannheim). The data sources were made available by the Zentralarchiv für Empirische Sozialforschung (Köln).

References

Adorno, T.W., Frenkel-Brunswick, E., Levinson, D.J. and Sanford, N.R. (1950), *The Authoritarian Personality*, New York, Evanston, London, Harper.
Allport, G.W. (1954), *The Nature of Prejudice*, Reading, Mass., Addison Wesley.
Amir, Y. (1969), Contact Hypothesis in Ethnic Relations, *Psychological Bulletin*, vol. 71, pp. 319–342.
Bergmann, W. and Erb, R. (1991), Antisemitismus in der Bundesrepublik Deutschland, *Ergebnisse der empirischen Forschung von 1946–1989*, Opladen, Leske + Budrich.
Bergmann, W. and Erb, R. (1996), Rechtsextremismus und Antisemitismus, in J.W. Falter, H.-G. Jaschke and J.R. Winkler (eds), *Rechtsextremismus, Ergebnisse und Perspektiven der Forschung*, Opaden, Westdeutscher Verlag.
Blalock, H.M. (1967), *Toward a Theory of Minority-Group Relations*, New York, John Wiley.
Bobo, L. (1983), Whites' Opposition to Busing, Symbolic Racism or Realistic Group Conflict? *Journal of Personality and Social Psychology*, vol. 45, pp. 1196–1210.
Brown, R. (1995), *Prejudice, Its Social Psychology*, Oxford, Blackwell.
Dalton, R. (1993), *Politics in Germany*, 2nd ed, New York, HarperCollins.
Dollard, J., Doob, L., Miller, N.E., Mowrer, O.H., and Sears, R.R., (1939), *Frustration and Aggression*, New Haven, CT, Yale University Press.
Eckert, R., Willems, H., and Würtz, S. (1996), Erklärungsmuster fremdenfeindlicher Gewalt im empirischen Test, in J.W. Falter, H.-G. Jaschke and J.R. Winkler (eds), *Rechtsextremismus, Ergebnisse und Perspektiven der Forschung*, Opaden, Westdeutscher Verlag.
Falter, J.W. (1994), *Wer wählt rechts? Die Wähler und Anhänger rechtsextremistischer Parteien im vereinigten Deutschland*, München, Beck.
Fuchs, D., Gerhards, J. and Roller, E. (1993), Wir und die Anderen, Ethnozentrismus in den zwölf Ländern der europäischen Gemeinschaft, in *Kölner Zeitschrift für Soziologie und Sozialpsychologie*, vol. 45, pp. 238–253.
Hargreaves, A.G. and Leaman, J. (1995), Racism in Contemporary Western Europe: An Overview, in A.G. Hargreaves and J. Leaman (eds), *Racism, Ethnicity and Politics in Contemporary Europe*, Aldershot, Edward Elgar.
Heckmann, F. (1992), *Ethnische Minderheiten, Volk und Nation, Soziologie inter-ethnischer Beziehungen*, Stuttgart, Ferdinand Enke.
Heitmeyer, W. (1987), *Rechtsextremistische Orientierungen bei Jugendlichen, Empirische Ergebnisse und Erklärungsmuster einer Untersuchung zur politischen Sozialisation*, Weinheim und München, Juventa.
Heß, U. (1996), *Fremdenfeindliche Gewalt in Deutschland*, München, Profil.
Hill, P.B. (1994), Räumliche Nähe und soziale Distanz zu ethnischen Minderheiten, *Zeitschrift für Soziologie*, vol. 13, pp. 363–370.
Hill, P.B. (1993), Die Entwicklung der Einstellungen zu unterschiedlichen Ausländergruppen zwischen 1980 und 1992, in H. Willems zusammen mit R. Eckert, S. Würtz und L. Steinmetz, *Fremdenfeindliche Gewalt, Einstellungen, Täter, Konflikteskalation*, Opladen, Leske + Budrich.
Hopf, C., Rieker, P., Sanden-Marcus M. and Schmidt C. (1995), *Familie und Rechtsextremismus, Analyse qualitativer Interviews mit jungen Männern*, Weinheim und München, Juventa.
Hyman, H. and Wright C. (1975), *The Enduring Effects of Education*, Chicago, IL., University of Chicago Press.
Jackman, M.R. (1973), Education and Prejudice or Education and Response-set? in *American Sociological Review*, vol. 38, pp. 327–339.

Jackman, M.R. and Muha, M.J. (1984), Education and Intergroup Attitudes: Moral Enlightenment, Superficial Democratic Commitment, or Ideological Refinement? *American Sociological Review*, vol. 49, pp. 751-769.

Jaschke, H.-G. (1994), *Rechtsextremismus und Fremdenfeindlichkeit, Begriffe, Positionen, Praxisfelder*, Opladen, Westdeutscher Verlag.

Krauth, C. and Porst R. (1984), Sozioökonomische Determinanten von Einstellungen zu Gastarbeitern, in K.U. Mayer and P. Schmidt (eds), *Allgemeine Bevölkerungsumfrage der Sozialwissenschaften*, Frankfurt am Main, Campus.

Lederer, G. and Schmidt, P. (eds) (1995), *Autoritarismus und Gesellschaft, Trendanalysen und vergleichende Jugenduntersuchungen 1945-1993*, Opladen, Leske + Budrich.

Lipset, S.M. (1959), Democracy and Working-class Authoritarianism, in *American Sociological Review*, vol. 24, pp. 482-501.

Melzer, W. (1992), *Jugend und Politik in Deutschland, Gesellschaftliche Einstellungen, Zukunftsorientierungen und Rechtsextremismus-Potential Jugendlicher in Ost- und Westdeutschland*, Opladen, Leske + Budrich.

Oesterreich, D. (1993), *Autoritäre Persönlichkeit und Gesellschaftsordnung, Der Stellenwert psychischer Faktoren für politische Einstellungen—eine empirische Untersuchung von Jugendlichen in Ost und West*, Weinheim und München, Juventa.

Rothbart, M. and John, O.P. (1993), Intergroup Relations and Stereotype Change: A Social-Cognitive Analysis and Some Longitudinal Findings, in P.M. Sniderman, P.E. Tetlock and E.G. Carmines (eds), *Prejudice, Politics, and the American Dilema*, Stanford, Cal., Stanford University Press.

Sears, D.O, and Funk, C.L. (1991), The Role of Self-Interest in Social and Political Attitudes, *Advances in Experimental Social Psychology*, vol. 24, pp. 1-91.

Selznik, G.J. and Steinberg, S. (1969), *The Tenacity of Prejudice*, New York, Harper and Row.

Sniderman, P.M., Brody, R.A. and Tetlock, P.E. (1991), *Reasoning and Choice, Explorations in Political Psychology*, Cambridge, Mass., Cambridge University Press.

Stouffer, S. (1955), *Communism, Conformity, and Civil Liberty*, New York, Doubleday.

Tajfel, H. and Turner, J. (1979), An integrative theory of intergroup conflict, in W.G. Austin and S. Worchel (eds), *The Social Psychology of Intergroup Relations*, Monterey, Cal.

Vanneman, R.D. and Pettigrew, T. (1972), Race and Relative Deprivation in the Urban United States, *Race*, vol. 13, pp. 461-486.

Wegener, B. (1984), Gibt es Sozialprestige? in *Zeitschrift für Soziologie*, vol. 14, pp. 209-235.

Weil, F. D. (1985), The Variable Effects of Education on Liberal Attitudes: A Comprative-Historical Analysis of Anti-Semitism Using Public Opinion Survey Data, in *American Sociological Review*, vol. 50, pp. 458-474.

Wiegand, E. (1992), Zunahme der Ausländerfeindlichkeit? Einstellungen zu Fremden in Deutschland und Europa, *ZUMA-Nachrichten*, vol. 31, pp. 7-28.

Wieviorka, M. (1994), Racism in Europe, Unity and Diversity, in A. Rattansi and S. Westwood (eds), *Racism, Modernity and Identity*, Cambridge, Polity Press.

Winkler, J.R. (1996), Bausteine einer allgemeinen Theorie des Rechtsextremismus, Zur Stellung und Integration von Persönlichkeits- und Umweltfaktoren, in J.W. Falter, H.-G. Jaschke and J.R. Winkler (eds), *Rechtsextremismus, Ergebnisse und Perspektiven der Forschung*, Opaden, Westdeutscher Verlag.

Winkler, J.R. (1997), Jugend und Gewalt in Rheinland-Pfalz, in S. Schumann and J. R. Winkler (eds), *Jugend, Politik und Rechtsextremismus in Rheinland-Pfalz*, Frankfurt am Main, New York, Lang.

Zentrum für Türkeistudien (ed.) (1995), *Das Bild der Ausländer in der Öffentlichkeit, Eine theoretische und empirische Analyse zur Fremdenfeindlichkeit*, Opladen, Leske und Budrich.

7 Dynamics of Political Values: Education and Issues of Tolerance

PAUL SNIDERMAN & ERICA R. GOULD

Each of us can, and frequently does, make different choices in different situations. We may favour greater government effort to help minorities on one occasion, and greater effort by minorities to help themselves on another. And it is not just on specific and transient issues that we citizens are willing to contradict ourselves. Our views on fundamental questions of the rights of citizens and values of democratic politics can vary from one occasion to the next. The very same person who supports the right of an unpopular political group to express its point of view publicly can turn on a dime and approve the refusal of a police department to issue a parade permit. (For a systematic exploration of the contestability of beliefs on democratic rights and values, see Sniderman, Tetlock, Glaser, Green & Hout, 1989, pp. 25–46).

The fact that citizens seemingly will take one side of an issue one day and the other the next raises, in the mind of any thoughtful observer, a cloud of questions. One of the most fundamental of these questions is what sense it makes to speak of citizens as capable of learning and internalising the values of a democratic politics. What does it tell us if citizens who, in some sense, have learned the value of tolerance are very far from always acting on it? Indeed, what does it mean to say that they have committed themselves to a value such as tolerance if in practice they only sometimes honour it?

This is, by our reckoning, a question of strategic importance. It is strategic because, depending on its answer, a host of other questions apparently of the first order of importance may not need to be even addressed. Consider the role of education. A small mountain of opinion surveys have accumulated purporting to show that the more and presumably the better an education people have had, the more likely they are to attach importance to freedom of expression and assembly (Sniderman, Tetlock, Hagen, Green & Hout, 1989); to value rationality in the form of science (Selznick & Steinberg, 1969); to appreciate the value of diversity in background and belief (Stouffer, 1979); to reject custom and habit as principles intrinsically of value in making social and political choices (Hyman & Wright, 1979); to repudiate sectarian conceptions of religious salvation (Glock & Stark, 1966); and to welcome innovation and change in modern life (Hyman & Wright, 1979); and, last but not least, to be tolerant toward minorities (for example, Selznick & Steinberg, 1969). But once the connection between the general orientations of citizens toward issues of tolerance and the actual choices they make on specific occasions is called into question, it becomes uncertain what importance should be attached to the role of education in promoting values of tolerance. What difference does it make if those with higher levels of education are more likely, because of this advantage, to support the values of political and social tolerance if, in their actual behaviour, they do not consistently act on these values?

The purpose of this paper, accordingly, is to explore how citizens go about the process of making actual choices related to issues of tolerance on specific occasions. How far, if at all, are their choices rooted in deeper-lying values bearing on tolerance? Why will the same person support claims on behalf of minorities on one occasion but decline to do so on another? Do the terms in which issues of tolerance are posed, particularly in the arena of politics, make a difference? How do arguments brought to bear on citizens on the occasion of a choice matter? Above all, does it really follow that because citizens make different choices about issues of tolerance on different occasions that their choices are not being guided by deeper-lying principles?

To address these questions, we shall first lay out a general approach to understanding public choices, and then derive from this general approach a specific account of the dynamics of choices bearing on tolerance of ethnic minorities.

A general theoretical framework for the analysis of public choice

Two models have dominated the analysis of public choice. The first, most systematically developed is the symbolic politics model (Sears, Huddie & Schaffer, 1986). It contends that citizens' choices about political issues, especially issues of tolerance, are controlled by general orientations. These orientations are acquired, principally through familial and peer socialisation, in childhood. Paradigmatic examples of early-learned orientations are ideological identification, political partisanship, and attitudes toward minorities. These orientations have three cardinal properties. Once acquired, they are enduring; they are general in their scope, applying to an array of specific choices; and they are controlling in their impact, imparting a distinctive stamp to the political choices that citizens make.

Thus the symbolic politics model, applied to issues of tolerance, yields a stream of predictions centred on consistency. Many whites, as children, acquire an aversion to blacks. This aversion, once acquired, persists, and the responses of adult whites to an array of issues dealing with blacks are driven by the aversion they acquired as children. The symbolic politics model thus postulates consistency over three dimensions—over time, across issues of race, and between whites' attitudes toward blacks and other orientations they have acquired. The latter is an implicit requirement of the symbolic politics model, since there would be no stable and consistent platform for responses to political issues in the absence of consistency between relevant orientations.

The second and more recent model, the constructivist model (see Zaller, 1992 or Wilson, 1992), is directly opposed to the first. Rhetorically, it poses the problem of choice in terms of a favoured metaphor. Citizens, asked to make a choice on a public issue, do not retrieve an already prepared answer from a mental 'file drawer.' On the contrary, they construct an on the spot position on the issue; they figure out what they think. And because they are figuring out what they think at the very moment when they are asked what they think, the answer they give depends heavily on considerations salient at that very moment.

The constructivist model thus rests on two premises. First, rather than supposing that people have acquired dispositions to choose consistently one or another side of political issues, it is assumed that most people have a mixed set of considerations, about as many pro as con, which they bring to bear when making most choices. Second, why, on a particular occasion, they make one choice or the other hinges on whether, at the moment of choice, a particular consideration happens to come to mind. In the absence of pre-organised orientations it follows that whether a pro or a con consideration comes to mind hinges, in turn, on the cues to hand at the moment of choice.

The constructivist model of public choice thus favours inconsistency on three dimensions. In public choices on issues of tolerance, citizens tend to be inconsistent over time, taking one side of an issue on one occasion, the opposite on another; inconsistent across issues, favouring one part of a package of policies to help minorities and opposing others, depending on the accidents of what comes to mind at the moment of choice; and inconsistent in their deeper-lying orientations, for the perfectly straightforward reason that most of the people are deeply ambivalent about most matters of importance.

Thus, the symbolic politics model insists on consistency—over time, across choices, and between underlying orientations; the constructivist model, on variability—over time, across choices, and over so-called underlying orientations. By contrast, the conception that we have been developing—a contextual model of choice—is meant to honour both the claims of consistency and variability.

Put in the broadest terms, we suppose that a proper theory of the process of making a choice about a public issue—such as, an issue bearing on ethnic minorities—must take account of three different sets of factors. We shall argue that how actual choices are made depends simultaneously on the characteristics of: (i) choosers; (ii) of the choice set; and (iii) of the context of choice. Later we shall specify the meaning, and illustrate the operation, of all three sets of factors in the course of our analysis. Here we want to emphasise that we are advancing not merely the weak claim that all three matter but the far stronger one that how each of them matters can depend on at least one of the others. Specifically, we mean to show that the impact of the context of choice can hinge on the characteristics of choosers and that the impact of characteristics of choosers can hinge on the characteristics of the choice set.

Education and tolerance of ethnic minorities: model and hypotheses

To extract specific predictions from the contextual model of public choice, two postulates and two distinctions are necessary (for a fuller exposition of the context theory of choice see, Sniderman, in press). The two postulates are:

1) Citizens tend to make public choices partly in the light of general and enduring orientations or values or, as we shall call them, choice priors.
2) Whether choice priors are brought to bear at the moment of choice depends on both the structure of a choice—specifically the number of legitimate alternatives open for selection—and the context of the choice—specifically whether arguments made in favour of a particular alternative are made at the moment of choice.

We thus assume that a proper account of how public choices are made must take account of the characteristics of choosers, the structure of choice, and the context of choice. As for distinctions:

1) It is necessary to distinguish between the acquisition of values and their activation. People may acquire a genuine commitment to a value, for example, political tolerance that over a series of choices predisposes them to be tolerant toward ethnic minorities. But whether for any specific choice they favour tolerance toward ethnic minorities depends on whether the value of political tolerance is activated at the moment of choice.

2) Values can play a dual role as choice priors: dispositional or situational. Viewed dispositionally, values represent a readiness to choose particular goals. To say that people differ in their values, so conceived, is to say that they can be rank-ordered by the degree, intensity, or extent of the importance they attach to a value; and of course, other things equal, this rank ordering is the best predictor of whether they will, on any given occasion, support the value. But other things are not always equal. For example, people's attention may be drawn to another value at the moment of choice. An individual who generally is predisposed to value the right to freedom of speech may, at the moment of choice, have his attention focused on the risk of public violence. The individual, may, in consequence, be more influenced by the situationally-invoked value of public safety even though this would normally not play a role. It is thus necessary to distinguish between dispositional values and situational factors.

Working with these postulates and distinctions, let us consider the role of education in the *activation* (as opposed to the acquisition) of values. A value like political liberty, if brought to bear, can influence responses to ethnic minorities: the more importance people attach to the right of citizens to express publicly political ideas that are unfamiliar, different, or critical, the more likely they are to respond positively to others who are, in appearance or background, unfamiliar, different, or foreign. But whether citizens bring to bear the values that they hold on actual choices that they make is by no means guaranteed. They may genuinely hold a value like political liberty but fail to see its bearing on a specific choice they are asked to make. Accordingly, our hypothesis is that the likelihood that a value like liberty is, at the moment of choice, activated is a systematic function of the amount of education that they have had.

The reasoning behind this introductory version of the activation hypothesis is straightforward. In general, the more education people have had, the more likely they are to be able to appreciate the bearing of the general values they hold on the specific choices that they make. Education increases their understanding of abstract ideas; the information they have to work with; their mastery of the rules of reasoning and inference. And just so far as education, for all these reasons, promotes cognitive consistency, it follows straightforwardly that it increases the likelihood that if people hold a value relevant to a choice bearing on tolerance, they will see its relevance and bring it to bear at the moment of choice.

The activation of values, however, depends not only on the characteristics of choosers but also on the structure of choice. We shall call choices in which only one of the alternatives open for selection is societally legitimated normatively one-sided. We shall call choices in which both of the alternatives open for selection are societally legitimated normatively two-sided (for a discussion of why the alternatives in public choice sets tend to be dualistic see, Sniderman, in press). Choices about tolerance considered in its own right are normatively one-sided. They are one-sided just so far as intolerance itself is not a societal norm. But if only one alternative is societally legitimate, then consistency pressures are one-sided. The more highly educated person who attaches a high degree of importance to political liberty is, by virtue of their level of education, more likely to see its bearing on a normative choice about tolerance of ethnic minorities. But although the level of education and commitment to political liberty are positively correlated, the correlation is far from perfect; which means that even though those who attach a low degree of importance to political liberty tend generally to be less highly educated, a substantial fraction of them are more highly educated. And the question, therefore, is whether they are especially likely to bring their orientation toward political liberty to bear on choices regarding minorities. The issue, notice, is not whether by virtue of attaching a low value to political liberty they are more likely to respond negatively to minorities. Indeed, they are. The question is whether, by virtue of being more highly educated, they are especially likely to do so. And the answer is that, just so far as only one of the alternatives open for selection is socially legitimate, they are not under pressure to maximise the fit between their view of political liberty and choices regarding minorities. And just so far as consistency pressures for normative choices are one-sided, the impact of education on the activation of values for normative choices tends to be *asymmetrical*.

By contrast, in normatively two-sided choices both alternatives are consistent with a competing value. Consider the most common case. Citizens are presented with a choice between two alternatives, one representing the position of the political left, the other of the political right. It is broadly true that those on the left, by virtue of their commitment to its values, tend to be drawn to the first alternative, while those on the right, by virtue of their commitment to its values, to the other. But the likelihood of either bringing their political outlook to bear at the moment of choice is a function of education. The more highly educated they are, whether they are on the political left or right, the more likely they are to appreciate the relevance of their political outlook at the moment of choice. And just so far as people on both sides are more likely, by virtue of being more highly educated, to maximise consistency between their political priors and their actual political choices, the activation of values is *symmetrical* for normatively one-sided choices.

But values can be brought to bear on the making of public choices by a different route. As the most casual observation confirms, they are invoked as a matter of routine by political leaders in an effort to influence public choice; and it is obviously worth considering who is most and least likely to be swayed as a consequence.

Invoking a value in a political argument is like waving a flag and attempting to rally support for the moment. But precisely the reason it is necessary to appeal to a value is because it would not otherwise be uppermost in the minds of enough people. Political argument is thus a means to win the support of those who otherwise would not be disposed to be supporters, and the question we now wish to explore is the role of education in political argumentation.[1]

Consider the dynamics of yielding. If one side of a political argument invokes a particular value in order to win support from those predisposed to favour the other side, who should be most vulnerable? Whether it is conservatives exposed to an appeal to a value favouring a liberal alternative, or liberals exposed to an appeal favouring a conservative one, the better either group understand what their political outlook requires of them, the more likely they should be to resist. Since education promotes understanding of the bearing of a general orientation on a specific choice, it follows that education should promote *the immunisation of* people against a value at odds with their ordinary dispositions at the moment of choice.

To formalise this train of argument, let us use the following notation: V_i, to denote a value invoked on a particular occasion, as contrasted with V_a, to denote a value acquired through socialisation; S_1, to denote that the structure of choice is one-sided (or normative), as contrasted with S_2, to denote that it is two-sided (or political); E, to stand for years (or level) of formal education; and, of course, T, to stand for a positive on an issue of tolerance.

Diagram 7.1 summarises graphically our model of value activation and immunisation. Since our concern is with the role of education in the activation rather than the acquisition of values, the trio of hypotheses take the form of conditional not main effects:

H1) The likelihood of people acting, on a specific occasion, consonantly with a value they have acquired increases with education.

H2) The activation of values conditional on education (H1) is itself conditional on the structure of choice. In the case of normative (or one-sided) choices, value activation tends to be asymmetrical; in the case of political (or two-sided) choices, symmetrical.

H3) The likelihood of people acceding to a counter-argument invoked at the moment of choice decreases with higher levels of education.

The first hypothesis is thus predicated on a first order interaction; the second and third, on second order interactions, as Diagram 7.1 illustrates.

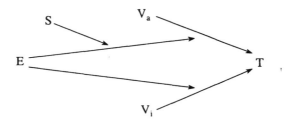

Diagram 7.1   A schematic model of value activation

Methods and data

Variation in response to issues of tolerance, obviously enough, runs across both individuals and across situations. Some individuals are consistently more likely than others to respond positively to issues regarding tolerance of minorities, and the very same individual, whether comparatively likely to respond positively or negatively in general, is more likely to do so in some situations, less likely in others. The two principal methods in social science, survey research and experimental design, are each capable of handling one aspect of this problem but not the other. General population public opinion surveys based on representative samples are the ideal instrument for mapping variation across individuals, but not across situations; randomised experiments, characteristically utilising narrowly constituted samples (such as students) are the ideal instrument for mapping variation across situations, but not across individuals.

It has accordingly been a principal objective of our research programme to introduce a new methodological approach to the study of public opinion capable simultaneously of mapping variance across both individuals and situations. This approach, developed through the support of the National Science Foundation,[2] capitalises on computer-assisted interviewing in general population surveys. In a computer-assisted (CATI) regime, a public opinion questionnaire takes the form of a computer program. Instead of requiring that for every experimental variation, an individual version of the questionnaire be physically produced in advance, the test item is 'composed' at the moment of application. A specific operator is developed for every facet varied (whether of wording, ordering, or formatting). At the moment of application, the operator selects at random from among the values assignable to each facet. Given the absence of physical constraints (in the form of having to print fixed in advance parallel versions of a survey questionnaire), each experiment can have multiple facets, each facet can take on multiple values, and individuals can be randomly assigned across as well as within experimental conditions. Yet, withstanding the complexity of experimental designs attainable, the actual manipulations are effortless for the interviewer and invisible to the interviewee.

This method has been applied and cross-validated in a continuing series of large-scale surveys undertaken in a number of countries. For the purposes of the present analysis we shall take advantage of surveys in the United States, but both the hypotheses we examine and the methods we apply are general.

Findings: symmetrical and asymmetrical effects of education

Normative choices: asymmetrical effects

Our focus initially is normatively one-sided choices, and more specifically still, normative choices regarding toleration of racial minorities. Accordingly, on each occasion of making a choice, the choice set consists of the alternative to respond positively or negatively to blacks. Both alternatives are open for selection, but the play of normative pressure is one-sided, favouring the former and opposing the latter. Our objective is to understand how, faced with an actual choice between a positive and a negative response to blacks, whites choose one rather than the other. Our starting point is a deliberately simplified conception of the choice making process. We shall take normatively one-sided choices to be a function of two characteristics of choosers—values they have acquired, in part through education, and their level of cognitive sophistication, as indexed by the amount of their formal education.

Political tolerance is a paradigmatic example of a value promoted by education and, if acquired, likely in turn to promote racial tolerance. The process of making a normative choice on any specific occasion can thus be expressed in terms of the following model:

$$Y = b_0 + b_1 x_1 + b_2 x_2 + b_3(x_1 * x_2) + e$$

where Y stands for response to a normative choice, such as, an evaluative judgement of a racial minority; b_0 for the intercept; b_1 for political tolerance; b_2 for education; b_3 for activation of political tolerance modelled as the interaction of education and tolerance; and e, for the error or disturbance term.

The model, graphically presented in Diagram 7.2, specifies three distinct ways that education can influence normative choices regarding tolerance, two familiar, the third not. For ease of identification, the former are represented by solid lines, the latter, by a dashed one.

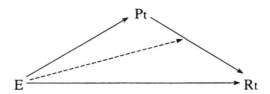

Diagram 7.2   Racial tolerance: education's multiple roles

The two standard causal roles are these. Education can promote racial tolerance directly by promoting its acquisition as a value in its own right. It can also promote racial intolerance indirectly, by promoting acquisition of a foundational value, such as political tolerance, which in turn promotes a commitment to racial tolerance. But in addition to the recognised causal contributions of education, our first hypothesis, if valid, suggests that it plays yet a third role. This third role is activation. If people have acquired a commitment to political tolerance, whether as a consequence of being more highly educated or by virtue of some other factor, they are more likely to appreciate its bearing on toleration of minorities because they have had the advantage of education. And they are, in consequence, more likely when making an actual choice to respond positively to ethnic or racial minorities.

Notice that, just so far as choices are normatively one-sided, a prediction of asymmetrical activation falls out of our formal model. The interaction term in the model treats the response to a normative choice as a multiplicative function of the degree of commitment to a foundational value and the number of years of formal schooling. This multiplicative term, when its arithmetic is worked through, captures the hypothesis that if a person has acquired a commitment to tolerance as a social and political value, he is more likely to see the point of it, the more highly educated he is. But the interaction term also entails that in normatively one-sided choices value activation is asymmetrical. If a person has failed to acquire a commitment to liberty as a primary value notwithstanding the fact that she is more highly educated, then she is not likely to make a yet more intolerant response to a minority group just because she is more highly educated.

To test the hypothesis of asymmetrical activation, we first constructed a measure to assess degrees of commitment to tolerance as a political and social value. This measure expressly focuses on support for 'allowing people to speak out for ideas that most people disagree with,' 'being tolerant of different groups even if their values and behaviour are very different,' and 'tolerating different beliefs and lifestyles.'[3] The question we want to explore, put generally, is under what conditions does support for political tolerance translate into support for racial minorities. As a measure of the latter, we focus on the evaluations of black Americans by white Americans. White's evaluations of blacks are gauged by a battery of evaluative judgements, positive as well as negative,[4] scored for ease of interpretation from zero (for most negative) to one (for most positive).

Our concern, specifically, is the activation of values as a function of the characteristics of choosers. Table 7.1, accordingly, reports responses to blacks as a joint function of degree of commitment to tolerance as a political value and level of education.[5] Consider first the independent effects of education and political tolerance, summarised in mean scores across columns and rows. Consistent with our formal model, both make a significant difference. The more highly educated people are, the more positive their evaluation of blacks ($f=11.587$, $p<.001$). Similarly, the more politically tolerant they are, the more positive their evaluation of black ($f=44.838$, $p<.001$). But the analytically pivotal term in the equation is the multiplicative function of education and political tolerance. The interaction term is statistically significant ($f=2.962$, $p<.02$), and contrasting the entries in the first and third columns, the pattern fits exactly the hypothesis of asymmetrical activation. Education increases the likelihood that politically tolerant whites will respond positively to blacks, without increasing the likelihood that politically intolerant whites will respond negatively to them. The activation effect of education is, as hypothesised for normatively one-sided choices, asymmetrical.

Normatively two-sided choices: symmetrical effects

Expressly political choices are characteristically normatively two-sided because they offer a choice between core values of competing orientations toward politics. And for choices of this kind education's activation effect is symmetrical rather than asymmetrical according to the second hypothesis.

Table 7.1 Normative choice: asymmetrical activation effects on positive evaluative judgements of blacks as a function of the interaction between education and political tolerance

		Political tolerance			
		Low	Mid	High	TOTAL
Education	Low	0.40	0.46	0.53	0.45
	Mid	0.43	0.46	0.65	0.52
	High	0.42	0.56	0.67	0.58
	TOTAL	0.41	0.48	0.61	

Source: 1991 Race and Politics Study: random digit telephone survey conducted by the Survey Research Centre at the University of California, Berkley. Target population = English speaking adults 18 years and over, in 48 contiguous states. 2,223 interviews were completed with a 65.3 per cent response rate. Interviews were conducted using CASES software. (N=1670)

The intuition here has two parts. The first is that democratic politics, as a realm of social interaction, is distinguished by the legitimacy of disagreement. The perspective from which citizens debate the merits of a public issue is itself part of the political debate. Those on the political left, just so far as they grasp the principles of the left, should differ from those on the right, and vice versa. The second is that, in making any particular political choice, the more cognitively sophisticated and aware citizens are, the more likely they are to bring their political principles to bear on publicly contested issues.

For political choices, if this line of reasoning is valid, education's activation effect should be symmetrical. To test this hypothesis the 'Equal Opportunity' experiment was conducted. In this experiment we focus on the acceptance or rejection of a claim for government assistance as a function of race. We define discriminatory behaviour as a greater readiness to reject a claim for government help made on behalf of an ethnic or racial minority than precisely the same claim made on behalf of a group that is not an ethnic or racial minority. Discriminatory behaviour, so defined, requires that a claim for assistance on behalf of the non-minority group cannot, viewed from any impartial standing, have more merit than the same claim made on behalf of a minority group, though the two may acceptably be judged as equal in merit.

Operationally, the 'Equal Opportunity' experiment assesses acceptance of claims for government assistance on behalf of blacks and women. It is worth emphasising that it is often argued that because blacks have had to bear the unique burden of slavery and legalised discrimination, the government is under a unique obligation to assist them. Occasionally, it is argued that the needs of women approach those of blacks, but to our knowledge no one argues that the oppression of women eclipses that of blacks. Hence a proportionately higher frequency of rejection of claims for government assistance on behalf of blacks than of exactly the same claims made on behalf of women is, at face value, proof of discriminatory behaviour.

The claim we focus specifically on is whether it is the government's responsibility to ensure citizens have an equal opportunity to succeed. To be precise, in one experimental condition a randomly selected half of the sample is asked:

> While equal opportunity for blacks and minorities to succeed is important, it's not really the government's job to guarantee it.
> Would you say that you basically agree or basically disagree?

In the other experimental condition the test item is the same in every respect except that instead of referring to 'blacks and minorities' it refers to 'women'. Notice that respondents are being asked only whether it is the government's responsibility to ensure equal opportunity to succeed. Affirmative action itself is not the issue. It is a matter of equal opportunity, not equal outcomes. Nonetheless, this experiment provides clear evidence of a continuing racial double standard: significantly more whites accept the claim to government assurance of equal opportunity when it is made on behalf of women (55.2 per cent) than when exactly the same claim is made on behalf of blacks (41.2 per cent).[6]

The analytic question of interest here, however, is the role of education in the activation of values on issues bearing on minorities. The second hypothesis holds that, since political choices are two-sided, activation effects as a function of education are symmetrical. Accordingly, Figure 7.1 plots the likelihood of acceptance of claims for government assistance as a function of a citizens' overall orientation on politics and their level of education, charting separately responses to women and to minorities.

The results, if it is appropriate for us to say so, are dramatic. On the one hand, those who are not as highly educated, whether conservative or liberal, are markedly more likely to accept a claim made on behalf of women than of blacks. Whereas, those who are more highly educated, whether liberal or conservative, treat claims made on behalf of women and blacks even-handedly. And their even-handedness, paradoxically, results from the activation of opposing values. Liberals, just so far as they have had the advantage of education and thus more insight into how their political principles bear on the choice before them, favour activist government without regard to who will benefit. And conservatives, just so far as they have had the advantage of education and thus more insight into how their political principles bear on the choice before them, oppose government activism also without regard to who benefits.

There is thus, as suggested by the results of the Equal Opportunity experiment, a profound irony to the role of education in making political choices bearing on ethnic and racial minorities. Since it increases the likelihood that people will actually act on their underlying values, education favours even-handedness, impartiality. But since people bring opposing values to political choices, education favours polarisation, not consensus, of positions on public policies proposed to assist minorities.

Political choices: asymmetrical effects

Our analytic model, to this point, follows standard practice. Therefore, we introduce a new paradigm now designed to permit the simultaneous analysis of individual predispositions and situational factors.

At an intuitive level, it is obvious that how people act on any particular occasion is a function simultaneously of the situation they find themselves in and of both the attitudes and aptitudes they bring to it. But how this complex of factors interact is very far from obvious. We wish therefore to take a new step and explore how, in the making of actual choices, the two systematically interact to constrain choice making processes.

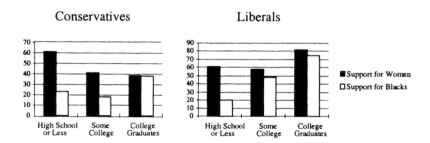

Figure 7.1 Political choice: symmetrical activation effects for judgements for governmental guarantees of equal opportunity for women and for blacks as a function of education and ideology

Source: 1986 Race and Politics Survey: a random digit telephone survey conducted from August to October 1986 by the Survey Research Centre at the University of California, Berkley. Target population = English speaking adults 18 years and over, residing in the five-county San Francisco-Oakland Bay Area. 1,113 interviews were completed with a 68.1 per cent response rate. Interviews were conducted using CASES software. Results presented are for non-Hispanic whites only. (N = 456; minimum base N = 20).

It is, to be sure, only an exploratory step, but incomplete and tentative as it is, it opens up a new window on the dual role of values in the making of political choices. Conventionally, values are conceived as organised and enduring predispositions to respond positively or negatively to general classes of objects. These predispositions differ in degree or intensity from one person to another. Individuals may accordingly be reliably rank-ordered, from most to least, in commitment to particular social and political values.

Values, so viewed, serve as decision priors, providing standing reasons to choose one alternative rather than another on any particular occasion of choice. But as any serious reflection makes plain, values may and frequently do play another and quite different role. As a general proposition, people often bring to occasions of choice systematic dispositions to favour (or oppose) one of the alternatives open for selection. But the choice they actually make can have much to do with the forces that bear on them at the moment of choice.

This is the commonsense view when it comes to politics. Arguments are at the heart of politics, and public arguments characteristically take the form of presenting what are conceived to be persuasive reasons to accept one alternative course of public action or to reject another. It is thus natural to think of politics as a domain of choice centring on strategic efforts by competing actors to invoke shared values to affect the process of choice, though there is a modest paradox to this conception. On the one hand, values invoked in the course of political argument tend be broadly shared, or there would be no point in appealing to them to maximise public support. Whereas, on the other, the reason it is necessary to appeal expressly to them is precisely because these values, though sufficiently potent to tip the process of choice, are not sufficiently salient to come automatically to mind in the absence of prompting. But this modest paradox notwithstanding, what we wish to explore are the dynamics of invoking shared values as a strategic manoeuvre in political argument.

How, exactly, do values invoked in the course of political argument affect the process of choice? Following the standard formulation, the choices that people make on any particular occasion are a function of the situation they find themselves in and of the attitudes and aptitudes they bring to it.

This formulation has the companionable virtue of inclusiveness. It also has the fatal vice of vagueness. In contrast, the model of political choice we are developing specifies the character of the connections among the three primary terms—values acquired through the course of socialisation, values invoked on an occasion of choice, and cognitive sophistication as indexed by education. As Diagram 7.1 made unmistakably clear, we are not simply contending that situational factors, in the form of values invoked on an occasion of choice, have an impact on choices above and beyond that of characteristics of individuals, in the form of values acquired through socialisation and cognitive sophistication. On the contrary, on the model of choice we are proposing, the relations among the primary terms are interactive, not additive.

One implication of a hypothesis of generalised interaction is that the impact of a value invoked at a moment of choice is conditional on the interaction of values acquired throughout the course of socialisation and from the level of cognitive sophistication. In turn, this hypothesis of a second- and not merely a first-order interaction has two distinct implications. First, among those whose values acquired through socialisation are consonant with a specific value invoked at a moment of choice, differences in responsiveness as a function of cognitive sophistication should be attenuated. Just so far as a compelling and clearly comprehensible cue is immediately at hand, the need to think through ideas to see their bearing on an immediate choice should be diminished, and in turn the importance of differences in cognitive sophistication should be diminished. Conversely, and second, among those whose values acquired through socialisation conflict with a specific value invoked at a moment of choice, responsiveness should be very much a function of cognitive sophistication. The better able they are to grasp the meaning and implications of the values they acquired in the course of socialisation, the better able they should be to resist the appeal of a competing value invoked at the moment of choice.

In our research programme we are carrying out a number of experiments, of varying degrees of complexity, on the interplay of values assessed both dispositionally and situationally. Here we shall report on the results of one experiment bearing directly on a central aspect of tolerance—acceptance of the claim that, in selling houses, it should be impermissible for the owner to refuse to sell because of the race of the person who wishes to buy.

The 'Open Housing' experiment is specifically designed to explore the dynamics of issues of tolerance when they come into play. The positions people take on an issue of equality, considered in isolation from competing considerations, might be sincere. But they may take a quite different position in the hurly-burly of real politics, not because they do not mean what they say when they confront the issue taken by itself, but because in the course of a political argument their attention has been directed to competing considerations.

Our objective is thus to mimic, in the course of a public opinion interview, the dynamics of political argument. The 'Open Housing' experiment was accordingly designed with three conditions. In the first experimental condition, the issue of open housing was presented in the standard 'neutral' form.[7]

Version 1: Neutral

> Suppose there were a community-wide vote on a general housing issue and that there were two possible laws to vote on. One law says that homeowners can decide for themselves who to sell their houses to, even if they prefer not to sell to blacks. The other law says that homeowners cannot refuse to sell to someone because of their race or colour.
>
> Which law would you vote for?

In the second experimental condition, the competing consideration of property values was deliberately invoked.

Version 2: Property Rights

> Some people believe that homeowners should be free to decide for themselves who to sell their house to, even if they prefer not to sell it to blacks. For example, some people might say it isn't that they don't want to sell to blacks; it's just that they don't want to be told what to do with their own property. In other words, they feel that because it's their property, they should have the right to sell to anyone they want to.
>
> How do you feel about this? Do you think homeowners should be able to decide for themselves who to sell their houses to, even if they prefer not to sell to blacks, or do you think homeowners should not be allowed to refuse to sell to someone because of their race or colour?

And in the third experimental condition, the question of a government's proper role was invoked.

Version 3: Role of Government

> Some people believe that the government should make an active effort to see that blacks can live anywhere they choose, including white neighbourhoods. Others believe that this is not the government's business and it should stay out of this.
>
> How do you feel? Is this an area the government should stay out of or should the government make an active effort to see that blacks can live anywhere they can afford to—including white neighbourhoods?

Our expectations, briefly, were as follows. The issue of mandated open housing presents a clear choice between liberal and conservative approaches to issues regarding minorities. Accordingly, in the neutral condition, whites should divide over the issue as a function of whether their overall political outlook is liberal or conservative. In contrast, in the other two experimental conditions, the more thoroughly they are anchored to their political outlook by virtue of better understanding it, the greater should be the likelihood of their resisting a competing value that has been invoked at the moment of choice.

As the first panel of Table 7.2 shows, liberals and conservatives divide over the issue of open housing in the neutral condition as a function of their political outlooks. Liberals are markedly more likely, conservatives significantly less likely, to support open housing. This first experimental condition corresponds to the standard treatment of issues in public opinion surveys. The objective of a neutral formulation, of course, is to eliminate as far as possible, pressures on a respondent to favour one or the other alternative. But precisely the point of political argument is to apply pressure, by giving persuasive reasons of one or another variety, to induce citizens to favour one rather than the other alternative. And studies of tolerance, we are manifestly suggesting, should be carried out in such a way as to throw light on how choices are made under the conditions that prevail in the real world.

With this in mind, consider the second panel of Table 7.3. It reports choices made about open housing when the value of property rights is invoked at the moment of choice. Invoking this value manifestly has a dramatic effect. Support for open housing plummets. And it falls pretty much across the board. But, look particularly at the response of more highly educated liberals. Consistent with the predictions of our model, they, distinctively, are immunised when the competing value of property rights is invoked at the moment of choice.

Property rights, manifestly, is a value that, if invoked, favours a limited view of government naturally congenial to conservatives. But, of course, one of the distinguishing features of political argument is that multiple values can be invoked. The 'Open Housing' experiment was thus designed to incorporate a third condition in which a value favouring an activist view of government naturally congenial to liberals would be invoked. Hence, the use of the explicit appeal to government activism on behalf of achieving equal opportunity expressly to remind liberals of the side of the issue that they should, as liberals, support.

Our findings, viewed in this light, are arresting. The results of the third experimental condition, rather than being the obverse of those of the second, are strikingly similar. Conservatives, opposed in principle to government activism on behalf of equality, not surprisingly reject mandatory open housing overwhelmingly in the third condition, just as in the second. What is perhaps surprising is that liberals do not rally in support of open housing, notwithstanding having received a reminder of the position that they, as liberals, should take. To be sure, an activation effect as a function of education is evident in the third condition. The most liberals with higher levels of education are more likely to take the liberal side than the least educated liberals; presumably due to a better understanding of liberalism by virtue of being more highly educated. But it is impossible, scanning the full surface of the third panel, to miss the political lesson to draw. In the third experimental condition, just as in the second, mandatory open housing is defeated.

Table 7.2 Political choices: The immunising effects of support for 'Open Housing' in the face of competing values as a function of education and ideology

Issue Framing	Education Level	Ideology		
		Liberal	Moderate	Conservative
Neutral	Low	0.67	0.45	0.45
	Medium	0.61	0.51	0.39
	High	0.67	0.61	0.57
		Liberal	Moderate	Conservative
Property Value	Low	0.26	0.17	0.15
	Medium	0.48	0.49	0.31
	High	0.62	0.31	0.30
		Liberal	Moderate	Conservative
Government Responsibility	Low	0.48	0.37	0.27
	Medium	0.32	0.26	0.30
	High	0.74	0.31	0.16

Source: 1991 Race and Politics Study: random digit telephone survey conducted by the Survey Research Centre at the University of California, Berkley. Target population = English speaking adults 18 years and over, the 48 contiguous states. 2,223 interviews were completed with a 65.3 per cent response rate. Interviews were conducted using CASES software. (N = 1156)

It is worth taking a moment to consider the implications of this result. The manipulations in the second and third experimental conditions were intended to invoke competing values, that of property rights to favour the conservative side, that of the social function of government to favour the liberal. As it turns out, the political consequence of invoking either is substantially the same—to favour the conservative side. This result, after reflection, led us to think though more carefully the nature of values invoked at the moment of choice on some issues involving tolerance toward minorities.

For each specific issue bearing on tolerance there is an array of ancillary arguments that may be invoked in order to influence the choices citizens make. What we had not appreciated, until working through the results of the Open

Housing Experiment, is the degree of variation across issues in the ecology of ancillary arguments.

The concept of an ecology of arguments is, we think, potentially useful for understanding why the dynamics of specific issues of tolerance can be so distinctive. On issues of tolerance that are normatively two-sided, there are publicly presentable arguments on both sides. But it does not follow that arguments are equally distributed on both sides. On the contrary, open housing seems a perfect example of issues of tolerance for which the distribution of arguments is skewed. More arguments against than for mandatory housing can readily be invoked in the course of public debate.

We invoke the notion of an ecology of issue arguments to call attention to the rhetorical environments of issues. They, quite as much as the preferences of individuals, are an integral part of the politics of tolerance. Indeed, in the case of the issue of open housing, we would suggest that the conservative side has the advantage over the liberal side on the issue of open housing primarily because the ecology of arguments favours their side. There are more, and more accessible, arguments that can be invoked against than for laws mandating open housing.

Open housing is not the only issue where the ecology of argument favours the conservative side. Affirmative action is another. But there are other issues of tolerance, concerned with alleviating distress or enlarging educational or economic opportunity, where arguments are more evenly distributed across both sides, or indeed, may even favour the liberal alternative. And the politics of these issues differs accordingly (for a general argument on the concept of issue pluralism see, Sniderman and Piazza, 1993).

Reprise

Economically summarised, our paper consists of two principal arguments: the first concerns the dynamics of education and tolerance; the second, the deeper consistency underlying the apparent variability of behaviour.

Education, it has been shown, promotes the acquisition of racial and ethnic tolerance as a value. And it does so both directly, by promoting its acquisition as a value in its own right, and indirectly, by promoting the acquisition of other values, such as political tolerance, which in turn promote racial tolerance. All this is familiar, and is, if not universally, at any rate consensually agreed. What we have wished to advance, by way of a contribution, is the hypothesis that education plays an additional, and so far unrecognised, role. Specifically, we have argued that above and beyond the part it plays in the acquisition of tolerance as a value, education can play a decisive role in the activation of tolerance at the moment of choice.

The activation, as opposed to the acquisition, of values is an unexplored corner of a theory of choice. And a strategic one; for it is patently obvious that people do not always act on their values, and it is accordingly essential to establish who is and who is not, and when they are and when they are not, likely to do so.

Broadly, two lines of argument emerge from our analysis. First, education influences the likelihood that citizens will grasp the bearing of their values on the choices that they, as citizens, are asked to make. Second, education influences the responsiveness of citizens to values invoked in the course of political argument.

Beginning with the first, it is necessary to take account of the structure of choice, and in particular, to distinguish between choices that are normatively one-sided and those that are normatively two-sided. Characteristically, choices about how to respond to minorities are normatively one-sided, in the specific sense that only one of the alternatives open for selection is societally legitimated. By contrast, choices about how to respond to public policies dealing with minorities tend to be normatively two-sided, in the specific sense that both of the alternatives open for selection are societally legitimate. And, as we have seen, the structure of choices matter, for if they are normatively one-sided, then the activation of values through education is asymmetrical; if two-sided, symmetrical.

As for the responsiveness of citizens to values invoked in political argument, our results have exposed a second role that education can play in moderating the connections between general values and specific choices. In speaking of values invoked in the course of debate, we have in mind the manoeuvres of political elites to win support for their side by appealing to widely shared assumptions as to what is desirable. And as we saw, just so far as citizens acquire a firmer understanding of what their values entail, they tend to be immunised against the appeal of competing values invoked in the course of political argument.

These specific findings on the dynamics of education and values noted, our results speak to the larger question of the variability of citizens' choices. It is perfectly obvious that the choices people make in politics can not be read straight off from the values they profess. The gap between the two is typically taken as evidence of the erratic and inconsistent character of their reasoning about public issues. To provide the basis for an alternative account, we have developed a model of public choice centred on the *interactions* of three terms: values acquired through socialisation, values invoked at the moment of choice, and cognitive sophistication. We emphasise the premise of interaction. Each matters, in addition to mattering on its own, by virtue of influencing how the other matters. It is our intuition that a sizeable portion of the apparently embarrassing capriciousness and inconsistency of ordinary citizen's judgements about politics, rightly understood, results from these non-linearities.

Appendix

The index of Racial Tolerance was built from the following questions:

Now I'll read a few words that people sometimes use to describe blacks. Of course, no word fits absolutely everybody, but, as I read each one, please tell me using a number from 0 to 10 how well you think it describes blacks as a group. If you think it's a VERY GOOD description of most blacks, give it a 10. If you feel a word is a VERY INACCURATE description of most blacks, give it a 0.
How about 'dependable?' On a scale from 0 to 10, how well do you think it describes most blacks?
How about 'intelligent at school?' (On a scale from 0 to 10, how well do you think it describes most blacks?)
How about 'aggressive or violent?'
How about 'lazy?'
How about 'smart with practical, everyday things?'
How about 'law abiding?'
How about 'boastful?'
How about 'determined to succeed?'
How about 'hardworking?'
How about 'friendly?'
How about 'irresponsible?'
How about 'keep up their property?'
How about 'complaining?'

Responses to these questions were equally weighted, summed and then scaled from 0 to 1, where 0 indicates racial intolerance and 1 indicates racial tolerance.

The index of education was built from the following question:

What is the highest grade or year of school you completed?
  The measure was trichotomised as follows: answers of 'eighth grade or lower,' 'some high school,' or 'high school graduate' were combined to be make the low educational level; answers of 'some college' made the middle educational level; answers of 'college graduate' or 'some graduate work or graduate degree' were combined for the high educational level.

The index of political tolerance was built from the following questions:

Now I'm going to read some statements about things some people consider important in life. Using a number from zero (0) to ten (10), please tell me how important each one is to you. If it's one of the absolutely most important things to you, give it a ten. If it's one of the least important things, give it a zero. (You're free to use any number between zero and ten, but remember, the more important something is to you, the higher the number you should give it.)

Dynamics of Political Values: Education and Issues of Tolerance 159

How about 'Tolerating different beliefs and lifestyles?' (On a scale from zero to ten, how important is that to YOU?)

(How about) Allowing people to speak out for ideas that most people disagree with? (On a scale from zero to ten, how important is that to YOU?)

As I read the following statement, please tell me how much you agree or disagree '(How about) We should be more tolerant of different groups in society, even if their values and behaviour are very different from our (Do you agree strongly, agree somewhat, disagree somewhat, or disagree strongly?)'

Responses to these questions were equally weighted, summed and then scaled from 1-3, with 1 being least tolerant and 3 being most tolerant.

The index of ideological self-identification was built from the following questions:

Generally speaking, would you consider yourself to be a liberal, a conservative, a moderate, or haven't you thought much about this?
Responses of liberal, moderate or conservative were included in this measure.
The 'Open Housing' index was built from a single question, asked in three different forms:

Suppose there were a community-wide vote on a general housing issue and that there were two possible laws to vote on. One law says that homeowners can decide for themselves whom to sell their houses to, even if they prefer NOT to sell to blacks. The other law says that homeowners cannot refuse to sell to someone because of their race or colour. Which law would you vote for?

Some people believe that homeowners should be free to decide for themselves whom to sell their house to, even if they prefer not to sell it to blacks. For example, some people might say it isn't that they don't want to sell to blacks; it's just that they don't want to be told what you do with their own property. In other words, they feel that because it's their property, they should have the right to sell to anyone they want to.

Some people believe that the government should make an active effort to see that blacks can live anywhere they choose, including white neighbourhoods. Others believe that this is not the government's business and it should stay out of this. How do you feel? (Is this an area the government should stay out of or should the government make an active effort to see that blacks can live anywhere they can afford to- including white neighbourhoods?)

Answers were coded on a scale from 0 to 1, with 0 indicating that homeowners should decide for themselves or the government should stay out of it and 1 indicating that the government should make an active effort to insure open housing.

The index of government guarantees of equal opportunity was built from the following question:

The next statements are about life in America today. As I read each one, please tell me whether you basically agree or basically disagree.
While equal opportunity for...
[VERSION 1] ...blacks and minorities...
[VERSION 2] ...women...
...to succeed is important, it's not really the government's job to guarantee it.

Individuals either agreed or disagreed with the statement.

The index of ideological identification in Figure 7.1 was built from the following question:

In general, when it comes to politics, do you usually think of yourself as a liberal, a conservative, a moderate or what?

The responses of self-identified liberals and conservatives were included in this experiment.

The index of education in Figure 7.1 was built from the following question:

What is the highest grade of school or year of college you COMPLETED?

Answers were divided into three categories: high school or less, some college and college graduates.

Notes

1 Arguments designed to invoke competing values, for perfectly obvious reasons, play a major role in public debate of political but not normative choices.

2 We thank the Political Science Program of the National Science Foundation (SES-8508937 and SES-8821575) for invaluable support.

3 See Appendix to this chapter for details on construction of all measures.

4 For a description of the components of the measure of racial tolerance and the method of their combination, see Appendix to this chapter (above).

5 Since the dependent variable summarizes evaluative responses to African Americans, results are presented only for white Americans.

6 For the cynically inclined it is perhaps worth noting that the same differences persist controlling for sex of the respondent: that is to say, the greater margin of support for assisting women is not a function of a greater willingness of women to support claims made on behalf of women.

7 The specific wording is taken from the General Social Survey.

References

Glock, C.Y. and Stark, R. (1966), *Christian Beliefs and Anti-Semitism*, New York, Harper & Row.
Hyman, H.H. and Wright, C.R. (1979), *Education's Lasting Influence on Values*, Chicago, University of Chicago Press.
Sears, D.O., Huddie, L. and Schaffer, L.G. (1986), A Schematic Variant of Symbolic Politics Theory, as Applied to Racial and Gender Equality, in R.R. Lau and D. O. Sears (eds), *Political Cognitiion*, Hillsdale, NJ, Erlbaum.
Selznick, G. and S. Steinberg. (1969), *The Tenacity of Prejudice*, New York, Harper & Row.
Sniderman, P.M. (in press), Taking Sides: A Fixed Choice Theory of Political Reasoning, in A. Lupia, M. McCubbins and S. Popkin (eds), *Elements of Political Reasoning: Understanding and Expanding the Limits of Rationality*, New York, Cambridge University Press.
Sniderman, P.M. and Piazza, T. (1993), *The Scar of Race*, Cambridge, Mass.: Harvard University Press.

Sniderman, P.M., P.E. Tetlock, J.M. Glaser, D.P. Green and Hout, M. (1989), Principled Tolerance and American Political Values, *British Journal of Political Science*, vol. 19, pp. 25–46.

Stouffer, S. (1955), *Communism, Conformity and Civil Liberties*. New York: Doubleday.

Wilson, T.D. and S.D. Hodges. (1992), Attitudes as Temporary Constructions, in L.L. Martin and A. Tesser (eds), *The Construction of Social Judgments*, Hillside, New Jersey, Erlbaum, pp. 37–65.

Zaller, J. (1992), *The Nature and Origins of Mass Opinion*, New York, Cambridge University Press.

8 Education, Attitudes towards Ethnic Minorities and Opposition to Affirmative Action

GENEVIÈVE VERBERK & PEER SCHEEPERS

Introduction

Until recently the United States dominated the study of trends in ethnic attitudes. Researchers claimed that the US ethnic-majority's attitude towards ethnic minorities had changed over the past decades (see Campbell, 1971; Schuman, Steeh & Bobo, 1985). Empirical research had shown a continuous decrease in blatant negative attitudes, indicated by a decline in the percentage of majority people who rejected the general principles of ethnic equality. In the 1940s, Schuman et al. (1985) found that most majority people supported enforced ethnic segregation and discrimination. In the 1980s most of the majority population thought that ethnic minorities deserve the same rights, treatment, and respect as the majority. However, such equality is yet to be realised and opposition to policies aimed at establishing it has remained consistent (Schuman et al., 1985). Thus, many US majority people subscribe to the general principles of ethnic equality but not to their implementation.

Several scholars have argued that this apparent contradiction could be explained by the existence of new, more subtle forms of negative attitudes, 'symbolic racism' (McConahay & Hough, 1976; Kinder & Sears, 1981; McConahay, Hardee & Batts, 1981), 'aversive racism' (Gaertner & Dovidio, 1986; Dovidio, 1993) and 'laissez-faire racism' (Bobo & Smith, 1994). Putting aside any differences in scope between these categories, what these categories of racism have in common is that negative attitudes towards ethnic minorities are disguised, subtle, and ostensibly non-ethnic. Furthermore, these negative attitudes do not represent an adherence to notions of biological inferiority but, rather, a belief in the cultural inferiority of ethnic minorities. However extensive the body of literature on these forms of racism may be, as yet no agreement has been reached on the definition of these concepts, their use in measuring forms of racism and finally the interpretation of the results gathered (Pettigrew, 1985; Sniderman & Tetlock, 1986a; Pincus, 1994).

In the Netherlands, most research on negative attitudes towards ethnic minorities has concentrated on the more blatant forms, which, contrary to in the United States, have not declined but have remained stable (Scheepers, Eisinga & Linssen, 1994). These blatant negative attitudes have been found especially among the elderly, regular church goers, less highly educated people, manual labourers and the self-employed (Scheepers, Felling & Peters, 1989, 1990; Scheepers et al., 1994). However, during the 1990s, opposition to affirmative action policies has been more widespread, particularly among the less highly educated, than blatant negative attitudes. This suggests that the Dutch population's opposition to affirmative action policies cannot be explained in terms of blatant negative attitudes towards ethnic minorities (Scheepers, Schmeets & Felling, 1997). Hence our central question is:

> to what extent can we explain this opposition (a) in terms of structural variables, such as the level of education, or (b) in terms of blatant negative attitudes towards ethnic minorities, or (c) in terms of other phenomena related to these negative attitudes towards ethnic minorities?

Certainly, the existence of more covert subtle negative attitudes towards other ethnic groups would provide another explanation for this opposition. Tajfel and Turner's social identity theory is of use here (1970, 1982a, 1982b; Tajfel & Turner, 1979). It rests on the basic assumption that people have a fundamental need to belong to a social group, and that they wish to achieve or maintain a positive self-identity. People first categorise those whom they consider belong to their own group, as well as those they consider to belong to other groups. Then, they compare their own group (the ingroup) with the other groups (the outgroups) in such a way that the ingroup is perceived to be superior to the outgroups. Because ethnicity is often the most obvious characteristic, these comparisons often occur along ethnic lines (Dovidio, 1993). The implicit assumption has been that most, if not all, people value their (ethnic) ingroup's characteristics positively and the outgroups' negatively. It is from here that we draw our hypothesis that a broader range of social groups *than those already mentioned* as holding blatant negative attitudes, hold negative attitudes but that these are possibly more subtle and covert.

The more subtle and covert forms of negative attitudes held by the Dutch ethnic majority towards ethnic minorities in the Netherlands have recently received increased academic attention (Essed, 1984, 1991; Kleinpenning,

1993; Pettigrew & Meertens, 1995; Verkuyten & Masson, 1995). These researchers found that, similar to in the United States, subtle negative attitudes have emerged in Dutch society, characterised by a belief in the cultural inferiority of ethnic minorities and ostensibly non-racist justifications. However, no agreed definition of concepts or a strategy for measuring these attitudes has yet been found, in the Netherlands or the US.

With this study, we aim to establish conceptual clarity by means of a systematic theoretical and empirical investigation of negative attitudes of the Dutch ethnic majority towards ethnic minorities. We do so by formulating and testing a theory of the relationship between blatant and subtle negative attitudes towards ethnic minorities on the one hand, and independent, intervening, and consequence variables on the other (see Davis, 1985). Thus, locating blatant and subtle negative attitudes within the social sphere, and allowing us to consider the consequences of these attitudes as well.

Theoretical issues

In recent decades, a body of literature has emerged in the social sciences centred, especially in the United States, on debates on negative attitudes towards ethnic minorities. The most influential studies are those concerning the concepts 'symbolic racism' (McConahay & Hough, 1976; Kinder & Sears, 1981; McConahay et al., 1981) 'aversive racism' (Gaertner & Dovidio, 1986; Dovidio, 1993) and 'laissez-faire' racism (Bobo & Smith, 1994).

Symbolic racism research is based on the assumption that old-fashioned racism may have declined, but that it has been replaced by a new form consisting of a combination of traditional American values and negative sentiments towards ethnic minorities (McConahay & Hough, 1976; Kinder & Sears, 1981; Kinder, 1986). These two forms of racism are supposedly expressions of different negative attitudes towards ethnic minorities. Old-fashioned racism refers to overt racism comprising a belief in the inferiority of ethnic minorities and support for ethnic segregation. Symbolic racism has been defined as the 'expression in terms of abstract ideological symbols and symbolic behaviours of the feeling that blacks are violating cherished values and making illegitimate demands on the racial status quo' (McConahay & Hough 1976, p. 38).

Aversive racism refers to beliefs of superiority without the overt and bigoted elements (Kovel, 1970). According to Gaertner and Dovidio (1986), aversive racial attitudes are held by many members of the ethnic majority group who possess strong egalitarian values. Aversive racism represents a conflict between feelings and beliefs associated with a sincerely egalitarian value system on the one hand and unacknowledged negative feelings and beliefs about blacks on the other hand (Gaertner & Dovidio, 1986). Because aversive racists are very concerned to appear unprejudiced, Gaertner (1978) concluded that the attitudes expressed in responses to most of the then currently available surveys would be considerably affected by social desirability. Later, Gaertner and Dovidio (1986) stated that it would not only be difficult, but possibly impossible to develop a valid and reliable questionnaire with which to assess aversive racism.

Bobo and Smith (1994) have argued that, in the US, Jim Crow racism—old-fashioned blatant racism—has been replaced by laissez-faire racism which asserts that the disadvantage experienced by ethnic minorities is rooted in their culture. Thus absolving the ethnic majority population of the responsibility for any disadvantage or poor living conditions experienced by many ethnic minority communities. Laissez-faire racists will actively oppose measures aimed at improving the status of ethnic minorities or supporting for principles of ethnic equality and integration. When ethnic discrimination occurs they tend to do nothing. The difference between Jim Crow racism and laissez-faire racism is that the first is based upon notions of the biological inferiority and the latter on notions of cultural inferiority (Bobo & Smith, 1994). Ethnic and cultural minority groups are still considered a threat; hence, the expression of the racism has mutated, from the now less acceptable blatant racism expressed in biological terms to the subtler laissez-faire form.

Recent research in this area has shown that these subtle negative attitudes also prevail in European societies (Barker 1981; Essed 1991; Kleinpenning 1993; Pettigrew & Meertens 1995). Barker (1981) has proposed that the expanding number of immigrants in the United Kingdom has caused the majority population to feel threatened, and that their culture requires protection against foreign influences. This new racism has replaced the traditional biological racism. Barker pointed out that the 'new' racist's defence of their way of life against that of other cultures is a central character feature because such individuals consider that cultural differences are incompatible. Similar to the theory of symbolic racism, the perceived threat posed by ethnic minorities is not based on a concrete personal threat but rather on a threat to the way of life, to the customs, values and norms of the ethnic majority. Verkuyten and Masson (1995) have studied this new racism among Dutch ethnic majority youth in the Netherlands. They concluded that new racism correlated positively with personal self-esteem, collective self-esteem, positive ingroup evaluation, social distance and frequency of voluntary interethnic contacts.

Essed (1984, 1991) introduced the concept of everyday racism, expressed not only in overt acts of racial intolerance and exclusion, but also in the small routine practices of day-to-day interaction in which racist motives and implications are covert. These routine practices, which are often unnoticed, activate and reinforce racism in contemporary society. Essed identified three features of everyday racism, marginalisation, problematisation, and containment of ethnic minorities. Marginalisation occurs when majority people unproblematically view themselves as the normative group, and consider that the ethnic minority member(s) have nothing to contribute and that they should adjust to ensure smooth ethnic relations. Problematisation means that ethnic minorities are considered the ones who have problems or cause them for the ethnic majority. Containment of ethnic minorities aims to avert or combat opposition to racism, by denying the existence and daily reality of racism and discrimination by most members of the majority group (Essed, 1991).

Kleinpenning (1993) distinguished four types of racism: biological racism, symbolic racism, ethnocentrism and aversive racism. In his view, biological racism refers to beliefs in the innate inequality between the majority and ethnic minorities; symbolic racism refers to feelings that ethnic minorities pose a social, economic and cultural threat; ethnocentrism is the combination of perceptions of superiority among the majority ingroup and the perception that ethnic minorities are inferior; and aversive racism refers to uneasy and uncertain feelings towards ethnic minorities. Using survey data from secondary school students belonging to the ethnic majority, Kleinpenning concluded that the different forms are separate steps in a single cumulative dimension of ethnic attitudes which proceeds from aversive racism via ethnocentrism and symbolic racism to biological racism. Aversive racism is the least extreme form and biological racism the most. Biological racists will also express the other less extreme forms (Kleinpenning, 1993).

Pettigrew and Meertens (1995) labelled the distinction between old and new forms as a distinction between blatant and subtle prejudice. Blatant prejudice consists of two components, the experience of threat from and the rejection of ethnic outgroups, and opposition to intimate contact with ethnic minorities. Subtle prejudice is composed of three components, all of which contain the socially acceptable rejection of minorities for apparently non-discriminatory reasons: the defence of traditional values, the exaggeration of cultural differences, and the denial of positive emotions towards ethnic minorities. Ethnocentrism proved to be the most important determinant of blatant as well as of subtle prejudice. Pettigrew and Meertens concluded that contrary to other European countries subtle prejudice is more widespread than blatant prejudice in the Netherlands.

Although the studies discussed above agree that a change has occurred, there is no consensus as to the content of these changes. What emerges from this overview is the need for theoretical and methodological clarity. Two striking examples illustrate the need for a consensus on the definition of the concepts used to measure contemporary ethnic attitudes. In the first differing definitions have led to remarkable differences of application. Kleinpenning (1993) has argued that aversive racism is the least extreme form of racism. He did so using items based on Bogardus' social distance scale (1925, 1963) to measure what is a component of subtle prejudice. Contrary to this, Pettigrew and Meertens (1995) used a social distance scale, but they measured opposition to intimate contact with outgroup members, a component of *blatant* prejudice. Thus quite similar items have been used to measure blatant prejudice and but also subtle prejudice. This difference in application is all the more noteworthy because, strictly speaking, social distance scales are not measures of attitudes towards ethnic minorities but of behavioural intentions (see for example Fishbein and Ajzen, 1975). We will return to this later. The second example highlights that concepts are not always interpreted consistently from study to study. Ethnocentrism, for example, has been interpreted differently by Kleinpenning (1993) and Pettigrew and Meertens (1995). Kleinpenning has argued that ethnocentrism is an intermediate step on the cumulative racism dimension and has placed it between aversive and symbolic racism. In contrast, Pettigrew and Meertens, have concluded that ethnocentrism is the main predictor of blatant prejudice as well as of subtle prejudice.

Even so, we do not consider the many definitions to be mutually exclusive. Indeed, to a certain extent, they are complementary. For example, Dovidio and Gaertner (1991) have argued that the various forms relate to different categories of people. Symbolic racism refers especially to attitudes expressed by conservatives while aversive racism captures the attitudes of liberals (Dovidio & Gaertner, 1991). Kleinpenning's (1993) empirical conclusions, for example, were developed exclusively from the attitudes of highly educated secondary school students. Furthermore, it is clear that the many of the approaches have a lot in common. For instance, old-fashioned racism, biological racism, and Jim Crow racism all refer to the overt form of racism in which a belief in the biological superiority of the ethnic majority goes hand in hand with a support for ethnic segregation. The concepts symbolic racism, new racism, and ethnocentrism all contain a belief in the cultural superiority of the ethnic majority. Furthermore, opposition to intimate contact with ethnic minorities is an aspect often present in these concepts.

We aim to develop a substantive grounded theory on ethnic majority attitudes towards ethnic minorities and the relationships between these groups. These attitudes will be explained using a theoretical framework which evolved during our investigations (for a similar approach see Strauss & Corbin, 1990). We do not limit ourselves to hypotheses based only on the research discussed above. Rather, we use it to alert us to what factors might be relevant, what we may expect to find and, importantly, what needs further exploration.

With this study, we wish to improve upon earlier attempts to theorise and measure ethnic majority group attitudes towards ethnic minorities in three ways. The studies of Kleinpenning (1993), Pettigrew and Meertens (1995), and Verkuyten and Masson (1995) were largely based on American concepts. However, due to cultural differences, theories and methodological approaches developed elsewhere cannot be applied without adaptation. The definition of negative attitudes and the construction of measurements should not be based on a literature review of current state of the field in other countries alone, but also on extensive local research. We avoid this pitfall by using the American studies but we adapt them in line with our local research, thus allowing us to arrive at a theoretically and empirically sound *locally* appropriate and applicable redefinition of these concepts. A second pitfall of earlier studies was a focus on either the majority or the minority group. Essed (1991) interviewed only black women. Kleinpenning (1993), Pettigrew and Meertens (1995), and Verkuyten and Masson (1995)[1] based their conclusions on respondents from the ethnic majority group alone. Our definition of the attitudes of the Dutch majority population towards ethnic minorities is based on both perspectives. After all, with regard to inter-ethnic relations both groups are involved. Each of the two groups provides a different perspective on the reality of the majority population's attitude towards ethnic minorities. In this study, we combine these two perspectives, allowing us to reach a more comprehensive view on our research problem. Third, instead of using only one methodological approach we combine theoretical perspectives, various data sources, and qualitative and quantitative methodologies. This tripartite approach enables us to avoid the possible problem of bias which arises if only one method is used (Denzin, 1978). Further, because this method allows us to collect more varied information we can draw conclusions on the nature of ethnic attitudes as well as on the extent to which these attitudes occur.

Re-defining the composite aspects of blatant and subtle negative attitudes

Here we describe our methodological approach. Central to this was the definition of the aspects that form our re-conceptualisation blatant and subtle racism. Each aspect is then dealt with in turn, after which we explain how they differ from other available aspects or terms. In the following section, we use this re-conceptualisation to hypothesise on the social location of blatant negative attitudes, and on the relation between blatant and subtle negative attitudes on the one hand and intervening and consequence variables on the other.

Approach

The methodology used in our study draws on elements of grounded theory (Glaser & Strauss, 1967; Strauss & Corbin, 1990) as elaborated by Wester (1984, 1991). The aim is a systematic definition based on a through examination of aspects of social reality. An important principle in this research approach is the reciprocal relationship of data collection, analysis, and reflection. These processes are strongly interrelated and alternate with each other (Strauss & Corbin, 1990). This reciprocal cycle of data collection, analysis and reflection means that the selection of respondents and data for analysis in any one phase is determined by theoretical considerations derived from the preceding phases. These theoretical considerations determine what is needed to construct and test the developing analysis. Based on this knowledge, it is possible to select new data with which to refine, confirm, or refute findings of previous phases.

Wester's (1991) step-by-step approach to conducting qualitative research based on grounded theory assists our research in a systematic and structured way. After reviewing the literature (see the section 'Theoretical issues'), in-depth interviews were held with members of ethnic minority groups. To gain a broad range of ethnic minority members' experiences, we selected our interviewees on the basis of theoretical considerations (Strauss & Corbin, 1990). Members of ethnic minority groups were selected who were able to describe blatant as well as subtle forms of negative attitudes expressed by the majority population. Another important factor affecting selection was their ability to describe these attitudes from both their own perspective and that of members of other ethnic minority groups. Twelve informants were invited to participate in the research project, 11 of whom accepted. We used semi-structured, in-depth interviews. The interviews were conducted in the last months of 1993 and each one lasted from 1 to 1.5 hours. All interviews were recorded. The data was analysed using version 3.1 of the program KWALITAN (Peters & Wester, 1990). KWALITAN was developed to assist with the systematic and structural qualitative analyses required by grounded theory methodology. We used its capabilities to develop sensitising concepts, with which we structured the subsequent interviews and analyses of our study.

Interviews were then held with respondents from the ethnic majority group, whose selection was also based on theoretical considerations. Respondents were selected at different times during our research. At every sampling point choices had to be made about who to sample in accordance with the required data. The emerging theoretical concepts formed the guiding principle for the sampling. In total, we approached 25 respondents from the ethnic majority group, 22 of whom accepted. Again, we used semi-structured, in-depth interviews. Interview schedules for these interviews were constructed based on the findings of the literature review and the interviews with the members of the ethnic minority groups. We interviewed this group in the first half of 1994. Interviews were of one to two hours duration each, and all were recorded. The transcripts were coded and analysed according to the themes emerging from the data.

This data pool was also analysed with the help of KWALITAN (Peters & Wester, 1990). Each interview-transcript was divided into relevant text segments, before carrying out the open coding of the text segments into categories required to formulate field-related concepts. These actions were guided by the research questions and sensitising concepts formulated previously. By comparing the concepts applicable to each category and by integrating categories and their properties, the data were reduced to the central concepts (Glaser & Strauss, 1967; Strauss & Corbin, 1990).

Blatant negative attitudes

Analyses of the interviews from both groups showed that blatant negative attitudes towards ethnic minorities are revealed by three often simultaneously occurring aspects. One of which is a *belief in the biological or cultural superiority of ones' own group*. Another can be called *problematisation*. Individuals who express blatant negative attitudes regard the presence of ethnic minorities in Dutch society as very problematic. Matters relating to ethnic minorities are mentioned together with criminal behaviour, educational problems, deterioration of norms and values, the housing shortage, and government economic policies. A third aspect concerns *the generalisation of perceived negative characteristics of ethnic minorities* on the one hand and *the individualisation of perceived positive characteristics of ethnic minorities* on the other. We found that negative evaluations, of ethnic minorities were applied to the whole outgroup without constraint. These general conceptions of ethnic minorities were usually abstracted from negatively evaluated elements that had been perceived in the actions of some ethnic minorities. They were often based on little or no direct experience. Instead, much weight was given to media representations or the stories of significant others. Positively evaluated characteristics were considered the exception rather than the rule.

These findings suggest that blatant negative attitudes are expressed explicitly and overtly, a finding supported by the studies discussed earlier. From our empirical interview data we conclude that in the Netherlands blatant negative attitudes towards ethnic minorities are revealed by three strongly associated aspects, *superiority, problematisation,* and *generalisation of negative characteristics and individualisation of positive characteristics.*

As already discussed, earlier research found *biological* superiority to be an aspect of old-fashioned racism, biological racism, and Jim Crow racism. Whereas, *cultural* superiority was considered to be characteristic of symbolic racism, laissez-faire racism, new racism, and ethnocentrism. We, on the other hand, combine these two forms of superiority into one. We do so because of the overt way in which these aspects came together to the fore in the interviews with both groups, confirming the significance of the dual action of these aspects

Essed (1984, 1991) identified *problematisation* as a characteristic of everyday racism. The results of the interviews with both groups indicated a strong relation between superiority and problematisation. Ingroup members who expressed feelings of superiority towards ethnic outgroups often openly described the behaviour and presence of ethnic minorities as problematic. Therefore, we consider problematisation to be an aspect of blatant negative attitudes towards ethnic minorities.

Generalisation of negative characteristics and individualisation of positive characteristics was mentioned in previous research (Essed, 1984). However its was not found to be characteristic of a specific form of negative attitudes. The high frequency as well as the overt way in which this aspect came to the fore in our interview data caused us to consider this aspect to be characteristic of blatant negative attitudes towards ethnic minorities.

Subtle negative attitudes

Subtle negative attitudes towards ethnic minorities are expressed implicitly and covertly. They are expressed in seven strongly associated aspects. A subtle negative attitude can be expressed through *paternalism*. Paternalism is when a member of the majority group is willing to provide members of ethnic minorities with whatever they think is needed but refuse to grant them responsibility or freedom of choice. These apparently positive intentions are implicitly aimed at maintaining the dominance of the majority culture. Three things are important here. Paternalistic individuals express their views in terms such as 'have to' and 'ought to', removing any element of choice for the individual or ethnic minority in question. They also blame ethnic minorities for the existence of racism and discrimination, and they implicitly perceive their culture as superior to those of the ethnic minorities.

Subtle racism is also expressed through the *exaggeration of cultural differences*. Members of the ethnic majority who hold subtle negative attitudes emphasise differences between their group and ethnic minorities, in such a way that members of ethnic groups feel marginalised and excluded. The differences perceived include codes of dress, language, rituals, norms of behaviour and systems of belief. In exaggerating these differences, the existence of a fundamental agreement on basic values, norms, and behaviour, is emphasised by the individual who assumes that all members of their group share common cultural features. The exaggeration of cultural differences takes on a different guise, *exoticism*. People with a subtle negative attitude often express their attraction to another culture by stressing the culture's colourful and unusual aspects. Nevertheless, the exaggerated way in which they express themselves makes them hard to believe.

We also found that majority people will be on their guard when interacting with ethnic minorities. We called this aspect *negative cautiousness*. Here, ethnic minority members perceive majority individuals to be overly conscious of and ill at ease in their presence. Such people find it hard to empathise with the customs and values of ethnic minorities, and find acceptance of these customs even harder.

Another aspect is *overvaluation of the unimportant*. People expressing subtle negative attitudes often stress that the presence of ethnic minorities enriches Dutch society. However, this is limited to unimportant matters such as: 'nowadays we have a wide choice of restaurants', or 'we can buy a lot of strange things in shops owned by foreigners, that we could not buy before', and 'our music is much more varied now'. It is not extended to more fundamental matters such as the raising of children or the lifestyles and norms and values of ethnic minorities. Such statements implicitly refer to the inequality between the two groups by reinforcing the fundamental norms and values of the majority group as the normative ones.

After analysis, the results of the interviews showed that most majority respondents did not have positive feelings towards ethnic minorities. These respondents did not express any favourable opinion on ethnic minorities. As with the blatant negative attitudes, while some of these respondents expressed negative attitudes, another group held no real positive or negative attitudes towards ethnic minorities. This group would not say 'I would like' or 'I would hate to have neighbours from an ethnic minority group'. Instead, they would say 'I would not have any problem with that' or 'I would not feel uncomfortable'. It seems that slightly negative or positive feelings were neutralised upon reflection. We call this aspect of subtle negative attitudes *neutralised feelings*.

Majority people with a subtle negative attitude also express what we have called *negative tolerance* towards ethnic minorities. This ostensible tolerance is expressed as indifference but only for as long as the majority person in question is not bothered by actions of the ethnic minority (member). Furthermore, this group attached great importance to the traditional values of the majority ingroup. These respondents were happy to give ethnic minorities freedom to maintain their own way of life as long as they did not undermine 'traditional values'. Furthermore, they displayed no form of positive tolerance to ethnic minorities. We consider tolerance to be positive when it is based on respect expressed in a readiness to impose restraints on oneself.

It should be noted that not all of these aspects are new to the field, and that some overlap with others already defined elsewhere. Paternalism, for example, is similar to Essed's (1991) pacification, an aspect of his definition of everyday racism. We found all the key aspects of Essed's pacification—patronising and moralising attitude and an expectation of thankfulness. However, in our study, the expectation of thankfulness was related more to problematisation than to paternalism. Some majority people expressed the opinion that members of ethnic minorities should be grateful instead of causing problems. Hence, the expectation of thankfulness does not form part of our definition of paternalism. Furthermore, for us, the apparently positive intentions of majority people implicitly aimed at the dominance of their own culture is specific to paternalism, whereas Essed viewed this as a general feature of everyday racism.

Our aspect, *negative tolerance* differs slightly from Barker's new racism (1981), Kleinpenning's symbolic racism (1993^2), Pettigrew and Meertens' subtle prejudice (1995), and Essed's repressive tolerance (1991). Integral to all of these was the willingness to grant ethnic minorities the freedom to maintain their own way of life as long as this did not undermine the ethnic majority's norms and values. What our aspect negative tolerance encapsulates that the above do not, is a lack of positive tolerance towards ethnic minority groups. By positive tolerance we mean a readiness to impose the same restrictions on oneself.

Based on the interviews with the majority group we consider *overvaluation of the unimportant* to be an aspect of subtle negative attitudes towards ethnic minorities. We did not come across this aspect in previous research. However, it could be related to new racism (Barker, 1981), symbolic racism (Kleinpenning, 1993), subtle prejudice (Pettigrew & Meertens, 1995), and everyday racism (Essed, 1991), because the defence of traditional values is also a central component of these forms of racism. Furthermore, Essed showed that an ability to dance and cook well was often mentioned as characteristic of black women. These stereotypes came also to the fore in our interviews. We classified them as the overvaluation of the unimportant.

Our aspect *the existence of neutralised feelings* is similar to that of the denial of positive emotions, found by Pettigrew and Meertens (1995) to be an aspect of subtle prejudice. Pettigrew and Meertens proposed that subtle prejudice often entails a disinclination to express positive feelings towards ethnic minorities. However, what came to the fore in the interviews with the ethnic majority group were *neutralised* feelings. Therefore, we propose that the disinclination to express either positive or negative feelings towards ethnic minorities is important. Thus, again the need for a new aspect: the existence of neutralised feelings.

The interviews with both the minority and the majority ethnic groups showed that members of the ethnic majority are ill at ease and wary when interacting with members of ethnic minorities. In addition, they have difficulty empathising with ethnic minority customs and values. We labelled this aspect *negative cautiousness*. Components of this aspect were also found in previous research (Gaertner & Dovidio, 1977; Gaertner, 1978; Barker, 1981; Essed, 1991; Dovidio, 1993; Verkuyten & Masson, 1995).

The aspect *exoticism* was brought to our attention by the respondents of the ethnic minority group. We believe this to be a totally 'new' aspect, which was strongly prevalent when we interviewed members from the ethnic majority group. We consider this aspect to be an aspect of subtle negative attitudes.

Table 8.1   Aspects of blatant and subtle negative attitudes of the ethnic majority towards ethnic minorities

Blatant Negative Attitudes		
	*	superiority
	*	problematisation
	*	generalisation of negative characteristics and individualisation of positive characteristics
Subtle Negative Attitudes		
	*	paternalism
	*	exaggeration of cultural differences
	*	exoticism
	*	overcautiousness
	*	overvaluation of the unimportant
	*	neutralised feelings
	*	negative tolerance

Pettigrew and Meertens (1995) proposed that subtle prejudice is revealed by three components, of which one entails *the exaggeration of cultural differences*. Essed (1991) also came across this aspect in interviews with black women. Because the exaggeration of cultural differences came to the fore in our interviews with the minority and the majority group we consider this to be an aspect of subtle negative attitudes towards ethnic minorities. The aspects just discussed occur more often than not together. They are summarised in Table 8.1.

The findings described in this section suggest that blatant negative attitudes are expressed in the aspects superiority, problematisation, simultaneous generalisation of negative characteristics and individualisation of positive characteristics. Subtle negative attitudes towards ethnic minorities are expressed in the aspects paternalism, exaggeration of cultural differences, exoticism, negative cautiousness, overvaluation of the unimportant, the existence of neutralised feelings, and negative tolerance.

The theoretical model and hypotheses

Together the central concepts form a theoretical framework. We developed an empirically grounded theory on the nature of blatant and subtle negative attitudes, on differences in the social location of blatant and subtle negative attitudes, as well as on the explanation and consequences of blatant and subtle negative attitudes.

The nature of blatant and subtle negative attitudes

Over recent decades, we have seen not only the emergence of a growing body of literature concerning subtle negative attitudes towards ethnic minorities, but also concerning the relation between blatant and subtle negative attitudes. Theorists of symbolic racism have concluded that although traditional racism and symbolic racism are correlated, the two forms are distinguishable (for example see, McConahay & Hough, 1976; Sears & Kinder, 1985; McConahay, 1982; McClendon, 1985). Kleinpenning (1993), and Pettigrew and Meertens (1995) concluded that blatant and subtle forms of negative attitudes towards ethnic minorities can be considered theoretically as well as empirically distinct from each other. Kleinpenning also concluded that the distinguishable forms (biological racism, symbolic racism, ethnocentrism and aversive racism) are embedded in a cumulative scale. This cumulative dimension proceeds from biological racism, via symbolic racism and ethnocentrism to aversive racism. Kleinpenning concluded that those members of the ethnic majority group who subscribe to blatant forms of racism would also subscribe to the more subtle forms.

The qualitative results of our study to date lend some support to the conclusions of the theorists of symbolic racism (for example see McConahay & Hough, 1976; Sears & Kinder, 1985), as well as Kleinpenning (1993), and

Pettigrew and Meertens (1995) in that blatant and subtle negative attitudes towards ethnic minorities are strongly related but nevertheless theoretically and empirically distinguishable. However, the results also gave ample reason to cast doubt on these results. We found that ethnic majority group members who express aspects of blatant negative attitudes express only some aspects of subtle negative attitudes, not all. Hence, subtle negative attitudes are not embedded as a whole in blatant negative attitudes rather certain ones match certain forms of a blatant negative attitude. Ethnic majority members with a predominantly blatant negative attitude, predictably, did not express any of the following aspects *exoticism, overvaluation of the unimportant, negative tolerance,* and *the existence of neutralised feelings.*

These findings led us to formulate our first explicit and challenging null hypothesis:

H1) The associations between aspects of blatant and subtle negative attitudes will be so high that both dimensions can not be empirically distinguished.

This is clearly in accordance Sniderman and Tetlock's statement '…the correlations (between old-fashioned and symbolic racism) are all quite high, that, in consequence, it may be difficult to distinguish between them empirically' (1986, p. 136). However, it clearly contradicts the hypotheses put forward by McConahay et al. (1981), Kinder and Sears (1981) and lately by Pettigrew and Meertens (1995) who claim that both dimensions are empirically distinct.

Next, we explicate our hypotheses on the relationship between these aspects of ethnic attitudes and a favourable attitude towards the ingroup. In the introductory section we explained that, in order to achieve and preserve a positive self-identity, individuals compare their ethnic ingroup with ethnic outgroups (see Tajfel 1970, 1982a, 1982b). They do this in such a way that they tend to perceive positive characteristics as typical of members of the ethnic ingroup, whereas negative characteristics tend to be attributed to members of ethnic outgroups. These two processes have been called respectively social identification and social contra-identification. The outcome of these processes is the combination of positive attitudes towards the ethnic majority and negative attitudes towards ethnic minorities. This combination of attitudes is often found in empirical research (Sumner, 1906/1959; Adorno, Frenkel-Brunswik, Levinson & Nevitt Sanford, 1950/1982; Levine & Campbell, 1972; Smooha 1987; Eisinga & Scheepers, 1989; Billiet, Carton & Huys, 1990; Pieterse, Scheepers & Van Der Ven, 1991; Billiet, Eisinga & Scheepers, 1996). Nevertheless, all these studies focus almost exclusively on the more blatant forms of negative attitudes. Based on social identity theory, we propose that subtle negative attitudes towards ethnic minorities correlate with positive attitudes towards the ethnic majority. Therefore, we formulate a second, two-part hypothesis, for blatant and subtle racism:

H2a) The more strongly the ethnic majority member holds blatant negative attitudes towards ethnic minorities, the more likely it is that they will express positive attitudes towards their group.

H2b) The more strongly the ethnic majority member holds subtle negative attitudes towards ethnic minorities, the more likely it is that they will express positive attitudes towards the ethnic majority.

Differences in the social location of blatant and subtle negative attitudes

Although McConahay & Hough (1976) contended that traditional racism receives mainly support from less educated majority people, they did not provide any empirical evidence for the relationship between education and the distinguished forms of racism. Meertens and Pettigrew (1990) concluded that, in general, less highly educated people are more liable to prejudice. They also concluded that blatant and subtle forms are located in specific educational categories. Blatant negative attitudes were especially found among less highly educated members of the ethnic majority, whereas those holding subtle negative attitudes tended to be more highly educated (Meertens & Pettigrew, 1990). However, univocal results on the social location of blatant and subtle prejudice in age categories were not found in the various countries.

The results of the analyses of the interviews with the ethnic minority group suggested that the form taken by the blatant and subtle negative attitudes differed depending on socio-economic level and educational background. In agreement with Pettigrew and Meertens (1995), we found that blatant negative attitudes are especially prevalent among less highly educated members of the ethnic majority, whereas subtle negative attitudes are especially prevalent among those with an intermediate level of education. Blatant negative attitudes predominated among those with a lower socio-economic background, whereas subtle negative attitudes were more common among those with a mid-level socio-economic background. We could not provide consistent results regarding the social location of blatant and subtle negative attitudes in categories of age and gender.

We find realistic conflict theory useful for relating these qualitative findings to more general theoretical propositions. Realistic conflict theory indicates which circumstances reinforce the mechanisms of social identification and social contra-identification. A central assumption of realistic conflict theory is that socio-economic competition for scarce resources between groups such as ethnic groups leads the formation of negative attitudes of the other group(s). The competition may be concrete, such as housing and labour, or abstract such as culture, power, and status (Coser, 1956). There is a distinction between actual competition, taking place on the societal level, and perceived competition, taking place on the individual level. The actual competition is transposed into perceived competition and is as such of overriding importance (Blalock, 1967). Realistic conflict theorists propose that members of a specific social group develop a sense of group identity while they work together towards shared goals. If members of the ethnic majority perceive that scarce resources are accruing to ethnic minorities, these resources are then perceived as lost resources. The perceived competition can be based on actual as well as on subjective considerations. Both considerations may affect perceived threat on the part of ethnic minorities, which in turn reinforce negative attitudes held towards them (Coser, 1956; Blalock, 1967; Levine and Campbell, 1972). It has been proposed that perceived threat is a major predictor of blatant negative attitudes towards ethnic minorities, that is, perceived threat may reinforce the mental process of social contra-identification as a result of which blatant negative attitudes may be strengthened (Studlar, 1977; Schäfer & Six, 1978; Hagendoorn & Janssen, 1983; Castles, 1984; Elich & Maso, 1984; Krauth & Porst, 1984). Moreover, this relation was later supported by empirical evidence (Eisinga & Scheepers, 1989; Billiet, Carton & Huys, 1990).

We assume that socio-economic background influences how the threat posed by an ethnic minority group is perceived. Members of the ethnic majority from a relatively low rung in the social stratification system are more likely to be confronted daily with this actual competition over scarce resources. Consequently, they are more likely to express their negative attitudes towards ethnic minorities in relatively blatant terms. There may be also categories somewhat higher in the social stratification system, who do not actually perceive this competition, however, they may fear this actual competition in so far as they expect the upward mobility of ethnic minorities. Consequently, they may express their negative attitudes towards ethnic minorities in relatively subtle terms. Therefore, our third, two-part, hypothesis is as follows:

H3a) Blatant negative attitudes towards ethnic minorities are especially prevalent among less highly educated members of the ethnic majority and among ethnic majority members with a lower socio-economic background.

H3b) Subtle negative attitudes towards ethnic minorities are especially prevalent among intermediately educated members of the ethnic majority and among members of the ethnic majority.

After we had elaborated the nature of our dependent variables, blatant and subtle negative attitudes towards ethnic minorities, and their relationship with the independent variables education and socio-economic background, we tried to build further on a nomological framework including the structure of relationships between these negative attitudes on the one hand and intermediate, and consequent variables on the other hand (Davis, 1985).

We also wished to explain the relationship between the independent variables education and social class on the one hand, and blatant and subtle negative attitudes. A conclusion to be drawn from the interviews with both groups is that these relations might be interpreted by the perception of a threat posed by ethnic minorities. Here again, realistic conflict theory may be useful for explaining the effect of such a threat in line with a number of classic and recent studies (Coser 1956; Blalock 1967; Levine & Campbell 1972; Olzak & Nagel, 1986; Olzak, 1989; Coenders & Scheepers, 1997). These theoretical and empirical notions on the explanation of the relation between education and social class on the one hand, and blatant and subtle negative attitudes on the other hand, lead us to our fourth two-part hypothesis:

H4a) Members of the ethnic majority with lower levels of education and those with lower socio-economic backgrounds perceive ethnic minorities as a greater threat than those with higher levels of education and those with a higher socio-economic background.

H4b) The more members of the ethnic majority feel threatened by ethnic minorities, the more likely they are to hold blatant and subtle negative attitudes towards ethnic minorities.

In addition to the perception of ethnic minorities as a threat, we add another classic intermediate variable to our model, authoritarianism. Hypotheses concerning this variable are based on classic theoretical contributions. These hypotheses are derived from the theoretical considerations of Adorno et al. (1950/1982) who demonstrated that authoritarianism is highly predictive of ethnocentrism. Adorno et al. stated that because of their blind submission to authorities, authoritarian people depend highly upon their social ingroup in order to derive a positive self-identity. Authoritarian people also condemn and disparage people who deviate from conventional norms and values of the ingroup. This means that authoritarian people are inclined to social identification and social contra-identification. It was found that socio-economic background and education level are associated with authoritarianism. Empirical research showed that less highly educated people and people from lower socio-economic backgrounds are more inclined to authoritarian attitudes than more highly educated people and those from higher socio-economic backgrounds (see Scheepers et al., 1990). Therefore, we consider authoritarianism to be an intermediate variable explaining the relation between socio-economic background on the one hand and blatant and subtle negative attitudes towards ethnic minorities on the other. Hence, we derive our fifth, two-part, hypothesis that:

H5a) Members of the ethnic majority with lower levels of education and from lower socio-economic backgrounds are more inclined to authoritarianism than members of the ethnic majority with higher levels of education and from higher socio-economic backgrounds.

H5b) The more authoritarian the members of the ethnic majority, the more they likely it is that they will hold blatant and subtle negative attitudes towards ethnic minorities.

We propose that a third variable, political intolerance, intermediates in the relationship between social class and education on the one hand and negative attitudes towards ethnic minorities on the other. In empirical research it is often found people with a lower socio-economic background are more politically intolerant than those with a higher socio-economic background (Selznick & Steinberg, 1969; Davis, 1975; Lipset, 1983; Weil, 1985; Gibson & Tedin, 1988; Jelen & Wilcox, 1990). This research reveals that differences in political intolerance can be attributed to differences in educational attainment. The effects could be interpreted as a form of socialisation within the socio-cultural context (see Selznick & Steinberg, 1969; Weil, 1985) and as a matter of perspective (see Konig, 1997). First, the effect of education could represent the influence of the dominant liberal culture. Second, people from lower socio-economic backgrounds could have a narrower perspective on social reality making them more politically intolerant than people with a higher socio-economic background.

Subsequently, political intolerance is assumed to influence the process of evaluation of other groups such as ethnic minorities (see Lipset, 1983; Wagner & Zick, 1995). It is assumed that ethnic minorities are most disliked by politically intolerant people. The above-mentioned leads us to our sixth, two-part, hypothesis that:

H6a) Less highly educated members of the ethnic majority and from lower socio-economic backgrounds are more politically intolerant than those with higher levels of education and from higher socio-economic backgrounds.

H6b) The more politically intolerant a member of an ethnic majority group is, the more likely they are to hold blatant and subtle negative attitudes towards ethnic minorities.

The effects of blatant and subtle negative attitudes

Substantial research has not only been undertaken on the predictors of blatant negative attitudes, but also on the effects of these attitudes. It was found that blatant negative attitudes are important for explaining behavioural intentions towards ethnic minorities (Schmidt, 1992; Scheepers, 1996). Rationally planned behaviour theory (Fishbein & Ajzen, 1975; Ajzen & Fishbein, 1991; Ajzen, 1991, 1993) has dealt with the interpretation of the relationship between attitudes and behaviour. It has been suggested that, although situational, normative, and individual characteristics will have their own effects, attitudes are major determinants of behavioural intentions. Behavioural intentions are assumed to guide and affect actual behaviour (Fishbein & Ajzen, 1975; Ajzen & Fishbein, 1991; Ajzen, 1991, 1993). Meta-analyses have provided considerable support for the theory of planned behaviour (Schmidt, 1992; Eckes & Six, 1994). Empirical analyses have shown that traditional racism as well as symbolic racism is an important indicator of possible resistance by members of the ethnic majority to affirmative action policies (McClendon, 1985, McConahay, 1982). Pettigrew and Meertens (1995) found that people who hold blatant negative attitudes are more in favour of a restrictive immigration policy than people who subscribe to subtle prejudice. The latter were more likely to favour a restrictive immigration policy than those holding no negative attitudes at all. Kleinpenning (1993) concluded that biological racists and symbolic racists are more strongly inclined to oppose affirmative actions than ethnocentrists and aversive racists. Based on the results of the interviews with the majority and minority groups, we conclude that the more negative the attitude towards ethnic minorities, the more individuals are inclined to oppose policies intended to establish ethnic equality. Considering this we come to our seventh two-part hypothesis:

H7a) The more negative the attitude towards ethnic minorities, the stronger the opposition towards policies intended to establish racial equality.

In agreement with Kleinpenning (1993) and with Pettigrew and Meertens (1995), we expect blatant negative attitudes towards ethnic minorities to be more indicative of the distinguished consequence variables than subtle negative attitudes, thus hypothesis 7b:

H7b) The effects of blatant negative attitudes on opposition to policies aimed to establish ethnic equality, will be stronger than the effects of subtle negative attitudes.

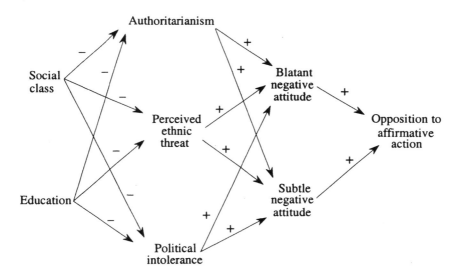

Diagram 8.1   Theoretical model for hypotheses 4 and 7

The derived hypotheses are displayed in Diagram 8.1. We will test this model empirically using survey data derived from a national sample of the ethnic majority population.

Data collection

This study is part of a larger longitudinal project on 'Social and cultural trends in the Netherlands' (Sociaal-culturele ontwikkelingen in Nederland: SOCON). As a part of this sociological research programme which covers a wide range of topics, data on ethnic relations were collected in 1985, 1990, and in 1995 (see Felling, Peters, Schreuder, Eisinga & Scheepers, 1987; Eisinga, Felling,

Peters, Scheepers & Schreuder, 1992; Eisinga, 1995; Eisinga, Felling, Konig, Peters & Scheepers, 1998). SOCON 1995 also includes measurements on subtle and blatant negative attitudes towards ethnic minorities that were defined and applied in the present study. Following a two-stage random-sample technique, designed to represent the adult Dutch population, 1009 respondents were selected from the general population. We consider this sample representative of the entire Dutch population because the sampling distribution closely matches real population distribution. Having defined the independent, intermediary, dependent, and consequence variables of our theoretical model, the variables now can be applied.

Dependent variables

Based on the research review as well as the qualitative data, we applied our dependent variables, blatant and subtle negative attitudes. Each aspect of these attitudes related to a list of field-related concepts from which we formulated the items. This provided us with a pool of 57 items to measure the aspects of the dependant variables. On the advice of experts in the field, we reduced the list of items to 27. We chose eight items intended to measure the aspects of blatant negative attitudes and 19 to measure subtle negative attitudes.

In each item the ethnic outgroup was associated with an attribute according to the aspect measured (see Fishbein & Ajzen, 1975). Because attitudes towards outgroups are likely to vary according to which outgroup is the focal point (see Hagendoorn & Hraba, 1987; Kleinpenning, 1993; Hagendoorn, 1995), a fundamental issue was on which ethnic outgroups should the items focus. Two options were available, restriction to one or to some specific ethnic outgroups which encapsulate the ethnic diversity in Dutch society (see Alba, 1994) or, we could use a term suitably representative of all ethnic outgroups. Because outgroups may change over time, the items needed to be durable enough to be applicable over the whole measurement period. Based on the interviews with the majority ethnic group we chose the term *ethnic minorities* as representative enough to encompass the most salient ethnic outgroups in Dutch society. To ensure that respondents' answers varied only in accordance with their beliefs, and not with reference to those outgroups they associate most with the term ethnic minorities, we offered all ethnic majority respondents the same reference points. These reference points were offered to all respondents at the introduction of the questionnaire.

We did not test for *the exaggeration of cultural differences* and *exoticism* because we felt quantitative research methods were inadequate to measure these two aspects of subtle racism. Due to the importance of the verbal and the non-verbal context in which *exaggerated cultural differences* and *exoticism* were expressed, we decided that the reliability and validity of measurements based on standardised items could be questionable.[3]

When formulating the items closed-ended questions were used because they allow the same reference point to be offered to all respondents (Converse & Presser, 1988). As Converse and Presser (1988) stated, when constructing items they should be clearly and shortly written in everyday language because complicated and very long items are likely to confuse the respondents. Because respondents may never have thought about the object of the items, we gave the respondents a 'never thought about' option. We did not choose for a separate 'no opinion' filter question because empirical research has shown that many respondents will choose this 'no opinion' option (see Converse & Presser, 1988).

After the standardised questionnaire was constructed, it was tested in a pilot study. Based on this it was evaluated and adjusted. The adjusted measurement of blatant and subtle negative attitudes towards ethnic minorities is presented in Table 8.2. The questions formulated to test the dependent variable positive attitude towards the ethnic ingroup replicated from Eisinga and Scheepers (1989) are listed in Table 8.2. Eisinga and Scheepers (1989) derived their list of questions with which to measure positive attitudes towards the ethnic ingroup on work by Adorno et al. (1950/1982) and Levine and Campbell (1972). It has been shown to be reliable and valid (see Eisinga & Scheepers, 1989; Scheepers et al., 1989).

We examined the results of the item analyses for the dependent variables positive attitude towards the ingroup, blatant negative attitude towards ethnic minorities, and subtle negative attitude towards ethnic minorities. The items dealing with these variables were simultaneously factor analysed.[4] Because of the factor's expected inter-correlations, we applied oblique rotation. The results of the analyses are presented in Table 8.3. As shown in Table 8.3, agreement with the items measuring the attitude towards the ethnic ingroup varies from 48.0 to 69.8 per cent. Agreement indicates a positive attitude towards the ingroup. The scores indicating a blatant negative attitude towards ethnic minorities ranged from 10.6 to 50.4 per cent. Items v2107 and v2109, which were intended to measure the generalisation of negative characteristics, received notably high levels of approval (42.8 and 50.4 per cent respectively). Disagreement with the items v2115 to v2119 and with item v2129 indicated subtle negative attitudes towards ethnic minorities. Disagreement with the remaining items intended to measure subtle negative attitudes was interpreted in the same way. The scores for answers indicating subtle negative attitudes ranged from 14.4 to 86.1 per cent.

Table 8.2 Ethnocentrism (answer categories: agree entirely; agree; do not agree, do not disagree; disagree; disagree entirely; never thought about)

Blatant Negative Attitudes towards Ethnic Minorities
Superiority
v2100   In general, Dutch people behave better than ethnic minorities do
v2101   In general, the customs of Dutch people are better than those of ethnic minorities
v2102   Because they don't know any better, ethnic minorities cling to their own way of life
v2103   In general, ethnic minorities shall not achieve the level of Dutch people
Problematisation
v2104   People from ethnic minority groups do cause a lot of problems in our country
v2105   Our social problems would be solved to a large extent, if all ethnic minorities were to return to their country of origin
Generalisation of negative characteristics and individualisation of positive characteristics
v2106   There are only few people from ethnic minority groups who really make an effort
v2107   Yet, there are many people from ethnic minority groups who make improper use of the Dutch social security system
v2108   There are only few people from ethnic minority groups who really want to adjust to the Dutch way of life
v2109   Yet, there are many people from ethnic minority groups who are engaged in crime

Subtle Negative Attitudes towards Ethnic Minorities
Paternalism
v2111   It is a good thing that we encourage ethnic minorities in their personal development
v2112   In order to be less discriminated against, ethnic minorities have to adjust to the Dutch way of life
v2113   In order to be able to develop themselves, ethnic minorities have to adjust to the Dutch way of life
v2114   It is important that we look after the interests of ethnic minorities
Overvaluation of the unimportant
v2115   Dutch people can learn many good things from ethnic minorities (disagree)
v2116   Our country would be better off if we were willing to accept the good things of other cultures (disagree)
v2117   The coming of ethnic minorities to the Netherlands is an enrichment to our cultural activities (disagree)
Existence of neutralised feelings
v2118* How often have you felt sympathy for ethnic minorities living in the Netherlands? (not often-never)
v2119* How often have you felt admiration for ethnic minorities living in the Netherlands? (not often-never)
(*answer categories: very often, often, not too often, a few times, never thought about)
Overcautiousness
v2120   In initial contacts with ethnic minorities, you have to be more on your guard than usual
v2121   With ethnic minorities you often don't know where you stand
v2122   I find it hard to show understanding for customs of ethnic minorities
v2123   I feel uncomfortable when ethnic minorities are around
v2124   When in contact with ethnic minorities, I'm very carefully with what I say
v2125   When in contact with ethnic minorities, I try to approach them extra positively
Negative tolerance
v2129   Out of consideration for other cultures, I am willing to adjust my way of life (disagree)
v2130   Living together with people from different cultures does not have to mean that I have to give up anything (disagree)

Positive Attitude towards the Ethnic Majority
v0657   We Dutch people are always willing to work hard
v0658   Generally speaking, the Netherlands is a better country than most others
v0663   Every Dutch citizen should honour our national symbols, such as the national flag and anthem
v0665   I am proud to be Dutch

Table 8.3 Ethnocentrism: frequencies, factor analyses and reliability

Items	agree	neutral	disagree	Valid Cases	h^2	Factor Loadings (>.20)		
Positive attitude ingroup								
v0657	48.0	33.8	18.3	832	.26			.47
v0658	64.7	21.2	14.1	831	.20			.38
v0663	59.7	23.5	16.8	833	.37			.56
v0665	69.8	22.9	7.2	828	.55			.77
Blatant negative attitude outgroup								
superiority								
v2100	10.6	29.9	59.4	836	.52	.68		
v2101	11.7	32.6	55.8	832	.49	.65		
v2102	18.3	30.1	51.6	818	.22	.41		
v2103	21.6	24.9	53.6	812	.34	.56		
problematisation								
v2104	32.9	33.4	33.7	835	.51	.66		
v2105	19.1	24.9	56.0	843	.59	.59	.25	
generalisation/individualisation								
v2106	14.0	31.3	54.7	801	.57	.67		
v2107	42.8	32.5	24.7	830	.59	.62	.21	
v2108	35.0	35.7	29.3	815	.48	.52		
v2109	50.4	31.0	18.6	819	.36	.57		
Subtle negative attitude								
paternalism								
v2111	86.1	10.7	3.2	821				
v2112	58.3	27.7	14.0	842	.40	.52		
v2113	64.5	24.4	11.1	845	.37	.44	.22	
v2114	49.4	32.8	17.8	816				
surplus value unimportant								
v2115	35.5	43.1	21.5	806	.42		.48	
v2116	35.4	32.4	32.2	817	.40		.57	
v2117	41.1	31.2	27.7	791	.50		.55	
neutralised feelings								
v2118	40.2	41.2	18.7	831				
v2119	24.8	47.4	27.7	833	.26	.23	.37	
negative cautiousness								
v2120	19.4	31.5	49.1	809	.43	.71		
v2121	25.6	34.7	39.7	804	.54	.75		
v2122	14.4	18.1	67.5	827	.34	.56		
v2123	10.9	19.9	69.2	834	.31	.59		
v2124	24.1	28.7	47.2	797				
v2125	30.0	40.3	29.7	804				
negative tolerance								
v2129	12.0	27.7	60.4	828	.25		.52	
v2130	32.2	30.9	37.0	820				

Percentage of variance explained: .41
N (after listwise deletion): 607

Factor correlation matrix:

	factor1	factor2	factor3
factor1	1.00		
factor2	.47	1.00	
factor3	.50	.24	1.00

Cronbach's alpha: .92 .73 .67

As expected, principal factor analysis with oblique rotation revealed a three-dimensional structure.[5] All items intended to measure a positive attitude towards the ingroup have a substantial loading only on one dimension, no other items loaded on this dimension. The items indicative of blatant negative attitudes towards ethnic minorities met the requirements. They all have a communality of more than .20 and a factor loading of more than .40. In addition, they all refer to the same dimension. Two of the items also loaded on a second factor (v2105 and v2107), however, given the low values of the loadings, this multi-dimensionality was not considered inconsistent. Only after eliminating items with low inter-item correlations, a communality of less than .20, a factor loading of less than .40, or substantial double loadings on both dimensions of negative attitudes, was the principal factor model considered appropriate. We noted that the seven items intended to measure the aspect *paternalism* or the aspect *negative cautiousness* refer to same dimension as the items that were indicative of the blatant negative attitudes. Thus supporting our expectation that members of the ethnic majority with a strong blatant negative attitude would also express paternalistic attitudes and be overcautious. Furthermore, examination of the factor pattern structure indicated that only six out of 17 items, indicating *the overvaluation of the unimportant, neutralised feelings and negative tolerance*, refer to the dimension subtle negative attitudes.

Thus, we concluded that there are three empirically distinguishable dimensions. The first is concerned predominantly with blatant negative attitudes towards ethnic minorities, but also includes a number of questions initially developed to measure subtle negative attitudes. The second dimension is concerned with subtle negative attitudes towards ethnic minorities, whereas the third dimension is considered indicative of a positive attitude towards the ethnic ingroup.[6]

These findings imply, however, that our first hypothesis is refuted. However, we still found a distinct factor that could be labelled subtle negative attitude. Even though some items had to be eliminated because double loadings on the blatant as well as the subtle dimension indicated that an empirical distinction would be difficult, and a number of the seven items taken from the larger pool of 17 (developed to measure subtle negative attitudes) were embedded in the principal factor blatant negative attitudes. Hence, a small number of the items developed to measure the subtle dimension, did in fact constitute a distinct principal factor. Some items in this dimension were derived from a previous study by Pettigrew and Meertens (1995).

The correlation coefficients at the bottom of the right-most column of Table 8.3 show that the three dimensions correlated. As hypothesised, blatant as well as subtle negative attitudes are related to a positive attitude towards the ingroup but this relation is stronger for blatant attitudes; Pearson correlations are .50 and .24 respectively. The Pearson coefficient for blatant and subtle negative attitudes is .47. The reliability coefficients indicate a high or reasonable degree of internal consistency for the items referring to each dimension. Cronbach's alpha's are .92, .73, and .67 respectively. These findings corroborate our second set of hypotheses.

Measurement of intermediate variables

The *perceived threat of competition from ethnic minorities, authoritarianism*, and *political intolerance* serve as intervening variables in our model. *Threat of competition* was applied using the method developed by Eisinga and Scheepers (1989) adapted with reference to the results of the in-depth interviews with majority people. To the measure perceived threat of economic competition we first used items which refer to the allegedly disadvantageous position of Dutch people compared to ethnic minorities in areas of housing, education, labour, and social security. Then we formulated items indicative of subjective fear of the loss of norms, values, and cultural habits of the ethnic majority. Finally, we formulated items intended to assess the subjective fear that ethnic minorities are able to exercise too much political and social power. The questions developed and the relative frequencies and the factor analyses of these variables are displayed in Table 8.4.

Agreement with the items presented in Table 8.4 indicates that ethnic minorities are perceived as a threat. The high percentage agreement with item v2151 'Dutch values and norms should not be lost in a multi-cultural society' is striking. More than 80 per cent of the respondents agreed with this item. Agreement with the other items varies from 17.1 to 35.6 per cent. The results of the principal factor analyses, listed in Table 8.2, showed that the items refer to one dimension. The communalities and factor loadings of the items satisfy the postulated criteria, with the exception of item v2151. Therefore, we excluded this item from the scale. The reliability of the scale amounts to .91.[7]

The questions formulated to measure *authoritarianism*, presented in Table 8.5, were derived from the work of Adorno et al. (1950). The separate items refer to characteristics of the authoritarian personality, such as authoritarian submission, conformity to conventional norms, and aggression towards those who violate these norms. The results of the principal factor analysis on the authoritarianism scale are also presented in Table 8.5. Agreement with the items varies from 22.8 to 41.3 per cent. Agreement on these items is indicative of an authoritarian personality. We found one empirical dimension. The factor loadings and communalities are all sufficient according to our statistical criteria. The reliability of the authoritarianism scale is .72.

The intermediary variable *political intolerance*, was measured by a set of six items, asking the respondent whether people should be free in their expression of opinion. These items, which were developed by Middendorp (1978, 1979), are presented in Table 8.6. According to 62.8 per cent of the respondents, freedom to occupy buildings should be restricted. However, only 16.3 per cent of the respondents think that the freedom to demonstrate for or

Table 8.4   Perceived threat of competition: items frequencies, factor analyses and reliability

	Item	agree	neutral	disagree	h^2	Factor Loading (>.20)
v0639	Regarding the distribution of houses, people from ethnic minorities get their turn before Dutch people do.	35.6	31.1	33.3	.36	.59
v0640	Education for children from ethnic minorities is at the expense of Dutch children.	17.1	23.6	58.8	.33	.58
v0642	The day will come that Dutch people will be fired to give jobs to people from ethnic minorities.	16.0	20.5	63.5	.48	.69
v0643	Dutch people are cut back on income to pay for the social security of ethnic minorities.	32.1	25.2	42.7	.52	.72
v2150	Living together with ethnic minorities is at the expense of our own culture.	15.8	23.0	61.2	.60	.77
v2151	Dutch values and norms should not be lost in a multi-cultural society	81.0	12.3	6.7	.61	.78
v2152	The coming of ethnic minorities to the Netherlands is a threat to our own culture.	18.0	20.1	61.9	.61	.78
v2154	Ethnic minorities are too much in charge	18.7	24.1	57.2	.69	.83
v2155	Ethnic minorities have too much power in Dutch society	14.3	22.5	63.2	.74	.86
v2156	If ethnic minorities will become more engaged in politics, Dutch people would not have anything to say.	23.1	18.1	58.8	.61	.78

Percentage variance explained .54
N (after listwise deletion) 741
Cronbach's alpha .91

against an issue should be restricted. Because five out of six items were found to yield a one dimensional Mokken scale, responses were combined to produce a five-point index ranging up to high political intolerance.

Measurement of a consequent variable

The questions formulated to test for the consequent variable *opposition towards affirmative action* are listed in Table 8.7. This measurement was largely based on previous research. Items v2176 and v2177 assessed the extent to which respondents agree with the Dutch government's affirmative action policies. Similar items were used in the Dutch National Election Study in 1994 (Statistics Netherlands, 1994).

Table 8.5   Authoritarianism: items, frequencies, factor analyses and reliability

Item		Frequency		h^2	Factor Loading (>.20)
	agree	neutral	disagree		
v0623 People can be divided in two distinct classes: the weak and the strong	32.5	19.8	47.7	.51	.72
v0626 Most of our problems would be solved if we could somehow get rid of immoral, crooked and feeble-minded people	41.3	26.1	32.6	.31	.56
v0627 What this country needs most, more than laws and political programmes, is a few courageous, fearless, devoted leaders in whom the people can put their faith	37.0	27.1	35.9	.44	.66
v0628 A person who has bad manners, habits **and** breeding can hardly expect to get along with decent people	22.8	25.6	51.6	.32	.56

Percentage variance explained .40
N (after listwise deletion) 902
Cronbach's alpha .72

Table 8.6 Political intolerance: items, frequencies, Mokken scale analyses

Item	Frequency everybody should be free	Frequency freedom should be restricted	H_i	Popularity

I will mention some cases about your country. Would you please tell me whether you think everybody in this country ought to be free to do what has been mentioned, or whether this freedom should be restricted in one way or another? Should you be free to:

v0223 say whatever you like in public.	81.4	18.6	.53	.19
v0224 write whatever you like in public.	74.9	25.1	.56	.25
v0225 demonstrate in favour or against something.	83.7	16.3	.48	.16
v0226 criticise openly members of the Royal Family.	64.9	35.1	.50	.35
v0227 refuse military service.	73.8	26.2		
v0228 occupy buildings (e.g. schools, factories or universities) in order to enforce justified demands.	37.2	62.8	.48	.63

H .51
Rho .73
N (after listwise deletion) 991

As Table 8.7 shows, the attitude of majority people towards affirmative action varies according to the area of society the affirmative action is intended for. Only 22.4 per cent of the respondents agreed with affirmative action in the labour market (v2176), whereas 73.6 per cent agreed when it was related to education (v2177). Fourteen per cent of respondents opposed affirmative action in the educational arena. However, 53.2 per cent opposed affirmative action in the labour market. We decided to concentrate on this majority.

Measurement of independent variables

The socio-structural characteristics socio-economic background and education are the independent variables in our empirical-theoretical framework. The typology of *socio-economic background* was constructed according to the EGP-classification (Erikson, Goldthorpe and Portocarero, 1979, 1983). Respondents were categorised in relation to their employment. For a number of respondents, the social class was unknown, in most cases because they have never been employed outside the household. These respondents were allocated separate categories. This produced the nine-fold classification scheme in Table 8.9 which was treated as a categorical variable (professionals, office workers, self-employed, skilled manual workers, semi- and un-skilled manual workers, retired persons, unemployed persons, housekeepers, and students). *Education* was taken to mean the highest completed level of education attained by the respondent. The highest level of education was treated as an ordinal-level variable and was classified into seven categories (elementary school, lower vocational school, lower secondary school, secondary vocational school, intermediate secondary school, higher secondary school, professional further education, and university).

Measurement of control variables

The direct and indirect relations between the distinguished variables in the model are controlled for additional effects of gender, age, religious denomination, region and the degree of urbanisation of the place of residence. The choices of these variables has been based on previous empirical research (see Konig, 1997).

To measure *religious denomination* we asked the respondent the following two questions: 'Do you consider yourself to belong to a particular religion or denomination? And if so, to which one?' The answers to these questions

Table 8.7 Opposition to affirmative action: items and frequencies

	Item	agree	neutral	disagree
v2176	People from ethnic minority groups are more often unemployed than Dutch people. The government has tried to rectify this by taking more ethnic minorities into their employment. Ethnic minorities have been given precedence in specific situations. To what extent do you agree or disagree with this policy?	22.4	24.5	53.2
v2177	Sometimes, people from ethnic minority groups have a educational disadvantage compared to Dutch people. The government has tried to rectify this by putting up the money for education to them. To what extent do you agree or disagree with this policy?	73.6	12.3	14.1

(N=852)

were coded into five categories: (1) no religious denomination, (2) Catholic, (3) Reformed, (4) Calvinist, (5) other denominations. Region was classified into four categories depending on geographical location: (1) North, (2) East, (3) West, (4) South. The classification for the degree of urbanisation is derived from a 12 point system used by Statistics Netherlands (1983, 1991), which is based on information about the number of inhabitants, economic sectors in which inhabitants are employed, and population density of the area.

The social location of ethnic attitudes: bivariate analyses

Procedures

In this section, we present descriptive statistics for the whole majority population on negative attitudes towards ethnic minorities and regarding opposition to affirmative action on the labour market. Subsequently, descriptive analyses are presented with respect to the differences between social categories on these variables. To do so we calculated the percentage of respondents with a value on the blatant negative attitude scale higher than the mid-value. These respondents agreed with at least one item indicative of blatant negative attitudes. We repeated this for subtle negative attitudes. We also calculated the percentage opposed to affirmative action for the total population, and for those belonging to distinguished social categories.[8]

Results

As expected subtle negative attitudes towards ethnic minorities are much more widely dispersed than blatant negative attitudes (Table 8.8). Forty-eight per cent of the respondents scored higher than the mid-value of this scale. This is considerably more than the percentage of respondents who expressed blatant negative attitudes (35.1 per cent). Opposition to affirmative action is also relatively widespread, with more than half of the respondents (53.1 per cent) opposed to affirmative action. Table 8.8 also shows the different levels of blatant and subtle racism, and opposition to affirmative action, between people with different levels of education.

Agreement with blatant and subtle negative attitudes is highest among the less highly educated. Sixty per cent of all people with only elementary or lower vocational school agreed with blatant and subtle negative attitudes. Opposition to affirmative action is also relatively high among these people (60.6 and 58.2 per cent respectively). Among the highly educated there is a relatively low percentage of agreement with blatant and subtle negative attitudes as well as of opposition to affirmative action. These findings are not new and are in accordance with hypothesis 3a. The results related to hypothesis 3b are striking. For people with an educational level no higher or lower than intermediate secondary school, the level of agreement with blatant negative attitudes is relatively low (20.0 per cent). However, agreement with subtle negative attitudes is more than twice as high (47.3 per cent). Moreover, we found the highest level of opposition to affirmative action among the people in this category (63.6 per cent). We consider this to lend support to hypothesis 3b. We now turn to the differences between socio-economic backgrounds.

The attitudes expressed by individuals from different socio-economic backgrounds show a wide level of variance (Table 8.9). A number of deviations from the general mean are worth mentioning. Manual workers and the self-employed express the greatest level of blatant negative attitudes. Retired persons and housekeepers also express these blatant attitudes to a large extent. Manual workers, the self-employed, and housekeepers also express subtle negative attitudes to a greater extent than the general population. These findings support our hypothesis 3a. Remarkably, office workers, who are generally considered middle-class, agreed less with blatant negative attitudes (25.2 per cent) than they did with subtle negative statements (49.6 per cent). We consider this to be support for hypothesis 3b.

The theoretical model: multivariate analyses

Procedures: linear structural modelling

The model (see Diagram 8.1) was tested using linear structural modelling (LISREL VIII). LISREL allows the general suitability of the model to be tested as well as to postulate the expected correlations between the dependent variables. To meet the assumptions of linearity, we dummified the independent variables socio-economic background and education into as many variables as they contain categories, minus one that serves as a reference category.[9] For reference categories we chose: students for socio-economic background, and university for the level of education.[10]

Multivariate regressions were performed to decide which variables contributed significantly to the variation in the intermediate, dependent and consequent variables. We considered parameters that have a t-value smaller than 1.96 to be non-significant. We specified and estimated the model in Diagram 8.1. We excluded non-significant parameters from the model and re-estimated the parameters of the restricted empirical model. Non-significant

Table 8.8 Percentage of agreement with blatant and subtle negative attitudes and percentage of opposition to affirmative action by education

	Agreement Blatant Negative Attitude	Agreement Subtle Negative Attitude	Opposition to Affirmative Action
Elementary school	62.8	64.3	60.6
Lower vocational school	60.8	63.1	58.2
Lower secondary school	35.3	52.0	52.9
Secondary vocational school	35.1	61.4	58.2
Intermediate secondary school	20.0	47.3	63.6
Higher secondary school	17.4	30.9	46.4
College	16.7	29.2	42.3
University	20.3	23.8	45.3
TOTAL	35.1	48.1	53.1
N	838	832	853
Cramer's V	.28	.23	.19

Table 8.9 Percentage of agreement with blatant and subtle negative attitudes and percentage of opposition to affirmative action by social class

	Agreement Blatant Negative Attitude	Agreement Subtle Negative Attitude	Opposition to Affirmative Action
Professionals	21.3	36.8	50.6
Routine non-manual	25.4	49.6	54.8
Self-employed	40.7	59.3	64.3
Technicans and supervisor manual work	36.0	48.0	44.0
Skilled and unskilled workers	42.1	53.3	56.5
Retired persons	47.3	46.2	49.0
Unemployed persons	32.7	44.9	40.8
Housekeeping	55.4	65.6	60.3
Full-time education	26.5	38.8	51.0
TOTAL	35.1	48.1	53.1
N	838	832	852
Cramer's V	.20	.17	.16

parameters were excluded by fixing them to zero. First, we fixed the parameter with the lowest t-value to zero. If this did not lead to a significant loss of fit we examined whether other parameters could be constrained. We continued until all non-significant parameters were excluded from the model.

We examined the modification indices to ascertain that we had not applied any false restrictions to the model by fixing any significant parameters to zero. The constrained parameters that significantly improved the fit of the model were un-constrained. We released the parameter with the highest modification index first. This led to the largest reduction in the Chi-square estimate. After re-estimating the model we examined whether other parameters were eligible for inclusion in the model until an adequate fit was reached and no other parameters led to a significant additional increase in the fit of the model. The Chi-square value and probability level p provided the overall suitability of the restricted model. The direct and indirect relations between the distinguished variables in the model were controlled for additional effects of gender, age, religious denomination, and region and the degree of urbanisation of place of residence. The procedure is outlined in the appendix to this chapter.

Results

Table 8.10 shows the LISREL standardised parameter estimates obtained under regression of the restricted final model. The Chi-square value of the final model indicates that this model accurately fits the data (Chi square=39.31, df=42). With hypothesis 4a we claim that the lower the level of education and socio-economic background of the member of the ethnic majority, the more likely it is that the individual will perceive ethnic minorities as a threat. This heightened perception of a threat is what leads to the expression of blatant and subtle negative attitudes as claimed in hypothesis 4b. Hypothesis 5a claims that the lower the ethnic majority member's level of education and socio-economic background the more inclined to authoritarianism they will be than those with a higher level of education and socio-economic background. This, in turn, induces them to express blatant and subtle negative attitudes towards ethnic minorities, as claimed in hypothesis 5b. Moreover, hypothesis 6a claims that the lower the educational level and socio-economic background of the member of the ethnic majority member, the more politically intolerant they will be. This, in turn, induces them to express blatant and subtle negative attitudes towards ethnic minorities, as claimed in hypothesis 6b.

The educational status of the respondent appears to have a significant effect on perceived threat, authoritarianism and political intolerance. The standardised parameters of the distinguished educational levels were interpreted in relation to the reference category for the level of education, university. All parameter estimates belonging to educational categories were positive, indicating that the reference category (those who completed university) is the least likely to perceive ethnic minorities as a threat, exhibit authoritarianism or political intolerance. Table 8.10 shows, conversely, that especially those with a lower educational level (those having completed up to the level of secondary vocational school) tend to perceive ethnic minorities as a threat. It turns out that people from all educational levels below university subscribe more strongly to authoritarian attitudes than the reference category. With regard to the third intermediary variable, we found that especially people with an educational level equal to or lower than vocational school tend to be more politically intolerant than those who have finished university.

From Table 8.10 we derive that the effect of education on perceived threat of ethnic minorities, authoritarianism and political intolerance is much stronger than that of socio-economic background. The differences between socio-economic categories with regard to perceived threat, authoritarianism and political intolerance are small: nearly all parameter estimates of the effects of social class on the intermediate variables prove to be non-significant. Nevertheless, we did not exclude these parameters from the model because exclusion resulted in a significant decrease of fit. These results lead us to accept hypotheses 4a, 5a and 6a. Members of the ethnic majority with a lower level of education and socio-economic background perceive ethnic minorities as a greater threat, are more inclined to authoritarianism and are more politically intolerant than members of the ethnic majority with a higher level of education and socio-economic background.

That both perceived threat and authoritarianism appear to have a strong impact on both dependent variables is especially important. Particularly the effect of perceived threat on blatant negative attitudes towards ethnic minorities is strong: the parameter estimate amounts to .69. And the effect of perceived threat on a subtle negative attitude is also worth mentioning: .51. The effect of authoritarianism on blatant negative attitudes is modest (.20) and there is no effect on subtle negative attitudes. Although the effects of political intolerance on blatant and subtle negative attitudes are small, they are statistically significant. The parameter estimates are .05 and .08 respectively.

The effects of the intermediary variables on the dependent variables are strong enough to negate nearly all the direct effects of education and socio-economic background on blatant and subtle negative attitudes. However, education still exercises an effect on subtle negative attitude that is not accounted for by perceived threat, authoritarianism and political intolerance. This evidence leads us to accept hypotheses 4b and 6b on the relationship between perceived ethnic threat and political intolerance on the one hand and

Table 8.10 Standardised parameter estimates of the structural equation model of the effects on opposition to affirmative action controlled for gender, age, religious denomination, and region and degree of urbanisation of place of residence

Independent Variable	Perceived threat	Authoritarianism	Political intolerance	Blatant negative attitude outgroup	Subtle negative attitude outgroups	Opposition to affirmative action
Education						
elementary school	.32*	.38*	.16*		.11*	
lower vocational school	.33*	.37*	.16*		.12*	
lower secondary school	.17*	.25*	.07		.12*	
secondary vocational school	.18*	.27*	.09		.18*	
intermediate secondary school	.01	.15*	.01		.10*	
higher secondary school	.01	.09*	.01		.01	
college	.04	.10*	-.03		.06	
university°						
Social class						
professionals	-.11	-.10	-.08			
routine non-manual	-.05	-.07	-.06			
small proprietors	-.03	.01	-.03			
technicans and supervisor manual work	-.05	-.01	.02			
skilled and unskilled workers	.02	-.01	-.09			
retired persons	-.05	-.04	.10*			
unemployed persons	-.05	-.09*	-.01			
housekeeping	.09	.04	.03			
full-time education°						
Perceived threat				.68*	.50*	.24*
Authoritarianism				.19*	.08*	
Political intolerance				.05*		
Blatant negative attitudes outgroups						
Subtle negative attitudes outgroups						.26*
r^2	.25	.31	.14	.70	.35	.22

Chi^2=39.31 (df=42, p=.59)
AGFI=.96
N=798

* = statistically significant p<.05;   ° = reference category

blatant and subtle negative attitudes on the other. However, hypothesis 5b has to be partially rejected because it turns out that authoritarianism has no effect on subtle negative attitudes.

Let us now turn to hypothesis 6a, which claims that the more negative the attitude towards ethnic minorities, the stronger the opposition towards affirmative action will be. This hypothesis claims that the effects of blatant negative attitudes on opposition to affirmative action will be stronger than the effects of subtle negative attitudes. In the column on the far left of Table 8.10, we can see that opposition to affirmative action is significantly affected by subtle negative attitudes towards ethnic minorities. The parameter estimate amounts to .26. Contrary to our hypotheses we do not find a significant effect

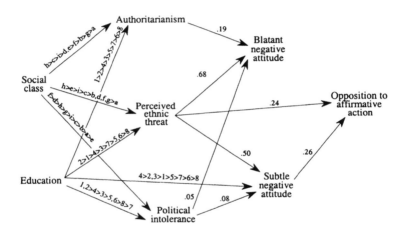

Diagram 8.2 Structural equation model of the effects on opposition to affirmative action controlled for gender, age, religious denomination, and region and degree of urbanisation of place of residence

Legend: Social class (a) professionals, (b) routine non-manual, (c) small proprietors, (d) technicians and supervisor manual work, (e) skilled and unskilled workers, (f) retired persons, (g) unemployed persons, (h) housekeeping, (i) full-time education. Education (1) elementary school, (2) lower vocational school, (3) lower secondary school, (4) secondary vocational school, (5) intermediate secondary school (O-level), (6) higher secondary school (A-level), (7) college, (8) university. (Chi^2=39.31, df=42, p=.59, AGFI=.96, N=798)

of blatant negative attitudes towards ethnic minorities on opposition to affirmative action. These findings lead us to accept partially hypothesis 6a and to reject 6b. What is remarkable is that perceived ethnic threat significantly contributes to the explanation of opposition to affirmative action: the parameter amounts to .24. The results of the LISREL analyses are displayed in Diagram 8.2.

An examination of Diagrams 8.1 and 8.2 along with Table 8.10 indicates that some other findings are worth mentioning. These are not directly related to our hypotheses but concern effects that were falsely fixed to zero in the theoretical model. Contrary to our expectations, education has direct as well as indirect effects on subtle negative attitudes. All parameter estimates are positive. This means that, once all other variables are controlled for, the people who have completed university are the least likely to subscribe to subtle negative attitudes towards ethnic minorities. Especially the parameter estimate for those who finished secondary vocational school is relatively high (.18).

Conclusion

We set out to find explanations for the empirical findings that people rather low in the social stratification system, strongly subscribe to negative attitudes towards ethnic minorities and consistently oppose affirmative action policies designed to reduce ethnic inequality. We ascertained that in the Netherlands, contrary to the United States, there has not been a longitudinal decline in blatant negative attitudes towards ethnic minorities. However, these blatant negative attitudes have not been widespread enough to account for the level of opposition to affirmative action, which, in the Netherlands is more widespread than in the US. Recent theoretical and empirical contributions suggested that there may be another dimension of negative attitudes towards ethnic minorities at work here, a subtle negative attitude held by people in the middle layers of the social stratification system, and that this might explain the widespread opposition to affirmative action.

To test for this other dimension, we developed standardised measurements for both blatant and subtle negative attitudes towards ethnic minorities. We did so by means of in-depth research, backed-up by a local test of these measurements, from which we improved the measurements and submitted them to a national sample representative of the Dutch population. We also developed a wide-ranging theoretical framework based on previous theoretical and empirical contributions as well as on our in-depth interviews with people from ethnic minority and the ethnic majority group. This framework included independent variables (education and socio-economic background), intermediate variables (perceived threat, authoritarianism, and political intolerance), dependent variables (blatant and subtle negative attitudes), and a consequent variable (opposition to affirmative action).

In doing so, we came across a vivid debate on the dimensionality of negative attitudes towards ethnic minorities, focusing on the question whether blatant and subtle negative attitudes could be empirically distinguished. Our results showed that many aspects of subtle negative attitudes towards ethnic minorities were highly related to blatant negative attitudes, indicating that subtle attitudes were embedded in blatant attitudes. However, we also found a strongly correlated but distinct subtle dimension, containing only a small number of aspects related to a subtle negative attitude. Whereas the items contained in the blatant dimension are overtly negative, the items in the subtle dimension are more covertly negative or non-positive. This is in accordance with previous findings by Pettigrew and Meertens (1995). Unfortunately, this empirical evidence is not clear enough to resolve this debate. We concluded that is rather difficult to distinguish between both dimensions.

Next, we set out to locate both blatant and subtle negative attitudes in categories of education and socio-economic background. Consistent with much previous research, we found that people with lower levels of education, those who were self-employed or carried out manual labour identified strongly with blatant and subtle attitudes. However, we found that people who had achieved intermediate educational levels as well as office workers also held distinct subtle negative attitudes. Following social identity theory, these findings imply that these intermediate categories are also likely to socially contra-identify with ethnic minorities: they simply use more subtle terms to express their attitudes.

We then used a multivariate analysis, to determine to what extent this bivariate relationship between educational and socio-economic categories on the one hand and blatant and subtle negative attitudes on the other could be interpreted in terms of our intermediate variables—perceived ethnic threat, authoritarianism, and political intolerance. It turned out that perceived ethnic threat, authoritarianism, and political intolerance accounted for most of the direct effects of education and socio-economic background on both aspects of negative attitudes. There was one exception, however: education retained a direct effect on a subtle negative attitude. Again, we found that, even after controlling for relevant variables, people with intermediate levels of education strongly expressed this attitude.

Finally, we focused on the direct effects of independent, intermediate and dependent variables on our consequent variable, opposition to affirmative action.[11] It appeared that there were no direct effects whatsoever of education and social class on opposition to affirmative action, indicating that these original relationships were accounted for by intermediate and dependent variables. In particular, perceived ethnic threat and a subtle negative attitude towards ethnic minorities appeared to be significant indicators, whereas a blatant negative attitude turned out to be non-significant, indeed, absent. Realistic conflict theory may well explain why people with low educational achievements oppose affirmative action: they perceive ethnic minorities as competitors for scarce resources, in particular labour. As such the implementation of affirmative action would be disadvantageous to them. We also found empirical evidence that even people with secondary educational levels perceived ethnic minorities to be a socio-economic threat, which may also account for the (bivariate) finding that these categories are opposed to affirmative action. However, the perception of ethnic threat was not a useful tool for interpreting the finding that people who achieved an intermediate secondary school level were strongly opposed to affirmative action. This finding might be interpreted particularly in terms of a subtle negative attitude.

The results presented here assess the impact of subtle negative attitudes on ethnic inequality. We recognise that some interesting and important questions remain unanswered. The logic of the empirical distinction between blatant and subtle negative attitudes as well as the consequences of these attitudes on variables other than affirmative action need future attention. Our findings highlight the need for future efforts examining ethnic inequality to account for blatant as well as subtle negative attitudes. In order to establish a better understanding of ethnic inequality in Dutch society.

Appendix

Table 8.1a   From theoretical model to empirical model: actions and fit of the model

Model	Chi^2	Degrees of Freedom	Significance
Theoretical model (Diagram 8.1)	87.32	48	.00
Step 1:set free perceived ethnic threat—>affirmative action	67.02	47	.03
Step 2:set free education—>subtle negative attitude	39.08	40	.51
Step 3:fixed to zero authoritarianism—>subtle negative attitude	39.23	41	.55
Step 4:fixed to zero blatant negative attitude—>affirmative action	39.31	42	.59

Notes

1   Verkuyten and Masson (1995) interviewed secondary school students from minority groups too. We do not consider this the same as what we have done because these interviews were aimed at describing the attitudes held by ethnic minorities towards other ethnic groups.

204 *Education and Racism*

2 Kleinpenning (1993) contended that symbolic racism entails the component that ethnic minorities are free to behave as they like within limits. To test for this component, he formulated a Likert-item. Based on low inter-item correlations this item was deleted from further analyses.

3 This idea contrast to that of Pettigrew and Meertens (1995) who tested for the aspect exaggeration of cultural differences using four standardised items. The questions with which they tested for the aspect exaggeration of cultural differences are as follows:
How different or similar do you think (outgroupers) living here are to other (nationality) people like yourself? (very different, somewhat different, somewhat similar, or very similar)
In the values that they teach their children?
In their religious beliefs and practices?
In their sexual values or sexual practices?
In the language that they speak?

4 We detail the methods of analyses. We first examined whether response-set effects occurred. It appeared that no respondents had to be excluded for this reason. Next, we looked at the frequencies of the separate items. After that, the items were re-coded to ensure that a high score on the item coincided with a high score on the theoretical concept. We then tested whether the items assumed to be indicative of a certain dimension referred statistically to the dimension concerned. For this purpose, we performed principal factor analyses on the items (FACTOR from SPSSx; Norusis, 1990), The appropriateness of the factor model was evaluated using conventional criteria (Kim and Mueller, 1984), We examined the correlation matrix for the items, Bartlett's test of sphericity, Kaiser-Meyer-Olkin measure of sampling adequacy, Kaiser's eigenvalues (minimum value 1.0), the discontinuity in the eigenvalue plot (scree test), the factor loadings (minimum value .40), the communalities (minimum value .20), and the interpretability of the model. Items which did not meet the criteria were excluded. The coefficient of homogeneity (Cronbach's alpha) was used to measure the internal consistency.
We used a listwise deletion of missing values. Thus respondents with one or more missing values on the items under consideration, were excluded from analyses. To reduce the number of excluded cases, the missing data were substituted. We substituted the missing data after decisions about the measurement scales were taken, but before the scale values were computed. Only for respondents who had a valid score on at least 60 per cent of the items referring to one theoretical concept did we estimate the missing codes by means of linear regression. We applied the missing data substitution program MDAT3 (Van Der Weegen, 1991), In order to test the appropriateness of the missing value substitution, we examined whether the Pearson correlation between the scale scores before and after missing data substitution is high. Subsequently, we obtained factor scores by using the default regression method in SPSSx (Norusis, 1990), The items referring to one concept, were summed to obtain a Likert scale.

5 The eigenvalues (minimum value=1), and the discontinuity in the eigenvalue plot (scree test) supported the three-factor solution (Kim and Mueller, 1983).

6 Strikingly, the wording of all items referring to the first dimension is in direct opposition to the items referring to the second dimension. Agreement with items of the first dimension, and disagreement with items of the second dimension, indicates a negative attitude towards ethnic minorities. Several scholars have argued that the representation of

positive and negative affects towards the same object in two separate dimensions may be due to measurement error (see Green, Goldman & Salovey, 1993; Green & Citrin, 1994; Van Schuur & Kiers, 1994; Billiet, 1997), Green and Citrin (1994) have described how non-random measurement error may attenuate the observed correlations between items worded in opposite to each other as a result of which factor analysis will unjustly reveal two separate dimensions. To check whether this is the case with regard to the results of our factor analyses, we applied LISREL VIII to the data (Green & Citrin, 1994), We compared a two-dimensional model with a one-dimensional model. The structure of two-dimensional model was based on the two first factors of our factor analyses. In the one-dimensional model not only random but also non-random error was allowed. Preliminary results of the LISREL analyses indicate that the two-dimensional model fits the data better than the one-dimensional. Then, we applied Mokken scale analyses to the data (see Van Schuur & Kiers, 1994), Contrary to the results of the LISREL analyses the results of the Mokken scale analyses are in favour of the one-dimensional model. Given these contrasting results at this moment, no definite conclusion is possible regarding the dimensionality of blatant and subtle negative attitudes towards ethnic minorities. Supplementary and profound analyses are necessary to resolve this problem.

7 We examined whether the items indicative of ethnic attitudes and the items indicative of perceived threat can be considered as empirically distinguishable. To do so, we simultaneously factor analysed the items dealing with blatant negative attitudes, subtle negative attitudes, perceived threat on the part of ethnic minorities and positive attitudes towards the ingroup. Examination of the factor pattern structure indicates that there is an eligible overlap in the items that go into the four factors. All of the items incorporated in the analyses to indicate perceived threat have a substantial loading only on the factor they were assumed to measure.

8 CROSSTABS from SPSSx: Norusis, 1990.

9 Using a one-way analysis of variance (MEANS of SPSSX, Norusis, 1990) we examined whether the relations between the other variables in our model could be represented in linear structural equations. The statistical analyses showed that the variables are mainly linearly related so the assumption of linearity is tenable.

10 We also dummified the control variables gender, religious denomination, and region. The categories man, no religious denomination, and north served as a reference category.

11 There were no substantial direct effects of the control variables on affirmative action.

References

Adorno, T.W., Frenkel-Brunswik, E., Levinson, D.J. and Sanford, R.N. (1950/1982), *The Authoritarian Personality*, New York, Norton and Company.
Ajzen, I. and Fishbein, M. (1991), 'Understanding Attitudes and Predicting Social Behavior. The Theory of Planned Behavior', *Organizational Behavior and Human Decision Processes*, vol. 50, pp. 179–211.
Ajzen, I. (1991), 'The Theory of Planned Behavior', *Organizational Behavior and Human Decision Processes*, vol. 50, pp. 179–211.

Ajzen, I. (1993), 'Attitude Theory and the Attitude-Behavior Relation', in D. Krebs, and P. Schmidt (eds), *New Directions In Attitude Measurement*, Berlin, Walter de Gruyter.

Alba, R.D. (1994), *Proposal for an ALLBUS Module on Attitudes Towards Ethnic Minorities in the Bundesrepublik*, New York, State University of New York.

Barker, M. (1981), *The New Racism*, London, Junction Books.

Billiet, J., Carton, A. and Huys, R. (1990), *'Onbekend of onbemind? Een sociologisch onderzoek naar de houding van de Belgen tegenover migranten*, Leuven, Sociologisch Instituut, Katholieke Universiteit Leuven.

Billiet, J., Eisinga, R. and Scheepers, P. (1996), 'Ethnocentrism in the Low Countries', *New Community*.

Billiet, J. (1997), *Controlling for Measurement Error in Substantive Social Surveys: an Evaluation of Some New Developments*, Paper presented at the annual meeting of the Dutch Sociological Association, Utrecht.

Blalock, H.M. (1967), *Toward a Theory of Minority Group Relations*, New York, Wiley.

Bobo, L. and Smith, R.A. (1994), *From Jim Crow Racism to Laissez-Faire Racism. An Essay on the Transformation of Racial Attitudes in America*, Paper presented at the Annual Meeting of the Sociological Association, Los Angeles.

Bogardus, E. (1925), 'Measuring Social Distance', *Journal of Applied Sociology*, vol. 9, pp. 299–308.

Bogardus, E. (1968), 'Comparing Racial Distance in Ethiopia, South Africa, and the United States', *Sociology and Social Research*, vol. 52, pp. 149–156.

Campbell, A. (1971), *White Attitudes toward Black People*, Ann Arbor, Institute for Social Research.

Castles, S. (1984), *Here for Good. Western Europe's new Ethnic Minorities*, London, Pluto.

Coenders, M. and Scheepers, P. (1997), 'Economische trends, immigratie en groeiende onverdraagzaamheid', *ADOJournaal*, vol. 4, no. 2, pp. 7–8.

Converse, J.M. and Presser, S. (1988), *Survey Questions. Handcrafting the Standardized Questionnaire*, Beverly Hills, Sage.

Coser, L.A. (1956), *The Functions of Social Conflict*, Glencoe, The Free Press.

Davis, J.A. (1975), 'Communism, Conformity, Cohorts, and Categories: American Tolerance in 1954 and 1972–73. *American Journal of Sociology*, vol. 81, pp. 941–513.

Davis, J.A. (1985), *The Logic of Causal Order*, Beverely Hills, Sage Publications.

Denzin, N.K. (1978), *The Research Act: a Theoretical Introduction to Sociological Methods*, New York, Mc Graw Hill.

Dovidio, J.F. and Gaertner, S.L. (1991), 'Changes in the Expression and Assessment of Racial Prejudice', in H.J. Knopke, R.J. Norell, and R.W. Rogers (eds), *Opening Doors, Perspectives on Race Relations in Contemporary America*, Alabama, The University of Alabama.

Dovidio, J. (1993), 'The Subtlety of Racism, *Training & Development*, vol. 47, no. 4, pp. 50–56.

Eckes, T. and Six, B. (1994), 'Fakten und fiktionen in der einstellungs-verhaltens-forschung: eine meta-analyse, *Zeitschrift fur Sozialpsychologie*, 253–271.

Elich, J.H. and Maso, B. (1984), *Discriminatie, vooroordeel en racisme in Nederland*, Den Haag, Ministerie van Buitenlandse zaken, Adviescommissie, Onderzoek Minderheden.

Eisinga, R.N. and Scheepers, P.L.H. (1989), *Etnocentrisme in Nederland: Theoretische en empirische modellen*, Nijmegen, Instituut voor Toegepaste Sociale Wetenschappen.

Eisinga, R., Felling, A., Peters, J., Scheepers, P. and Schreuder, O. (1992), *Religion in Dutch society 90: Documentation of a National Survey on Religious and Secular Attitudes in 1990*, Amsterdam, Steinmetz Archive.

Eisinga, R. (ed.) (1995), *Social and Cultural Trends in the Netherlands*, Nijmegen, Instituut voor toegepaste Sociale Wetenschappen.

Eisinga, R., Felling, A., Konig, R., Peters, J. and Scheepers, P. (1998), *Religion in Dutch Society 95: Documentation of a National Survey on Religious and Secular Attitudes in 1995*, Amsterdam, Steinmetz Archive.

Erikson, R., Goldthorpe, J. and Portocarero, J. (1979), 'Intergenerational Class Mobility in Three Western European Societies: England, France and Sweden', *British Journal of Sociology*, vol. 30, pp. 415–441.

Erikson, R., Goldthorpe, J. and Portocarero, J. (1983), 'Intergenerational Class Mobility and the Convergence Thesis: England, France and Sweden', *British Journal of Sociology*, vol. 34, pp. 303–343.

Essed, P. (1984), *Alledaags racisme*, Amsterdam, Feministische Uitgeverij Sara.

Essed, P., vertaald door Gircour, R. (1991), *Inzicht in alledaags racisme*, Utrecht, Het Spectrum.

Felling, A., Peters, J., Schreuder, O., Eisinga, R. and Scheepers, P. (1987), *Religion in Dutch Society 85: Documentation of a National Survey on Religious and Secular Attitudes in 1985*, Amsterdam, Steinmetz Archive.

Fishbein, M. and Ajzen, I. (1975), *Belief, Attitude, Intention and Behavior, an Introduction to Theory and Research*, Massachusetts, Addison-Wesley.

Gaertner, S.L. and Doviodio, J.F. (1977), 'The Subtlety of White Racism, Arousal, and Helping Behavior', *Journal of Personality and Social Psychology*, vol. 35, pp. 691–707.

Gaertner, S.L. (1978), 'Nonreactive Measures in Racial Attitude Research: a Focus on 'Liberals' ', in P.A. Katz (ed.), *Towards the Elimination of Racism* (pp. 183–213), New York, Pergamon Press.

Gaertner, S.L. and Dovidio, J.F. (1986), 'The Aversive Form of Racism', in J.F. Dovidio, and S.L. Gaertner (eds), *Prejudice, Discrimination and Racism* (pp. 61–90), New York, Academic Press.

Gibson, J. and Tedin, K. (1988), 'The Etiology of Intolerance of Homosexual Politics', *Social Science Quarterly*, vol. 69, no.3, pp. 587–604.

Glaser, B.G. and Strauss, A.L. (1967), *The Discovery of Grounded Theory*, Chicago, Aldine.

Green, D., Goldman, S. and Salovey, P. (1993), 'Measurement Error Mask Bipolarity in Affect Rating', *Journal of Personality and Social Psychology*, vol. 64, no.6, pp. 1029–1041.

Green, D. and Citrin, J. (1994), 'Measurement Error and the Structure of Attitudes: are Positive and Negative Judgements Opposites?', *American Journal of Political Science*, vol. 38, no.1, pp. 256–281.

Hagendoorn, L. and Janssen, J. (1983), *Rechtsomkeer, rechtsextreme opvattingen bij leerlingen van middelbare scholen*, Baarn, Ambo.

Hagendoorn, L. and Hraba, J. (1987), 'Social Distance toward Holland's Minorities: Discrimination against and among Ethnic Outgroups', *Ethnic and Racial Studies*, vol. 10, no. 3, July, pp. 317–333.

Hagendoorn, L. (1995), 'Intergroup Biases in Multiple Group Systems: The Perception of Ethnic Hierarchies', in Stroebe, W., Hewstone, M. (eds), *European Review of Social Psychology*, New York, Wiley, pp. 199–228.

Jelen, T. and Wilcox, C. (1990), 'Denominational Preferences and the Dimensions of Political Tolerance', *Sociological Analysis*, vol. 51, no.1, pp. 69–81.

Kim, J.O. and Mueller, C.W. (1984), *Factor analysis, statistical methods and practical issues*, Beverly Hills, Sage.

Kinder, D.R. and Sears, D.O. (1981), 'Prejudice and Politics: Symbolic Racism Versus Racial Threats to the Good Life', *Journal of Personality and Social Psychology*, vol. 40, pp. 414–431.

Kinder, D.R. (1986), 'The Continuing American Dilemma: White Resistance to Racial Change 40 Years after Myrdal', *Journal of Social Issues*, vol. 42, pp. 151–171.

Kleinpenning, G. (1993), *Structure and Content of Racist Beliefs. An Empirical Study of Ethnic Attitudes, Stereotypes and the Ethnic Hierarchy*, Utrecht, ISOR.
Konig, R. (1997), *Christelijke religie en antisemitisme in Nederland 1990*, Kampen, Kok.
Kovel, J. (1970), *White Racism, a Psychohistory*, New York, Vintage Books.
Krauth, C. and Porst, R. (1984), 'Sozioökonomischen Determinanten von Einstellungen zu gastarbeitern', in Mayer, K.U. and Schmidt, P. (eds), *Allgemeine Bevölkerungsumfrage der Sozialwissenschaften* (233–266), Frankfurt, Campus.
Levine, R.A. and Campbell, D.T. (1972), *Ethnocentrism: Theories of Conflict, Ethnic Attitudes and Group Behaviour*, New York, Wiley.
Lipset, S.M. (1983), *Political Man*, Londen, Heinemann.
McClendon, M.J. (1985), 'Racism, Rational Choice, and White Opposition to Racial Change: A Case Study of Busing', *Public Opinion Quarterly*, vol. 49, pp. 214–233.
McConahay, J.B. and Hough, J.C. (1976), 'Symbolic Racism', *Journal of Social Issues*, no. 2, pp. 23–45.
McConahay J.B., Hardee, B.B. and Batts, V. (1981), 'Has Racism Declined in America? It Depends on Who is Asking and What is Asked', *Journal of Conflict Resolution*, vol. 25, pp. 563–579.
McConahay, J.B (1982), 'Self-Interest Versus Racial Attitudes as Correlates of Anti-Busing Attitudes in Louisville: Is it the Buses or the Blacks?', *The Journal of Politics*, vol. 44, pp. 692–720.
Meertens, R.W., Pettigrew, T.F. (1990), *Subtle vs Blatant Prejudice, a Four Nation Comparison*, Paper presented at the European Association of Experimental Social Psychology conference.
Middendorp, C.P. (1978), *Progressivenss and Conservatism*, Den Haag, Mouton Publishers.
Middendorp, C.P. (1979), *Ontzuiling, politisering en restauratie in Nederland*, Meppel, Boom.
Olzak, S. and Nagel J. (1986), *Competitive Ethnic Relations*, Orlando, Academic Press.
Olzak, S (1989), 'Labor Unrest, Immigration, and Ethnic Conflict in Urban America, 1880–1914', *American Journal of Sociology*, vol. 94, pp. 1303–1333.
Peters, V. and Wester, F. (1990), *Qualitative Analysis in Practice*, Nijmegen, Department of Research Methodogloy, Social Science Faculty, University of Nijmegen.
Pettigrew, T.F. (1985), 'New Black-White Patterns: How Best to Conceptualize Them?', *Annual Review of Sociology*, vol. 11, pp. 329–346.
Pettigrew, T.F. and Meertens, R.W. (1995), 'Subtle and Blatant Prejudice in Western Europe', *European Journal of Social Psychology*, vol. 25, pp. 57–75.
Pieterse, H., Scheepers, P., Van Der Ven, J. (1991), 'Religious Beliefs and Ethnocentrism, a Comparison Between the Dutch and the White Church-Going South Africans', *Journal of Empirical Theology*, vol. 4, pp. 64–85.
Pincus, F.L. (1994), 'Does Modern Prejudice Exist? A Comment on Pettigrew and Roth', in F.L. Pincus and H.J. Ehrlich (eds), *Race and Ethnic Conflict. Contending Views on Prejudice, Discrimination, and Ethnoviolence* (69–73), Boulder, Westview Press.
Schäfer, B. and Six, B. (1978), *Sozialpsychologie des Vorurteils*, Stuttgart, Kohlhammer.
Scheepers, P., Felling, A. and Peters, J. (1990), 'Social Conditions, Authoritarianism and Ethnocentrism: A Theoretical Model of the Early Frankfurt School Updated and Tested', *European Sociological Review*, vol. 6, pp. 15–29.
Scheepers, P., Felling, A. and Peters, J. (1989), 'Ethnocentrism in the Netherlands: A Typological Analysis', *Ethnic and Racial Studies*, vol. 12, pp. 289–308.
Scheepers, P., Eisinga, R. and Linssen, E. (1994), 'Etnocentrisme in Nederland, Verandering bij kansarme en/of geprivigileerde groepen?', *Sociologische Gids*, vol. 41, pp. 185–201.
Scheepers, P.L.H. (1996), 'Sociaal-politieke reacties, etnocentrische en extreem-rechtse reacties', in H. Ganzeboom (ed.), *Sociale segmentatie in 2015*, Den Haag, Wetenschappelijke Raad voor Regeringsbeleid (forthcoming),

Scheepers, P. and Schmeets, H. and Felling, A. (1997), 'Fortress Holland: Support for Ethnocentric Policies among the 1994-Electorate of the Netherlands', *Ethnic and Racial Studies*, vol. 20, no. 1, pp. 145–159.
Schmidt, H. (1992), 'Vorurteile und diskriminierendes verhalten: Eine meta-analyse', *Gruppendynamik*, vol. 23, pp. 389–414.
Schuman, H., Steeh, C. and Bobo, L. (1985), *Racial Attitudes in America, Trends and Interpretations*, Massachusetts, Harvard University Press.
Sears, D.O. and Kinder, D.R. (1985), 'Whites' Opposition to Busing: On Conceptualizing and Operationalizing Group Conflict', *Journal of Personality and Social Psychology*, vol. 48, pp. 1141–1147.
Selznick, G. and Steinberg, S. (1969), *The Tenacity of Prejudice*, New York, Harper & Row.
Smooha, S. (1987), 'Jewish and Arab Ethnocentrism in Israel', *Ethnic and Racial Studies*, vol. 10, no. 1, pp. 1–26.
Sniderman, P.M. and Tetlock, P.E. (1986), 'Symbolic Racism: Problems of Motive Attribution in Political Analysis, *Journal of Social Issues*, vol. 42, pp. 129–150.
Statistics Netherlands (1983), *Typologie van de Nederlandse gemeenten naar urbanisatiegraad op 28 januari 1971*, 's Gravenhage, Staatsuitgeverij.
Statistics Netherlands (1991), *Bevolking der gemeenten van Nederland op 1 januari 1991*, 's Gravenhage, Staatsuitgeverij.
Statistics Netherlands (1994), *Nationaal Kiezersonderzoek 1994: kerncijfers*, Voorburg/Heerlen, Centraal bureau voor de Statistiek.
Strauss, A. and Corbin, J. (1990), *Basics of Qualitative Research*, Newbury Park etc., Sage.
Studlar, D.T. (1977), 'Social Context and Attitude toward Coloured Immigrants', *British Journal of Sociology*, vol. 20, pp. 168–184.
Sumner, W.G. (1906/1959), *Folkways*, Boston, Ginn, 1906; New York, Dover Publications.
Tajfel, H. (1970), 'Experiments in Intergroup Discrimination', *Scientific American*, vol. 223, pp. 96–102.
Tajfel, H. (1982a), 'Social Psychology in Intergroup Relations, *Annual Review of Psychology*, vol. 33, pp. 1–39.
Tajfel, H. and Turner, J. (1979), 'An Integrative Theory of Intergroup Conflict', in W.G. Austin, and S. Worchel (eds), *The Social Psychology of Intergroup Relations* (pp. 33–47), Monterrey, Brooks/Cole.
Tajfel, H. (1982b), *Social Identity and Intergroup Relations*, Cambridge, Cambridge University Press.
Van der Weegen, T. (1991), *MDAT3: Substitutie van missing data*, Nijmegen, Katholieke Universiteit Nijmegen, Faculteit Sociale Wetenschappen, Research technische Afdeling.
Van Schuur, W. and Kiers, H. (1994), 'Why Factor Analysis Often is the Incorrect Model for Analyzing Bipolar Concepts, and what Model to use Instead', *Applied psychological measurement*, vol. 18, no. 2, pp. 97–110.
Verkuyten, M. and Masson, M. (1995), ' "New Racism", Self Esteem, and Ethnic Relations among Minority and Majority Youth in the Netherlands', *Social Behavior and Personality*, vol. 23, pp. 137–154.
Wagner, U. and Zick, A. (1995), 'The Relation of Formal Education to Ethnic Prejudice: its, Validity and Explanation', *European Journal of Social Psychology*, vol. 25, pp. 41–56.
Weil, F. (1985), 'The Variable Effects of Education on Liberal Attitudes: a Comparative-Historical Analysis of Anti-Semitism Using Public Opinion Survey Data', *American Sociological Review*, vol. 50, pp. 458–474.
Wester, F. (1984), *De gefundeerde theorie-benadering. Een strategie voor kwalitatief onderzoek*, Nijmegen.
Wester, F. (1991), *Strategieën voor kwalitatief onderzoek*, Muiderberg, Coutinho.

Author Index

Adorno, T.W. 11, 43, 57, 63, 110, 111, 112, 116, 144, 177, 180, 185, 189
Ajzen, I. 168, 184, 184
Alba, R.D. 184
Allport, G.W. 11, 114
Amir, Y. 115, 135
Ashford, S. 48, 54

Bagley, C. 21
Barker, M. 166, 174, 175
Batts, V. 163
Becker, J. 54
Ben Birka, J. 34
Berger, S. 34
Bergmann, W. 99, 102, 120
Beswick, D.G. 21
Billiet, J. 48–61, 66, 70n, 177, 179, 205n
Bishop, G. 69
Blalock, H.M. 105, 179, 180
Bobo, L. 65, 106, 163, 165, 166
Bogardus, E. 168
Brody, R.A. 121
Brown, R. 115

Campbell, A. 163, 177, 179, 180, 185
Carton, R. 48, 51, 61, 177, 179
Castles, S. 179
Cayrol, R. 34
Citrin, J. 205n
Coenders, M. 180
Converse, J.M. 185
Corbin, J. 168, 170, 171
Coser, L.A. 179, 180
Crosby, F. 15
Csepeli, G. xii

Dalton, R. 99
Davis, J.A. 165, 180, 181
De Baets, A. 47, 53, 55
De Graaf, P. 63, 66
De Moor, R. 81, 91n
De Witte, H. xiii, 8, 48–54, 56, 63, 64, 66

Dekker, H. xii
Dekker, P. 53, 54, 56, 61
Delooz, P. 53
Déloye, Y. 34
Denzin, N.K. 169
Dewaele, A. 63, 67
Dollard, J. 105
Doob, L. 105
Dooghe, G. 47, 55
Dovidio, J.F. 4, 163–6, 168, 175
Dowden, S. 41
Dronkers, J. 66
Drouin, V. 41
Duckitt, J. 21, 24, 48
Durkheim, E. 43

Eckert, R. 99, 103
Eckes, T. 184
Eisinga, R. 49, 54, 56–2, 65, 164, 177, 179, 183, 184, 185, 189
Ekehammar, B. 6, 66–8
Elchardus, M. 59
Elich, J.H. 179
Erb, R. 99, 102, 120
Erikson, R. 192
Essed, P. 164, 166, 167, 169, 172, 174, 175

Falter, J.W. xiii, 102
Farnen, R. xii
Felling, A. 54, 56, 164, 183, 184
Fishbein, M. 168, 184, 184
Flap, H. 63, 66
Frenkel-Brunswik, E. 11, 177, 105
Fuchs, D. 105

Gabennesch, H. 65
Gaertner, S.L. 163, 165, 166, 168, 175
Gardiner, G. 24
Gerhards, J. 105
Gevaert, A. 67
Gibson, J. 181
Glaser, B.G. 170, 171

Glaser, J. 10, 79, 137
Glock, C.Y. 21, 25, 138
Goldman, S. 205n
Goldthorpe, J. 191
Gollwitzer, P. 60
Green, D. 10, 79, 137, 205n
Grunberg, G. 41, 43
Guimond, S. 68

Hagendoorn, L. xii, xiv, 4, 11, 57, 80, 179, 184
Hampel, R. 21
Hardee, B.B.163
Hargreaves, A.G. 99, 105, 107
Haslam, A. 10
Heß, U. 102
Heitmeyer, W. 99, 102, 106
Heunks, F. 82, 90
Heyns, B. 83
Heyvaert, P. 59
Hill, P.B. 21, 99
Hogg, M. 10
Hopf, C. 111
Hough, J.C. 38, 163, 165, 176, 178
Hout, M. 10, 79, 137
Hraba, J. 184
Huddie, D.L. 138
Huys, R. 61, 177, 179
Hyman, H.H. 6, 21, 144, 137, 138

Inglehart 91n

Jackman, M.R. 64, 144
Janssen, J. 57, 179
Jaschke, H.-G. xiii, 99
Jasinska-Kania, A. xii, 9, 75, 78, 79, 83, 91n
Jelen, T. 181
John, O.P. 114

Kaldenbach, H. 64
Kellman, H. 24
Kerkhofs, J. 48, 53, 91n
Kiers, H. 205n
Kim, J.O. 204n
Kinder, D.R. 163, 165, 176, 177
Kindermans, S. 69
Kleinpenning, G. 4, 80, 164, 166–9, 174, 176, 184–6, 192, 204n
Kohn, M. 63–6

Konig, R. 181, 184, 193
Koralewicz, J. 91n
Kovel, J. 165
Krauth, C. 103, 179
Krupp, B. 21

Lau, R.R. 65
Leaman, J. 99, 105, 107
Lederer, G. 111
Lehman 57
Lemaine, G. 34
Levine 177, 179, 180, 185
Levinson, D.J. 11, 177
Licari, F. 65
Linssen, E. 164
Linssen, H. xii
Lipset, S.M. 116, 181
Loosveldt, G. 53
Luijkx, R. 63

MacNeil, L.W. 22
McClendon, M.J. 176, 184
McConahay, J.B. 38, 163, 165, 176–8, 184
Marody, M. 91n
Marx, G.T. 21
Maso, B. 179
Masson, M. 166, 169, 175, 203n
Mattyssen, M. 6
Mayer, N. 33–6, 43
Meertens, R.W. 50, 165–9, 174–8, 184–5, 188, 202, 204n
Meloen, J. 57
Michiels, K. 67
Middendorp, C.P. 54, 189
Middletown, R. 21
Miller, N.E. 105
Milner, D. 22, 24
Mowrer, O.H. 105
Mueller, C.W. 204n
Muha, M.J. 64, 144

Nagel, J. 180
Nevitte, N. 79, 80, 82, 83, 90, 177
Norusis 204n, 205n
Nowicka, E. 76–8, 91n

Oakes, P. 10
Oesterreich, D. 111
Olzak, S. 180

Palmer, D. 68
Parkin, F. 25
Percheron, A. 39
Peri, xii, 30n
Peters, J. 54, 164, 170, 171, 183, 184
Peters, V.
Pettigrew, T.F. 24, 38, 50, 106, 164–9, 174–8, 184, 183, 188, 202, 204n
Piazza, T. 30n, 157
Pieterse, H. 177
Pincus, F.L. 165
Porst, R. 103, 179
Portocarero, J. 192
Presser, S. 185

Quinley, H.E. 21

Raaijmakers, Q. 54, 67, 69
Reicher, S. 10
Rezsohazy, R. 48
Robinson, J.P. 41
Roller, E. 105
Rosseel, E. 68
Rothbart, M. 114
Rotter, J. 62

Salovey, P. 205n
Sanford, N.R. 11
Schäfer, B. 179
Schaffer, L.G. 138
Scheepers, P. xii, xiv, 16, 49, 50, 54, 56–8, 60, 65, 164, 177, 179–85, 189
Schizzerotto, A. 30n
Schmeets, H. 165
Schmidt, C. 111
Schmidt, H. 184
Schönbach, P. 21, 24, 60, 65
Schooler, C. 64, 66
Schreuder, O. 183, 184
Schumann, H. 163
Schumann, S. xiii
Schweisguth, E. 41, 43
Sears, D.O. 138, 163, 165, 176, 177
Sears, R.R. 105
Selznik, G.J. 21, 25, 38, 144, 137, 138, 181
Sheatsley, P.B. 21
Sherif, M. 25

Sidanius, J. 24, 65
Six, B. 179, 184
Smith, R.A. 163, 165, 166
Smooha, S. 177
Sniderman, P.M. xiii, xiv, 4, 10, 30n, 38, 79, 121, 137, 140, 142, 157, 164, 177
Srole, L. 57, 59, 62
Stark, R. 138
Steeh, C. 163
Steinberg, S. 21, 25, 38, 144, 137, 138, 181
Stember, C.H. 21
Stephan, C.W. 24
Stephan, W.G. 24
Stiepel, G. 61
Stouffer, S. 102, 116, 137
Strauss, A.L. 168, 170, 171
Studlar, D.T. 179
Sumner, W.G. 50, 52, 177

Taguieff, P.-A. 35
Tajfel, H. 56, 111, 112, 164, 177
Tax, B. 64
Tazelaar, F. 63, 66
Tedin, K. 181
Tetlock, P.E. 4, 10, 24, 79, 121, 137, 164, 177
Timms, N. 48, 54
Todorov, T. 41
Tournier, V. 39
Turner, J. 10, 111, 112, 165

Van de Werfhorst, H. 66, 68
Van den Broek, A. 81, 83, 90
Van der Ven, J. 177
Van der Weegen, T. 204n
Van Praag, C. 53, 54, 56, 61
Van Schuur, W. 205n
Van der Leyden, L. 47
Vanneman, R.D. 106
Verbeeck, G. 53
Verberk, G. xiii, xiv, 17, 50
Verkuyten, M. xii, 165, 166, 169, 175, 203n
Verma, G. 21
Vink, R. 54
Vogt, W. 6
Volleberg, W. 69
Vos, L. 54

Wagner, U. 21, 24, 61, 65, 181
Wegener, B. 103
Weil, F. D. 102, 144, 120, 181
Wester, F. 170, 171
Wetherell, M. 10
Wiegand, E. 99
Wieviorka, M. 99, 106
Wilcox, C. 181

Willems, H. 99, 103
Wilson, T.D. 139
Winkler, J.R. xiii, xiv, 12, 103, 120
Wright, C.R. 6, 144, 137, 138
Würtz, S. 99, 103

Zaller, J. 139
Zick, A. 61, 65, 181

Subject Index

affirmative action 15, 17, 149, 157, 164, 182, 191–6, 199–203
age 4, 8, 9, 12, 37, 41, 47, 55, 56, 67, 78, 79, 82–8, 102–3, 121–2, 178, 199, 200
alienation 4
anomie 56–8, 62, 106, 107
anti-Semitism 46, 87, 96, 98, 99, 102–4, 120
authoritarian attitudes/disposition *see* disposition
authoritarianism 4, 17, 43, 44, 56–9, 63, 69, 70n 91n, 111, 119, 127, 180, 181, 189, 191, 197–9, 202

blatant prejudice *see* prejudice
blatant racism *see* racism
blatant racist syndrome *see* racist

choice 13, 137–138, 151
    bilateral structure of 14
    normative 13, 144, 145
    one-sided normative 13, 14, 144–7, 147, 148, 158
    (two-sided) political 14, 15, 139, 171, 148, 150, 151
cognitive abilities/capacities/skills 1–3, 6–9, 40, 65, 66, 68, 69, 120
cognitive complexity 3, 22, 24, 65
cognitive sophistication 3, 6–8, 24, 25 65, 154, 153
collective representations 11
colonialism 8, 42 *see also* nationalism
competition 25, 26, 49, 85, 86, 89
    perceived 2, 7, 13, 18, 179, 189
conformism 26–29, 63
conformist 67
conformity 4, 189
conservative political views 4, 8, 40, 45, 85, 88, 111, 150, 154, 168;
    see also political preferences
conservative disposition *see* disposition

contact with migrants/minorities 12, 80, 89, 114, 115, 125, 12, 80, 89, 114, 115, 125, 169, 168
cultural differences *see* differences

differences 34, 39, 43, 44, 94, 102, 181
    cultural differences 2, 172, 173, 175, 204n
    perceived group differences 11, 12, 112, 124
    social differences 2
disposition 13, 82, 90, 115, 125, 141
    attitudinal 12, 13
    authoritarian attitudes 13, 43, 44, 58, 110, 111, 112, 113, 115, 116, 180, 181, 198
    conservative disposition 13, 82
distrust 82, 85, 86, 89
    see also political mistrust

education
    curvilinear effect of 16
    extrinsic effects of 7, 9
    general 5, 67, 68, 69
    higher level of 3–5, 8, 13–15, 17, 18, 21, 36, 40, 41, 43, 44, 61,63, 64, 119, 182

    lower level of 2, 13, 21, 36, 38, 40, 41,44, 56, 61, 117–119, 180, 198
efficacy 9, 82
ethnic minorities *see* minorities
ethnic tolerance *see* tolerance
ethnocentric attitudes 52
    beliefs 54
ethnocentrism 50, 54, 169, 168, 176
exotic 16
exoticism 173, 175

gender 83, 102

identity 177, 179

215

identity (*continued*)
    national identity 34
    social identity 56, 57
    social identity theory 56, 111, 112, 164, 178, 202
ingroup 11, 49, 50, 56, 111, 112, 125, 164, 177, 185
    ingroup favouritism 112
    ingroup identification 112

liberal 15, 86, 112, 127, 156
localism 4, 56–8

minorities 4, 12, 16, 18, 34, 36, 39
    ethnic 4, 10, 33, 39, 83, 85, 98
moderate 3, 54

national pride 112, 113
nationalism 8, 42, 54
see also colonialism
nationalist 52, 54

occupational position/status 63, 64, 66, 119
outgroup 11, 25, 56, 78, 80, 95, 98, 99, 111, 112, 125, 164, 177, 184
outsider 11

personality 110, 111, 127
    authoritarian 63
    dispositions 4
    factors 4, 111
political liberty 13, 14, 141, 144
    mistrust 33
political preferences *see* preferences
political tolerance *see* tolerance
preferences
    political 3, 8, 39, 40, 43, 44, 55
    pre-existing 8, 15
    value preferences 4
prejudice 1, 11, 12, 17, 21, 22, 94
    blatant 3, 169, 168
    content of 4
    effect of education on 1–3, 21, 25, 26, 28, 30, 38, 62, 65, 70, 77, 90, 119, 120, 125, 198 *see also* education
    expression of 3, 45
    racial prejudice 21, 24, 38, 94, 95, 102, 105, 106, 111, 124, 125, 127

prejudice (*continued*)
    subtle 3, 169, 168, 174, 175, 182
    two views of prejudice 1
primary socialisation 8, 39, 111, 144
professional status *see* status
property rights 153, 154, 155, 160
    values *see* values

qualitative analysis 170

racial prejudice *see* prejudice
racial tolerance *see* tolerance
racism 3, 17, 22, 34–6, 47–50, 52, 66, 70, 75, 82, 93, 99, 106, 164, 169, 176
    aversive 80, 90, 163, 165–7, 176
    blatant 4, 16, 17, 50, 70, 78, 166
    everyday 49, 50, 53, 55, 56, 58, 60–2, 68, 69, 166, 167, 172, 174
    subtle racism 4, 16, 17, 50, 61, 70, 169, 172, 184, 194
racist 5, 34, 50, 60, 166, 169, 182
    blatant racist syndrome 16
realistic conflict theory 25, 178, 179, 203
reducing prejudice/racism 3–9, 13, 24, 45, 101, 107; *see also*
    effect of education on prejudice
religion 37, 38, 54, 66, 85, 193
religious orientation 37, 169, 193
republican model 7, 8, 34, 41, 42
    egalitarian republican model 8
right wing beliefs/political preferences
    see conservative political views

social class 103, 116, 178–181, 192, 195–8, 200, 202
social differences *see* differences
social distance 9, 10, 77, 78, 83–12, 88, 89, 96, 98, 121–3, 168
social life 9
    causal dynamics of 9
socially desirable behaviour/response 4, 61
socio-economic
    background *see* social class
    insecurity 12, 13, 109
    status 116
status
    professional 7, 9, 26–8, 83, 84, 87
    see also occupational position/status
    socio-economic *see* socio-economic

Subject Index

stereotype 22, 23, 49, 58, 64, 174
    negative 16, 25
subtle prejudice *see* prejudice
    racism *see* racism
superiority 16, 75, 78, 165, 169, 168, 172

threat (perceived)
    economic 4, 49, 66, 105, 106, 203
    of minorities 17, 49, 58, 105, 166, 179, 189, 198, 202, 205n
tolerance 9, 10, 13, 14, 25, 38–40, 79, 80, 82, 86
    detached 16
    ethnic 3, 5, 6, 83, 90
    political 14, 102, 141, 146, 147, 159
    racial 5, 6, 14, 80, 89, 146, 159, 160n
    specific lessons on 5
    towards ethnic minorities 9, 41, 44,

tolerance (*continued*) 77, 78, 82, 90, 173
trust 82, 90

urbanisation 9
urbanism 102–4

values 3, 13, 22, 24, 26–28, 34, 38, 42, 66, 82, 91n, 111, 112, 137, 138, 140–3, 146, 150, 151–3, 156–8
    see also Republican model
    egalitarian 165, 166
    property 15, 153
    transmission of 7–9, 22, 24, 41, 44, 45, 63, 65
value preference *see* preference

xenophobia 33, 34, 38, 45, 79, 89
xenophobic attitudes 37, 40, 41, 44, 45